C000294668

AS FAR AS WE CAN

A Journey from Barnsley to Australia and Back

MIKE PADGETT

Grosvenor House
Publishing Limited

All rights reserved
Copyright © Mike Padgett, 2021

The right of Mike Padgett to be identified as the author of this
work has been asserted in accordance with Section 78
of the Copyright, Designs and Patents Act 1988

The book cover is copyright to Mike Padgett

This book is published by
Grosvenor House Publishing Ltd
Link House
140 The Broadway, Tolworth, Surrey, KT6 7HT.
www.grosvenorhousepublishing.co.uk

This book is sold subject to the conditions that it shall not, by way of
trade or otherwise, be lent, resold, hired out or otherwise circulated
without the author's or publisher's prior consent in any form of binding or
cover other than that in which it is published and
without a similar condition including this condition being imposed
on the subsequent purchaser.

A CIP record for this book
is available from the British Library

ISBN 978-1-83975-515-6

For Tony and Lol

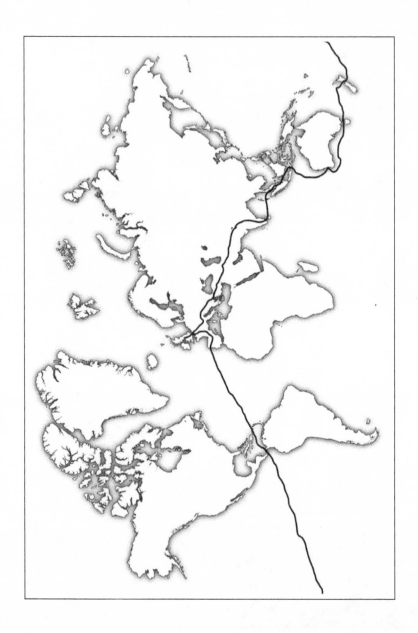

Contents

Foreword

Traditionally, the rite of passage of world travel or the Grand Tour was the sole province of the rich and titled. More recently the young gap year cohort supported by the umbilical cords of mobile phones and internet communication have taken their place. These three lads from Barnsley fit neither category, which makes this book a particular joy.

In a world currently starved of travel and adventure by a pandemic it is refreshing to be able to share an extraordinary journey undertaken by ordinary people. Not that Mike Padgett is by any means 'ordinary'. Now retired, he has made his mark in this east Yorkshire village of Sancton leading conservation campaigns and serving the community. He is often seen riding his treasured motorbike or, during lockdown, running and cycling in all weathers for exercise. Just the person to share an adventure with – you can rely on Mike.

Members of the village film club also know Mike from the film *Kes* and the iconic football scene. The first to be picked by the overbearing games teacher (Brian Glover) is Padgett - "Padgett, you're inside right" because he is the good footballer and teacher wants to win. As real life and fantasy coincide it is perhaps not stretching credibility too far to consider *As Far As We Can* as what might have happened next to at least some of the characters. Certainly, Barry Hines, the author of the novel on which *Kes* was based would be pleased to see his former pupil, Mike Padgett, in print and continuing his tale. As are we all. This is an adventure to be enjoyed, whatever your age.

Rob Thomson
February 2021

Preface

As a child I used to look out of the window when it was raining and imagine I was somewhere else. At first the neighbours across the street were concerned to see my glum face and used to ask my mother if I was all right. 'He's happy enough,' she would say. 'He likes to be outside exploring.'

That feeling of wanting to get out and look around became more urgent the older I got. When I'd explored my street, I wanted to explore all the other streets on my council estate. When I'd done that, I wanted to explore Barnsley town centre. And on it went until one day in my late teens I knew that the only way to satisfy the desire to see as much as possible was to travel around the world.

Most of my mates wanted to travel around the world as well but there was always a reason not to pack it all in and go: a steady job, a pension, a girlfriend, too busy having a laugh, no Barnsley Bitter for sale overseas. All good excuses. So, when I set off to Australia with two companions in a converted van in 1973, I promised to keep a diary intending one day to write a book about the travels for my family and friends.

It's taken forty-seven years to finally sit down and fulfil that promise. I hope that this book captures some of the spirit and joy of that year long adventure.

1

Magic

Mashhad: 23 January 1974

We parked the van on a quiet backstreet, wound down the windows and smiled at any young Iranian woman who looked our way. As usual Tony quietly made the most impact, I was happy with my score, and I think Lol was happy with his but you could never tell with Lol. When our egos had been sufficiently massaged, Lol climbed into the back and put the kettle on for the morning brew up, Tony jogged across the road to a kiosk to buy cigarettes and biscuits, and I lifted the engine cover and checked the oil level. There was no need for discussion. We'd been on the road for ten weeks now and we knew what had to be done and who had to do it.

The kettle had just begun to whistle when a young Iranian student in denim jeans and jacket invited himself into the van and sat down on our bed. I was a bit suspicious of him at first but I think he was just practising his English, and he was helpful, telling us unprompted the answer to two things we had been thinking about (and a third thing that only Lol had on his mind).

The student said, 'You will always find the best food in the market place. If it gets too cold for you to sleep in your vehicle the cheapest and best hotels can be found in the old part of the city. You will find a good brothel a hundred kilometres along this road on the left.'

That was all he said. He declined our offer of a cup of tea, shook our hands and hopped out of the van. He seemed like a good guy but we still counted our 8-track tapes.

Tony finished washing up and as we put on our sunglasses ready for an hour of sight-seeing there was a tap-tap on the windscreen. We expected to see the young Iranian student again or maybe the local beggars but this time it was a well-groomed youth with a hard face and perfect white teeth who smiled at us through the window. He was about our age, his English was excellent, even better than the young student's, and he had the patter of a good salesman.

'My name is Magic Mohammed,' he said. 'Welcome to Mashhad. It is a wonderful city in the middle of great change. Women are becoming more educated and every young man wants a Porsche Carrera.'

Tony, being a car man, liked Magic Mohammed straightaway and invited him into the van for a smoke. We told him we had travelled overland from England through Europe and Turkey and mentioned the scary rumours we had heard about Afghanistan, hoping he might dispel some of our fears. We even showed him the long knife we kept hidden under the driver's seat in case of bandit trouble. I wasn't sure whether it was the knife or our bold itinerary that made him flash those perfect white teeth again.

Mohammed enjoyed talking and he didn't seem in a rush to leave. Thankfully, there was a lull for a few seconds and Lol, not one for small talk, said it had been good to meet up but we had to get going. Mohammed looked at his slim gold watch.

'The Afghanistan border will be closed by the time you get there. Please come and join me for tea at my brother's house. His name is Ali. You will be most welcome and you can stay the night with us, if you like. We have good quality smoke. And we have something that could be to your advantage when you arrive in India.'

And he flashed those perfect white teeth again. We had been on the road long enough to know that occasionally adventure came dipped in bullshit.

'That's great,' we said in unison. 'Lead the way.'

We might have looked like three hippies, Lol with his thick ginger beard, waistcoat and cheesecloth shirt, Tony with his long blond hair and David Cassidy good looks, and me with my Joe Cocker hair and chin, but we weren't aimless and carefree. We had a plan. Not so long ago we were two gas fitters and an electrician cutting pipes and running cables on building sites in Yorkshire. Now we were on the road to Australia, and about to sample a bit of magic.

Ali's apartment was bare except for a Persian carpet covering half the floor, a room divider, a stereo unit in a wooden surround and a few wall posters of Eastern skylines. Three bearded, long-haired youths were sitting in a corner listening to Ozibisi. Two were rocking and chanting to the rhythm and the third was beating a Tom-Tom drum, eyes closed, in a world of his own. I had heard the album before. It was doing well in England when we left.

Ali was a slimmed down version of Mohammed and even more handsome. His teeth were just as perfect and with his short black hair and blue beard he looked like a barber's shop model. I admired his good looks, but

I didn't fancy him, quickly reminding myself of the good times I'd had with my girlfriends. Ali showed us a trick where he flamboyantly passed a bead from one hand to the other and then asked us to guess which hand it was in. I had seen something similar a couple of years ago when I was down in London for the weekend with a friend. It took place on a street corner on King's Road. A man, looking round suspiciously, pulled a tray out from under a newspaper stand and started sliding three upturned tumblers around, asking passers-by to 'find the lady'. A small crowd gathered and somebody had a go and won a few pounds. It looked easy and one smiling black guy got sucked in, winning every call at first then losing more and more. When he lost £20 in one bet, I went up to him and told him it was a con. The next thing a bloke in the crowd shoved his face into mine and said, 'You've ten bob in your pocket and that's all you'll ever have. Fuck off.'

Now we played pass the bead and Ali rolled a joint. I didn't inhale deeply and nothing happened. I'd managed to avoid smoking dope in Delphi and I was hesitant and a bit sceptical. Tony, who told us he'd smoked many times and taken pills in nightclubs in Manchester, didn't inhale too deeply either, not wanting to rush the hit. But Lol, who was almost as inexperienced as me, sucked on the weed as though it was a Park Drive tipped and when he stood up to go to the hole in the floor, he could hardly walk.

'Me legs are like chuffin lead,' he said and Tony and I laughed as he tried to climb over the edge of the Persian carpet and drag his lower limbs to the toilet.

Mohammed and Ali, foxed by the Yorkshire accent, looked on in confusion at Lol's battle with gravity. The three African lads in the corner were so far into their music that if Lol had stripped naked and back-flipped all the way to the toilet they wouldn't have noticed.

Lol was gone a long time and I went looking for him. I tapped on the toilet door.

'Has tha fon thi legs, yet, Lol?'

There was no response and I tapped again. Then I heard the bolt slide and Lol came out, unsteady, chin on his chest. When we were back sitting cross-legged on the floor, he closed his eyes and I could tell he'd been crying again.

August 2018 - Squires Bike Café, Yorkshire

Friday morning and Squires Bike Café just off the A1 is quiet. By eleven o'clock it will be packed. A few hardy riders are enjoying their bacon sandwiches and coffee outside where the early morning sun catches the picnic benches. I turn in and park the bike well away from any other bike so Tony will see me when he pulls in.

It's been 45 years since we set off to Australia in the VW van. Tony and I have stayed in touch throughout that time even when we both got married and moved away from Barnsley. We've been on many bike rides together during those years – France, Spain, Ireland, Wales, Scotland, and of course England including many trips around our home county of Yorkshire. We always said riding kept us young.

A few bikes come in, mostly solitary, and they park in neat order, the riders casually securing helmets to bike frames and removing ear plugs before ambling into the café for breakfast. In between these sedate arrivals, a red sports bike comes in loud and fast and squeezes into the nearest gap. The young rider flicks down his side-stand and walks away without looking back as though he has just wrestled a bull to the floor. He pulls off his helmet, sticks his mobile to his ear, and strides towards the café laughing into the air. I try to imagine the adventure he is sharing and I have to smile.

I hear the familiar sound of Tony's bike and recognise the Rossi replica helmet as he turns into the café and parks his machine next to mine. Tony takes off his helmet, runs his fingers through his grey hair and pushes up his sunglasses. He looks the part, as always.

'Good ride, Tony?'

'It's a bit chilly for August, old lad,' he says and we shake hands.

We find a quiet table inside the café and I fetch the drinks. Tony warms his hands on the steaming pot of coffee.

'I'm really looking forward to going up to Scotland.'

'Me too,' I say. 'We've never ridden up the west coast. All those beautiful roads through the mountains and the lochs.'

'Let's hope the weather stays good.'

'Did you have a look on Facebook?'

'Yes. Nothing.'

'Well, it'll be good fun searching for him,' I say. 'Any excuse for a long ride.'

'Do you think we'll recognise him, if we find him?'

'Will he recognise us?'

We haven't seen or heard from Lol for over forty years. A few years ago, someone told Tony they thought he'd got married, had a massive heart attack and moved overseas. With this November being the 45th anniversary of the start of our journey, we thought it was about time we found out if Lol was still around and if he was, get together to celebrate the occasion. After a lot of searching, we were told by an old friend that Lol was indeed still alive and had a house in Barnsley and a place in Spain.

A couple of weeks ago I rode over to the Barnsley address we'd been given, intending to make a surprise visit, but no one answered the door. An initially suspicious neighbour, after listening to my story, told me Lol was away. He thought he'd either gone to his place in Spain or he was up in Scotland in a log cabin he rented. It was somewhere north of Ullapool on the coast, he thought. But he wasn't sure.

Now Tony pulls the fat off his bacon and presses his sandwich until the tomato sauce seeps out. One of the staff behind the counter shouts number seventeen and a rider stands up and collects his full breakfast.

'Lol never said much to me when we were travelling,' Tony says. 'I never knew for certain why he went travelling.'

'Me neither. Mind you. I never really knew why you went travelling. I'm not even sure why I went travelling, either. I wasn't sure then and I'm still not sure now. It just seemed the right thing to do.'

We laugh at the freedom and naivety of our youth and the place goes quiet and for a minute I think it's something we said. We look up and everyone's eyes are on two attractive young women in full leathers who have just walked in and are shaking their long hair loose. I look at Tony and he looks at me and both of us sigh. They are about the same age as we were when we set off to Australia.

'When you think about it,' Tony says, 'we didn't talk to each other much at all when we were on the road.'

'We were young lads. Too busy looking for women and adventure.'

2

Where it Began

In the Spring of 1973, my best friend and fellow gas fitting apprentice Trev and I finally finished the two motorbikes we had been building for over a year in our garage and we couldn't wait to take our shiny new machines on a long run to test their reliability. We had talked of riding all the way to France during our three-week holiday to stretch the bikes and our minds. Neither of us had been abroad and the thought of cruising on foreign tarmac excited us.

I'd known Trev since junior school. Both of us failed our eleven-plus and ended up at Longcar Central School and then joined the Gas Board together. Trev was a wiry, bony lad and pound for pound the strongest kid I ever knew. He was also mentally tough and I think he got that from his dad. While everyone at senior school was letting their fringe grow long and having a modern square cut at the back, Trev would be called in off the streets by his dad every second Sunday and given a brutally short haircut. I think that's what turned Trev into a rebel. When he left school, he grew his hair long and if there had been a Hell's Angel's chapter in Barnsley, he would have been president.

Our motorbikes were choppers with extended forks and fat back tyres. Mine was blue, a BSA Golden Flash 650 motor in a sprung hub frame. Trev's was black, based on a Triumph 500 Bonneville. On the garage wall for inspiration, we had the iconic Easy Rider poster showing Peter Fonda and Dennis Hopper cruising the American highway on their choppers.

The finished bikes felt good. We had test ridden them over short distances, mainly to Sheffield and back, me in my green beret, Trev in his stars and stripes bandana. We once set off to Scarborough but only got as far as Malton because it started to rain and we didn't want to get our shiny bikes wet.

Our days in the garage fine-tuning the bikes were full of excitement and the planned trip to France was drawing near. Then along came Lol.

Lol was a gas fitter at the same depot as Trev and me, three years older at twenty-four, and fully qualified. He never said much to anybody in the yard, eager to get out and earn his bonus, often picking up his job sheet in silence and driving away while the rest of us stood around chatting. And he had a reputation for looking after number one. We'd all been told about the time he was working as an apprentice to an old fitter and he'd been sent to the fish shop to get fish and chips for them both. When he came back, he said to the old guy, 'Bad news. I dropped your bag,' and he handed over a broken bit of fish and a few scruffy chips. And the fitter didn't even get a refund.

I only worked with Lol once. I was his apprentice for the day. When I left a matchstick in his tin of flux (we used a spent match to paste the flux onto the fittings), he told me he'd warned his last apprentice that the next time anybody did that he would punch them. I thought that was a bit out of order, and not being one to back down, I said it's a good job it was me, then.

Lol had been engaged to his fiancée for two years. A date had been set for the wedding and in anticipation of a homely life together he had taken out a mortgage on a newly-built semi-detached bungalow in a quiet cul-de-sac within walking distance of the gas depot. Twenty-four years old and ready to settle down for ever. Then we heard his fiancée had run away with the manager of a big store in town. Lol never said anything but you could tell he was devastated. He had a pale complexion to start with and now it was like lard. In a man's world of blowlamps, grease, pipes and hammers, nobody talked to him about his loss or asked him how he was feeling.

No doubt in need of friendship, Lol teamed up with me and Trev, taking us in his little red Hillman Imp to the nightclubs in Wakefield and Sheffield, and it was on one of those nights out when he put his head in his hands and started crying. I could see his back heaving and I put my arm around his shoulder. He never spoke a word.

One day, Lol said he wanted to get away from everything and he asked if he could follow Trev and me to France in his Hillman Imp. The more the three of us talked about travelling abroad, the more the idea developed into a bigger adventure. I had read how a journalist in London, sick of the daily routine of work, planned to ride a motorbike to India and beyond. The idea excited me. Work as much overtime as I could, save every penny, pack in my job and go east. I felt as though I'd grown wings, poised on the edge of the white cliffs of Dover ready to soar into the sky. We kept dreaming and bought a map of the world. We read motorbike magazines and travel magazines and we learned about Marco Polo and the Hippie Trail to Nepal.

One night we took our folding camp beds over to Lol's unfurnished bungalow, now with a sold sign hammered into the little front lawn, and after a few cans of lager and countless replays of Silver Machine by Hawkwind, our ideas became wilder.

'Why not head for Australia or New Zealand?' Lol said. 'Go as far as we can to t'other side of the world.'

I said, 'Now that sounds like fun. And then come back t'other way so we'd have gone all the way round the world. It'd be a right adventure.' I turned to Trev. 'We could get a new motorbike each, all the same model, something like a Honda 250 twin,' I was nodding to Trev, trying to encourage him. 'They're cheap and reliable and easy to handle. And we could stay on camp sites to save money.'

Trev said he wasn't keen on that idea. He didn't want to go on a little Japanese 250 twin. Lol said he would prefer to go by car. We went quiet.

I said, 'Okay then. What about cycling to Australia?'

Lol said, 'Cycling?' and Trev wouldn't even look at me.

'We could use trains and boats and buses where we had to,' I said. 'Hitchhike a lift on the back of lorries if necessary. It'd be a cheap option. I've read about people doing it on their Jack so I'm sure the three of us could do it together.'

Lol, not known for undertaking physical exercise, pulled out his AA Road Map of Great Britain 1973 from under his camp bed and using his thumb and index finger as a divider, worked his way slowly south.

'Mmm,' he said after double-checking the distance. 'It'd tek us two bloody weeks to get to Dover.'

We all went quiet again. I was fit and liked exercise but I also wanted to get to Australia while I was still young.

Lol said, 'How about buying a campervan, then? No hotel bills. Share the driving.'

I thought it was a great option, not as exciting as going by motorbike, but I could see the van taking us to places a motorbike couldn't reach. Trev didn't like the idea. I knew it was because his heart was set on riding his Triumph. He couldn't drive and had no intention of learning. He would be a mere passenger, and Trev wasn't a passenger. We saw less and less of Trev and when he left the gas board to set up his own business, he went his own way.

So, now it was just me and Lol and we spent hours in his bungalow planning to pack it all in to go travelling round the world. Then one night in the King George Hotel in Barnsley, a new face came on the scene. A guy called Tony, somebody neither of us had met before, came up and said he'd heard we were planning to go to Australia in a camper van before the end of the year. It was then that I realised our adventure was no longer a dream, a wish, a game. It was real. With consequences.

'Travelling is in my blood,' Tony said. 'I wouldn't mind joining you if there's room in your van.'

Tony was twenty-one, the same age as me, and he lived with his parents in a little detached bungalow in Ward Green, a posh estate on the outskirts of town. He was a fresh-faced guy, an electrician working for a small electrical company where his dad was the foreman, and he had long blond hair and a baby-smooth chin. He was an only child, gentle and kind, and easy to get on with.

Tony said, 'I've been abroad quite a few times. When I was a child, I went to Majorca every year with my mom and dad.'

Instead of mam he said mom.

'And I went to Spain for a period last year with another guy. We worked in a bar for three months.'

When he said he had recently started seeing a new girlfriend, Gloria (apparently, they'd had eyes on each other for years), we wondered why he was so keen to travel abroad again. My hunch was that he was testing his new relationship. Or maybe he thought he could do better, which was hard to believe once we met Gloria.

On the outside, Tony was neither ambitious nor flash but he had a quiet love of sports cars and he talked about film stars and rock stars as though he knew them personally. I thought perhaps he was hoping to find fame and fortune on the road. Whatever the reason, his motivation seemed more complicated than Lol's simple desire to escape the misery of rejection. Tony seemed genuine. We liked his easy-going manner and he became traveller number three.

I wasn't sure what was motivating me to travel. Like Tony, I had a girlfriend. Well, a part time girlfriend. Her name was Jean. She worked in the office at the water board in Wakefield. She dressed like a hippie and had the face of a model but we weren't in love. I didn't need to test our relationship and unlike Lol, I wouldn't have been heartbroken if she'd run off with someone else, and neither would she if it was me doing the running off. We had great times in bed together but both of us were looking elsewhere for love.

I couldn't think of a clear and simple reason why I wanted to look over the wall around my home town but a few thoughts kept surfacing in my head, thoughts a bit too heavy to share with two relative strangers.

The first was around illness. I was a good footballer. I'd made the Barnsley Boys Under 15 squad when just fourteen, having captained the Under 11's, and signed schoolboy forms with the club. Then just weeks before my fifteenth birthday, I was diagnosed with rheumatic fever. I knew it was serious when my mother started crying and I remember thinking as the ambulance took me to hospital, if those bells go off, I'm done for. The cardiologist mentioned a heart murmur and I was confined to bed for three weeks, the first two flat on my back, no pillows, fed by nurses. I was in hospital for five weeks in total and the straightforward path to professional football that I'd taken for granted looked to have come to an end. While in hospital, I watched, through the window opposite my bed, a pair of magpies flying in and out of their nest high up in a big ash tree. Each time they flew away, I went with them. Their freedom and sense of purpose put things in perspective. Nature is a great leveller and I've always felt part of it. I thought come on. It's no use moping around. Get out and get on with it. The sky is big.

The second thought was to do with the film Kes. The film was adapted from the book, A Kestrel for a Knave, by northern writer Barry Hines, and it was filmed in Barnsley. It shone a light on the education of kids like me. It was an international success and I thought if Kes can travel around the world, what's stopping me?

The third was to do with the subservience I saw at work. I remember one example in my first year as an apprentice. I was carrying old Tom Smith's tool bag over my shoulder on our way back to the depot to pick up a roll of lead pipe. Tom was coming up for retirement after fifty years at the company. We'd bought our beef sandwiches ready for our break and I was looking forward to meeting up with my fellow apprentices back at the yard for a chat and a quick game of cards. We were about a mile and a half from the depot when Tom stopped dead and looked at his watch.

'It's twelve o'clock,' he said. 'Dinner time,' and he sat on the wall overlooking the canal and bit into his sandwich.

'You're joking, Tom,' I said. 'We're only ten minutes off the yard.'

'Dun't matter. Twelve o'clock is dinner time. I'm not going to start breaking the rules now.'

Tom died three months after retiring.

The final thought that wouldn't go away had been in the background for a few years and was to do with the way my parents lived. Sometimes I used to look down on my dad, watching him race the pigeons he kept behind the Royal Arms Hotel every Sunday morning no matter what. Training them every day in between shifts at the pit and a pint in the pub, letting them out to fly, bringing them back down to feed, locking them up again.

Pit, pigeons, pub. It seemed a waste of life. My mother had to force him to take her out to the pictures for a night off, or persuade him to sit with other couples in the pub lounge instead of leaving her on her own while he played dominoes with his mates in the bar. My mother, like a lot of miners' wives, learned to manage and it was a struggle. The way my parents coped with their hardworking lives had a big effect on me. There was a good chance the world would close in on me too before long and I thought better get out while you can before the routine of survival takes over.

Initially we considered buying a Land Rover Defender to take us on our adventure. If we were going to do some serious overlanding, we wanted to look like serious overlanders. But we were advised that a Defender would be uncomfortable on a long journey and would need constant maintenance. We calculated our likely mileage and the terrain we would encounter and opted for a VW camper van. We'd read how these vehicles were loved by travellers around the world and we would never be far from a VW garage. That weekend we saw a two-year old VW converted van advertised in the Sheffield Star for nine hundred pounds ono. The van looked good under the street lights and when the owner invited us in to his kitchen to talk through the documents and history, he sounded genuine. We agreed to buy the van pending an AA inspection. The owner said he couldn't guarantee holding on to it and if someone else came up with the money in the meantime he would have to let it go. The three of us went outside to discuss the purchase. It was our first big decision and it only took a minute.

We were excited about the van and proud of the way we had worked together to complete the purchase. I could just about afford my three hundred pounds share providing I worked overtime for the next few weeks and didn't go out. My mam said if I was short, she had a few pounds spare in the little brass tin she kept in the top kitchen cupboard out of sight of my dad. But I could never borrow anything from my mam. I knew it would take her months to build the savings back up again, and maybe years, if the rumours were true and the miners were getting ready to strike for a decent pay rise.

I could have sold my motorbike but I'd only just finished it and hardly had the chance to take it anywhere. Ken, a fellow gas fitter, offered to look after it for me in his garage while I was away and said he might consider buying it off me if ever I was desperate. I would have to be desperate. One day, I thought, if I ever come back home, that bike might take me on another big adventure.

Ken was a good friend of mine. He went to Holgate Grammar School and joined the Gas Board as an apprentice the same year as me. I didn't know Ken before the gas days although it's possible we would have seen each other as we walked down Racecommon Road to the bus station from our separate schools, the noisy Longcar lot on the left of the road, the aloof grammar school lot on the right.

Ken was a few months older than me and first to get a car, a bright yellow Ford Anglia with wide wheels, spotlights, and leatherette sports steering wheel. We would drive to Blackpool and Scarborough and have some great fun chatting up the girls and finding out who we were. Ken was known for being tight with his money and for keeping his head down at the first sniff of trouble. One night we were in the Palatine pub in Blackpool and there was a fight and somebody was arrested. Gang members of the guy arrested went round every table asking customers to give any spare change they had to help get their friend out of jail. I asked no questions and gave them the money to avoid having my head kicked in. To my amazement Ken pretended to look through his pockets and then told the big Scottish guy holding out his hand that he had no change. We refer to that night as the moment Ken's avarice overcame his cowardice.

When Ken got married, our lives took a different path. I used to rib him about settling down. Having a mortgage around his neck for the next twenty-five years. Keeping the front lawn neat and tidy. Making sure his car was as expensive as the neighbour's. Washing it on the drive every Sunday morning. It was strange in a way. Ken ached to go travelling around the world and I had a longing to find the right girl and settle down.

There were no side windows in the van. It had a two-ring gas cooker, a bed for two small adults (two inches of foam on top of a sheet of plywood above the rear engine), and a five-gallon water carrier. Tony built and fitted a rack that covered the whole roof and he installed an 8-track stereo into the dashboard. I fitted a third seat in between the two front seats and Lol's uncle, a mechanic, fitted an engine cut-out security switch under the driver's seat. We bought two jerrycans for spare fuel and a folding spade from the Army Stores on Eldon Street and Tony fastened two spare wheels and tyres on to the roof rack. A small selection of spare parts and a first aid kit together with one of my mother's old carving knives, which we kept under the middle seat for self-defence, completed the van preparation.

And finally, the route and the leaving date were agreed. We will follow in the footsteps of Marco Polo and head for Nepal before sailing to Australia from India, leaving Barnsley on Wednesday 28 November. We worked out how much it would cost in fuel and food to get to India, assuming it would take us around four months. Then from India we hope to find a merchant ship and work our passage across the Indian Ocean to Australia. The AA provided us with an itinerary, including a warning to drive through

Afghanistan as quickly as possible, and they wished us the very best of luck.

Tony quit the electrical firm where he worked, and Lol and I handed in our notice at the Gas Board, doing our best to show loyalty in case we ever wanted our jobs back. On our last day at work, the office staff and gas fitters pinned a map of the world to the noticeboard in the yard so they could keep a track of our journey and we promised to send them a postcard from every country we visited.

The week before our departure date, we bought the *Barnsley Chronicle* and laughed with embarrassment and pride at the photograph showing the three of us thumbs up and smiling in our VW converted van. The headline read:

Overland to Australia

Marco Polo's route across Europe will be retraced over the next six months - by three Barnsley men in a converted van. They plan to travel overland to Australia.

They hope to begin their journey on Wednesday. From France, they will thread their way through Europe and into Turkey as far as India or Nepal before taking the ship to Australia.

They plan to stay there for about a year and if they like the country may settle there.

If they decide to come home, they will turn the journey into a round-the-world trip by coming back through America.

Why Australia? 'We heard so much about the place,' Mike said. 'We went through a lot of ideas and came up with this one. We aren't going specifically to Australia. We want to go as far as we can and see as much as we can along the way.'

We looked at each other and Lol said, 'No going back now, lads.'

*

On the morning of 28 November, I packed the tins of beans, packets of dried soup, bottles of shampoo and toilet rolls into the cupboard above the two gas rings, double-checked the roof rack security ropes holding down the spare wheels, the jerrycans and the folding spade, and went back inside to collect my flying jacket.

'Right,' I said. 'That's it. Time to go.'

My mother wouldn't let me linger in the front doorway to say goodbye. She was a superstitious woman, unlike my dad (except when it came to having the same numbers every week on his Vernons pools). My mother always said a door was a symbol of mystery, fortune or danger to come. Or the end of something. To stand in the doorway was to loiter in the in-between world. Not a good place, she said. I didn't believe half of it and I know my dad thought the only reason not to hang around at the front door was to keep the cold out. I kept moving and everyone followed me up the garden path, my mother, dad, two brothers, David and Jonathan, and two sisters, Sandra and Anne. We hugged and cried and said goodbye, and a few of the neighbours looked on from their front gates, an honour usually reserved for funerals. Jonathan was only three, a late surprise for my parents, and saying goodbye nearly broke my heart. I could justify leaving home to everybody except him.

I left the estate and drove to the other side of town to pick up Tony. Everyone there had been crying, as well. His mother and dad looked as though they couldn't believe their only child was leaving to go to Australia. Tony's girlfriend, Gloria, hugged him and kissed him goodbye and through tears asked me to make sure he ate well.

The excitement of finally setting off to the other side of the world took over and by the time we reached Lol's house we were singing in carefree harmony to Crosby, Stills, Nash and Young, Teach Your Children.

I parked the van right outside Lol's parents' kitchen window and we were about to jump out and share the goodbyes when the front door opened and Lol came out carrying his little beige travel bag. He shut the door behind him and his head was down. We could see his mother and dad through the window but they didn't look up from their breakfast. They didn't even wave him off when we drove away. It was just as though he was setting off to work. He looked sloughed at the cold send-off, on the verge of crying, but he didn't say anything and neither did we. He put his bag in the back of the van, climbed into the middle seat and said, 'Let's get off, then.'

August 2018 - Squires Biker Cafe

'Shall we get off, then? Scotland here we come.'

Tony nods and we both automatically check our mobiles. Nothing urgent. I drink the last of my tea and we say cheers to the lasses behind the counter.

'I'll just nip to the loo,' I say.

'I'll be outside.'

'I don't know how you manage to ride with a belly-full of coffee in your bladder.'

'It's never bothered me.'

'I thought it might be prostate trouble but I've had it checked. It's a nuisance. I can't go two hours on the bike now without having to stop.'

'Did you have the finger up the old…?' Tony doesn't finish his sentence. He would never say arse or anything that sounded like swearing, especially in a busy café where a woman might overhear. Instead, he gestures to show where the doctor's middle finger would go and I look round in case somebody is watching and wondering what we are talking about.

'Yeah,' I say. 'Just like that.'

Outside and the sun is stronger now but the air is still chilly. Bikers are arriving every few minutes and the parking area is beginning to glisten with chrome and colour. Tony sees me rubbing sun tan lotion on my nose and cheeks.

'What's that tha putting on all over thi kite?'

Even though both of us left Barnsley more than twenty years ago, we always slip into the dialect when we disagree on something. It's a filter, softening the words, stopping a difference of opinion escalating into an argument.

'Sun screen,' I say. 'I'm hoping we're going to get plenty of sun.'

'I don't bother with anything like that,' Tony says pulling on his balaclava. 'Or ear plugs.'

'I've had skin cancer. I don't want another one.'

I told him about my skin the last time we went out for a ride but it can't have registered. I can only see his eyes and I know he is working on a reply.

'It's too late for that now, old lad,' he says.

I smile and put the sun screen away. I've brought enough for both of us. He'll probably ask me for some later if it gets hot.

'Are you leading,' I say. 'Or do you want me to go first?'

'Go for it.'

Tony pulls on his helmet. I push my ear plugs in and put my hand on his padded shoulder.

'Same as usual. If we get split up, I'll pull in and ring your mobile.'

We are always getting split up, especially when I'm the lead rider. Busy roundabouts are our speciality. Tony has all the racing gear and his bike looks mean with its orange wheels but he's not the sharpest at roundabouts. We ride out of the cafe and for the first few miles we hardly see a car. There are plenty of bikers, nodding in solidarity, heading to the café like bees to a hive. A couple of bikes overtake us and I wonder if it's the two young women we saw in the café. Something to talk about when we next stop.

3

Into Europe

1-7 December 1973

It had been a long day motoring through France and across the German border. Miss Collins, my long-suffering French teacher at school, had been right when she said Frenchmen wore berets and rode bicycles, though if ever I saw her again, and assuming she didn't run away screaming, I'd let her know the cycles now have little motors driving them.

It was getting cold in Europe. Last night in Nancy the temperature dropped so low the shampoo bottles froze solid and the van's ceiling was decorated with ice nodules from our breath. We thought there would be sunshine everywhere once we left England and none of us had brought warm clothing apart from a flying jacket each. The only way to survive the cold night had been to fasten the three sleeping bags together and share body heat. It had also been a good way to get to know each other. We still hadn't probed each other's reasons for leaving home to travel around the world. Maybe we had consciously avoided discussing the topic, scared by the thought of living so close together in a van for months, hoping our own personal motivation would keep us united all the way to Australia.

The mental effort involved in driving on the right and handling foreign money, together with the tension built up over the last few weeks as we prepared to leave our homes and secure jobs behind, had tired us out. When we arrived in Baden-Baden late in the afternoon on Saturday 1 December, we found out that life was about to get even more stressful. There were posters on every lamp post and traffic lights warning drivers of a twenty-four-hour driving ban starting at three o'clock on Sunday morning. It was, according to the traffic police we quizzed, due to the oil crisis.

We had read in the papers back home about the Arab oil embargo and the potential for petrol shortages. OPEC (Organisation of Arab Petroleum Exporting Countries) had threatened the nations they saw as supporting Israel during the Yom Kippur war, which ended a month before we set off. It looked as though only the United States of America, the United Kingdom, the Netherlands, Canada and possibly Japan would be affected so we hadn't taken much notice. The crisis must have worsened and we wondered how many other twenty-four-hour driving bans we might come across during the rest of our journey.

The ban meant we were not allowed to drive until three o'clock on Monday morning. It was going to be a long, cold Sunday, especially with no heater in the van. As I sat in the driver's seat, the candle flickering on the cooker top in the fast-fading afternoon light, I could see Lol lying on the bed in his flying jacket resting his eyes and as usual rubbing his feet together with the accuracy of a metronome. I nudged Tony and we shook our heads at his old-man's habits. Lol's ginger beard was getting thicker and over the last few days he seemed to have aged, or maybe it was the cold, artificial light.

To kill time and keep warm during our enforced delay we sat at a table in the same café for nearly the whole of Sunday, spending three precious marks. When the café closed at eight o'clock, we zipped up our jackets and went straight across the road into a cosy hotel. We bought one coke each, sat in a corner as far away as possible from the bar and kept our heads down. By midnight, we were the only customers. We knew the manager and staff were talking about us and eventually their stares made us zip up our jackets again and leave. On our way out I gave the unresponsive manager a cheery bonsoir and Lol added ta-ta for na. I don't think the staff understood or appreciated the rhyming joke.

Outside it was freezing cold and we had to knock the snow off the van doors before we could open them. We suffered the cold for an hour, wearing our sleeping bags and every piece of clothing we owned.

Lol said, 'This is getting dangerous,' and he wrapped a towel around his head. There was never a crease in Lol's clothes where there shouldn't have been a crease and always one where there should have been and even the towel looked tidy.

We were too cold to laugh at his home-made turban and when it got to half past one, feeling light-headed and numb, we decided to start the engine and turn on the heater. If we were caught by the fuel police, we would plead ignorance. I turned the ignition key and the engine spun freely but wouldn't start.

'What's wrong with this thing?' I said. 'It must be the cold. It's got to the engine.'

Tony said, 'Let me have a go.'

We swapped seats, glad to be moving our limbs. Tony turned the key and the engine spun freely for a minute but there was still no life.

'Strange,' he said. Tony never swore.

Lol said, 'Tha might have flooded it. Let me have a go.'

We all swapped seats again and Lol sniffed the air for petrol. After a few minutes of silence and praying, he turned the key. Nothing.

We kept trying, each of us using our own technique, and it was two o'clock before I realised I'd left the engine security cut-out switch turned on, the one Lol's uncle had fitted under the driver's seat. By that time the battery was dead.

When it finally got to three o'clock, legal drive time, we took turns to push the van in an attempt to bump start the engine. We tried for an hour, the wheels skidding in the snow, and were flagging in the sub-zero conditions when a German youth in an Audi saloon appeared out of the night and gave us a tow. Eventually the van started and we shook his hand so hard he had to ask us to let go.

Driving so early in the morning, deep in the white Black Forest, sitting side by side, wrapped in our warm flying jackets, felt like being in a tiny aeroplane. For mile after quiet mile, we never saw another vehicle and our tyres rolled over the snow without a sound. The light from our headlights, dispersed by the whiteness, sharpened the night and made the trees look as hard as fossils.

We were marvelling at the silence and serenity when we came across a Mercedes stuck in a ditch and two people at the roadside looking on helplessly. The car's headlights were still on and steaming in the falling snow. We left our engine running and headlights on dip to illuminate the scene and could see that one of the rear wheels of the Mercedes had spun itself deep into the ditch, spraying the surrounding snow with soil and grass. There was blood on the driver's chin and the snow at his feet was spotted red. Both he and his female passenger were wrapped in heavy fur coats and smelled of alcohol.

There was no need for an explanation, a request for help, or a translation. We attached one end of our tow rope to the rear of the Mercedes, the other end to the rear of the van, and with Tony driving, and me and Lol, and to a lesser extent, the injured driver, pushing hard against the back of the van, we pulled the Mercedes out of the ditch and back on to the road. The driver said, 'Thank you boys, thank you boys, thank you boys. You are Great British people,' and he pressed ten German marks into my hand. We remembered the young German Audi driver and thought favour repaid.

*

I fell asleep in the back of the van while Tony was driving and woke up in Zurich, apparently having missed some great scenery and lots of young women. Dog tired, cold and ready for a bit of comfort we booked into the Bergidyll hotel in Andermatt and had a glorious, relaxing hot bath.

When I opened my eyes the next morning, snug and warm in the soft bed, with more than enough room to spread-eagle my six-foot frame, I realised just how cramped and hard it had been sleeping on the board above the engine at the back of the van that we lovingly called a bed for three. Lol was still fast asleep in his bed, obviously enjoying the luxury as much as me, and it took a few gentle shoves to stir him.

Tony said, 'Be careful. You know what he can be like when he wakes up.'

It was good advice. For all three of us, being woken by someone other than your girlfriend or your mam was an unknown experience and the result was unpredictable. It was an early lesson and we learned quickly.

We strolled down for breakfast, no cooking for us this morning, and had coffee and bread rolls with jam. Heaven. I stole a packet of jam for later and we tipped the waiters to get rid of the loose change weighing down Lol's kitty bag.

Tony said, 'How are we doing for money, Lol?'

'All right, as long as we dun't stay in hotels like this again.'

'Can't we invest in some more foam for that bed, then?' I said. 'It's killing me.'

Lol said, 'Put some more air in t'back tyres.'

We burst into laughter, not so much at the joke, more at the pleasure of seeing Lol step out from under the dark cloud that had been hanging over him for months.

We posted letters and cards home, including a card to the gas fitters and staff at the yard, and set off, singing with excitement. Well, Tony and I were singing. Lol doesn't sing. He taps his thighs with his thumbs and you have to know what to look for otherwise you'd miss it. But I could tell he was happy. We were all happy. Italy was next which meant we were a twelfth of the way to Australia.

The good mood didn't last long. We passed a big red road sign saying Gotthard Pass was closed for the winter. Tony checked the map while I tried to get more news from a nearby tourist information centre. Lol calculated the potential cost of the diversion and said we had no choice but to catch the train ferry through the Alps.

What an experience it was. Belted up in the locked van, strapped to the deck of an open trailer, in the dark tunnel surrounded by spooky sounds, we were like little kids on a ghost train. The ride lasted twenty minutes and cost twenty-six Swiss francs. We dropped through four thousand feet of beautiful snowclad mountainside and the sun burst through the clouds for the first time since setting off from Barnsley. The train ferry was expensive but we agreed it had been worth every franc just to witness the natural glory.

*

The needle on the fuel gauge was close to red as we drove through the Italian border and we stopped to fill up at the first petrol station we came across. The signage was difficult to read and we still hadn't worked out whether benzine was diesel or petrol or a general term for fuel. Lol used his calculator and concluded that two-star petrol was around twenty pence a gallon. The wide boy on the pumps filled our tank and then tried to con us out of a thousand lira. Although it was only a few pence, it was a good job he didn't argue because Lol had one of those cold looks on his face and I could see him pinning the attendant against the pumps.

On the road to Rapallo, we saw a family of peasants looking weather-beaten and happy collecting wood on a remote mountain side. I wondered what the Italians would do without wood. It's used everywhere and anywhere.

Many of the villages and small towns we passed through were no better than slums, mostly drab pink and blue blocks of functional flats with cheerless washing strung across the narrow gap between them. In contrast, the roadway constructions through the mountains were fantastic feats of engineering and looked incredible even set against the natural beauty of the mountain slopes. One bridge appeared to have collapsed and been abandoned partway through construction. I wondered who was paying for it.

Outside the railway station in Rapallo, Lol cooked beans and eggs and grilled the meat we had bought last night in Andermatt. The beans and meat were frozen solid, as was the water inside and outside the van. It was Lol's last shift as chef. We had decided to share the time-consuming cooking duties between the three of us from now on. We also agreed who would take on the other main duties based on our preferences and skills. I am to be in charge of van maintenance, Tony is to take care of route planning, and Lol will look after the finances.

A quick, cold walk through the nearby streets confirmed there were no women around and we suspected it would be even worse at night. We returned to the freezing van, bored and in need of shelter. Lol got grease on his cardigan when he leaned against the van's sliding door mechanism, and he wasn't happy. It was his best cardigan, the one he kept neatly folded under his pillow. He told us it had been a birthday present from his ex-fiancée during better times. Tony and I still laughed.

I filled the kettle from a tap outside the railway station but the water smelled so bad we decided, for the first time, to use the water purifying tablets we'd got from the Army Stores on Eldon Street back home. The tea tasted better for the sterilization but to be on the safe side I took two penicillin tablets. I had a few left over after recently completing five years of antibiotic treatment for rheumatic fever. I almost wished the doctor had prescribed another year's worth. It felt a bit scary not having to take any more after taking one a day for all those years.

We arrived in Venice early evening and after driving around for an hour we found somewhere safe by the sea about half a mile from the centre and parked up for the night. Venice looked a little less spectacular than I had imagined. But this was the real thing. I couldn't wait to see the place in daylight. Tony lit the candles and we wrapped ourselves in our sleeping bags. We talked of home, though not longingly, and Lol had a Benson and Hedges and Tony dragged on a Peter Stuyvesant menthol. I'd only started smoking a few months ago and managed to resist the temptation to join them.

Tony was missing Gloria. I could tell because he kept playing Carol King and James Taylor records about lost love. Lol was as steady as ever although lately he had been doing silly little things like using the wrong key for the van.

Must write to Jean. And to Trev. Hope he's getting out on his Triumph. Hope Ken is looking after my BSA chopper bike and not revving the hell out of the newly reconditioned engine. Tired. Didn't think it would be this cold. Worse than back home. And everyone looks so poor. Would rather travel by night and sightsee by day but better not say anything – getting on okay. Only argued a couple of times and smoothed things over instantly. Think we're going to succeed. Yugoslavia tomorrow. Wonder what's in store for us. Happy birthday Dad.

I woke up at half past ten and didn't rise till noon and only then because Tony made us all a cup of tea. All of us slept well. We must be getting used to the cold, cramped bed. I told Lol and Tony it was all right for them. I had to get used to sleeping with my feet sticking over the edge of the plywood.

Through the van window, Venice looked just as drab and damp as it did when we arrived last night. After our egg and beans, we kicked a ball about on a stretch of derelict land. Tony surprised me. He was quick and had decent ball control for a non-player. Lol couldn't even stop the ball and we nearly lost it twice to the sea. I felt tired after only ten minutes. It doesn't take long to get out of condition.

We walked through the drizzle into the centre of the city and saw lots of students merrily going their way. All around, happy young Americans danced and ran and jumped in the puddles. They must see more than I see. To me it was dirty and smelly with uncared for buildings butt up against each other in stagnant water. Most of the buildings looked as though they were dying with only the ground floors surviving as brightly decorated shops. There was almost as much rubbish floating around the waterways as there was on the canal at the bottom of Old Mill Lane in Barnsley. But at least there was no sunken, rotting barge and the glossy gondolas looked well-cared for.

In St Mark's Square, pigeons landed on tourists, pigeons squatted, and pigeons fluffed their feathers in the cold. I couldn't understand how a country could allow a once beautiful city to degenerate into a grey, tired and sorrowful mess. Lol was even less impressed. Tony wasn't as critical and he kept talking about the light and the colour. When he said he had gone to art college straight after school we teased him about setting up his easel, putting on his beret, and sizing up the buildings with his thumb and finger. He laughed and made fun of himself but we could see he was a little embarrassed and we soon stopped.

We met a guy from London on his way back from India with his Japanese girlfriend. I don't know what they had been up to but he looked knackered. He wore a shabby, off-white linen suit, a gold earring, and his blonde hair was ragged and sun-bleached. The girl was dressed in faded, patched denim jacket and jeans and she wore a leather Bronco hat.

We told them we were on our way to Australia.

'Spend some time in India, man,' the guy said. 'It's far out. We've been freaking out there for three years.'

The Japanese girl crinkled her eyes and smiled.

'You'll fall in love with the country,' she said.

Tony asked them where they were going.

The guy said, 'England, eventually. We're in no rush, are we babe? It'll take as long as it takes. All you need is love, man.'

They gave us the peace sign and wandered off.

Tony said, 'How cool are they?'

'Super cool,' I said. 'Just floating around waiting for something to happen.'

Lol said, 'They'll not get far bart money.'

We got lost a few times and were directed by smiling girls with busy arms and strange words. When hunger forced us back to the van, we found an Aussie VW campervan parked next to us. Their side door was open and we could see three girls and one guy packing away their kettle and books. We said hello and smiled. They were from Australia, on their way to England.

'Wow,' I said. 'That really is cool. We're doing the same journey only the other way round. You're going that way. We're going that way.' I tried to point east and west. I think I got my directions wrong but they got the drift.

We talked about Australia and England and they warned us to be prepared for the cold in Yugoslavia and Greece.

The guy said, 'You think you get cold weather in England. Just wait until you get to Yugoslavia, mate.'

The van set off and we watched the guy and the three girl passengers wave goodbye out of the window. I expected Lol to say something and I didn't have to wait long.

'Lucky bastard,' he said and we laughed at his miserable face.

Tony said, 'No offence, gents, but I think I've picked the wrong van.'

*

For once, we sailed straight through customs and arrived in Yugoslavia at half past eight in the evening, knackered. The four Aussies had advised against taking out insurance or buying petrol coupons. Too expensive, they said. Lol reckoned we had saved at least fifteen pounds.

We parked in Rijeka close to the harbour wall where yachts and boats were moored just yards away. We had dinner in the front seats, and watched the rocking boats and pedestrians passing by. Tony went to bed and I went for a walk with Lol. There were plenty of young people around the harbour and in the centre of town, all well behaved and polite, and among the walkers were a few courting couples, which was a good sign. We looked around for a place where they might meet up, perhaps a square or a pub, but there was no sign of a hub. Just as we were thinking of returning to the lonely van, we came across a student commune. At last, lots of girls, plenty of stares and a few smiles. It was noisy. People were talking earnestly in small groups and pairs. Occasionally, there was a loud laugh followed by high hand slapping. We felt like joining in. It was good to be among so many happy people our age.

On our way back to the van we were drawn, like the Bisto Kids, to the smell of hot chestnuts roasting on a mobile brazier on a street corner.

I said, 'I could murder a hot chestnut, Lol. Reminds me of bonfire night.'

'Come on, then. Let's live dangerously. We can just about afford three portions.'

Tony was awake when we got back and I made us all a cup of milk made from Marvel. It was a grand supper.

We woke up the next day to find the van surrounded by dockers' cars. Thankfully they hadn't blocked us in. They must have seen the GB badge and taken sympathy on us. We shopped around for bread and had toast for the first time on our journey. The van smelled of burnt crumbs and hot margarine and we soaked it up.

The road out of Rijeka passed through more beautiful mountains and we looked up in awe. None of us had seen anything like it before. When we saw a poor, old man walking the mountain road alone, we stopped and gave him two cigarettes. He nodded, that was all, and we felt good.

We drove hundreds of miles through a wooded plateau and saw very few people. Passing through Karlovac we saw sturdy bull carts driven by men with identical rugged expressions on identical faces. It felt like we were a hundred years back in time.

The drive along the rough road was tiring but the scenery was so different to anything we had ever seen before that none of us moved from the front seats. With Lol's permission, we treated ourselves to an expensive meal of ham, eggs and beans at a transport café. The drivers and staff were friendly, staring long enough to show interest but not to interfere. I hoped we did the same. In the toilet, I checked my beard. It wasn't as rugged as the whiskers on the drivers' chins but it was coming on.

While Lol was driving, I started reading 'The Thief Who Came to Dinner'. It was an unusual story about a computer expert who was bored by his day job and decided to be a jewellery thief by night. I liked it. If I hadn't chosen to travel, I could have fancied doing that for a bit of adventure.

It was getting dark when we arrived in Beograd and the city looked hard. All the office blocks and tower blocks were lit up with harsh light, and we had to shield our eyes from the oncoming car headlights. We decided to carry on and were pulled up by a traffic cop for turning left when the traffic lights said straight on only. When we realised what we had done we apologised and played the stupid foreigner.

'We from England,' I said. 'Lost.'

The cop shone his torch inside the van and looked at the gear on our roof rack.

'Where are you going?'

'Australia,' Lol said.

Tony gave one of his innocent young boy smiles and said, 'Skopje.'

'Keep on this road. Skopje is straight on.'

I think the cop liked us. Perhaps he was impressed by our adventure. Maybe it was the kind of thing he had always wanted to do. He turned off his torch and stepped back.

'That is fifty dinars in your pockets,' he said. 'Good luck and good-bye.'

I thought it's amazing how such a little act of generosity from someone in authority can cheer you up.

The road out of Beograd was busy at first, well-lit and easy to follow but then as the traffic thinned out the blackness of the countryside made driving dangerous. Somehow, it was always me who ended up driving at night. I wondered if Lol and Tony had bad eyes.

My head was aching by the time we stopped at the small town of Verika Plana, on the Morana river. The place was quiet and we parked up for the night on a patch of rough waste ground under a street light just off the main street.

I slept solid and woke up from a dream where I was being rocked like a baby in somebody's arms. When I opened my eyes, Tony was gently and slowly driving the van off the waste ground. It was eight o'clock and Lol was fast asleep. Locals had gathered around the vehicle, reaching over each other to get a look at us through the windows, and then stepping out of the way at the last minute to let us drive off the grass.

It was cold and snow was still on the ground. We drove a few yards to a motel to get fresh water and we came across three hippies huddled around the rear of their GB plated VW camper van. They had the engine out and were dismantling it on the frozen ground.

Tony said, 'Hi. Are you guys from England?'

He tapped out three cigarettes from his pack of Peter Stuyvesant and handed them round. The hippies must have been freezing but they nodded and lit the cigarettes with steady, oily hands.

'Piston trouble by the looks of it,' one of them said without even a shrug.

I tried to identify the parts on the ground but some were half-buried in the snow. The repair was beyond my mechanical know-how and I kept my mouth shut.

Lol said, 'Good luck,' but they didn't answer.

In a nearby market, peasants were buying and selling goods, moving their varied wares by horse and bull drawn carts. The place was noisy with trading but there was no shouting or aggression despite, or maybe because of, the poverty. The Yugoslavs appear to be bleak, rugged, happy, quiet, hard-working and homely people. Their country looks bleak, rugged, desolate and repetitive.

When we arrived in Skopje in the snow later that dark afternoon, we couldn't understand why all the traffic lights and house lights were turned off. We thought it must have been a local energy saving idea but the streets were almost in total darkness and it looked a dangerous way to save power. It was only when we saw people queuing for kerosene and petrol at every dimly lit garage that we realised there must have been a power cut. As Lol said, we would never make good detectives. Tony checked our map and itinerary and confirmed that our next destination was the town of Bitola near the Greek border.

The roads were remote and our eyes were on the fuel gauge, which had been on reserve for the last twenty miles. Just as we were approaching an isolated, single road village the engine spluttered and jerked to a halt.

'Bugger,' Lol said as he tried to steer the van on to the grass verge.

Tony and I got out and pushed the van off the road.

I said, 'I can't see there being a garage in this one-horse town.'

Tony said, 'I'll get the jerry can off the roof and go and see if I can find some petrol somewhere. Somebody might be kind enough to sell us a gallon.'

'I'll come with you,' I said. 'Are you staying here, Lol? Keep an eye on the van?'

'Can do.'

Tony climbed on to the roof and when he lowered the jerry can to me, he had a slack look on his face like Stan Laurel. The weight of the can caught me by surprise. It was full of fuel. We had carried it all the way from home and forgotten about it.

We drove for hours, the snow-covered mountains all around lit by the moon. It felt like we were in one of those old cowboy films where the outline of Indians appears in silhouette on top of the ridge. As the moon moved through the sky, the landscape changed and began to look like shots of the moon itself, blue and earie, silent and lifeless.

Lol pulled his sleeping bag over his head and fell asleep in the back. I had a long conversation with Tony about girls and life ahead and life past. It felt good to share a few inner thoughts and I realised Tony was a great kid.

August 2018 - To Alston

A caravan has overturned on the A1(M) and we slow down like everybody else as we pass the wreckage. The towing car is still attached and upright. The home on wheels is almost flattened and the carriageway, littered with clothes and domestic leisure goods, looks like the beginnings of a fly-tip. Two Highways Agency men in hi-vis jackets are sweeping the debris on to the hard shoulder and another is throwing sand on to an oil spill. Something else to talk about when we next stop.

The ride should improve once we get to Scotch Corner and turn west towards the lakes. My old knees and fingers are feeling the cold despite thermal underwear and heated grips. Rain clouds have settled in front of the sun and oncoming cars have their headlights on. A few have windscreen wipers going. I switch my lights on and a few seconds later Tony's headlamp lights up my mirrors. The temperature is dropping the further north we ride.

To liven up the ride we turn off the A66 near Barnard Castle and head off on the B6277 for Alston, the highest market town in England. The quiet roads are lovely, if a bit damp, winding and undulating and I'm riding about twenty yards behind Tony. We're doing around thirty miles per hour and I brake gently as we approach a blind bend. Tony doesn't slow down and I can't believe he's going to try to take the bend at that speed. I hold my breath then he sits up, his rear wheel locking, creating a puff of black smoke from his tyre. He misses the turn, rides straight through an open gate and comes to a skidding halt on a farm track. I wait for him in a layby and when he takes off his helmet, he tries to look unperturbed but I can tell from his wavy smile he knows he has been lucky.

'Bloody hell, Tony. Didn't you see the bend sign?'

'No. Missed it. No problem. Did you like my off-road skills? Never looked like coming off.'

'God. If a car had been coming the other way.'

We stop at a café in Alston and I'm still shaking my head. One car, just one car and that would have been the end of Tony.

Opposite the café there is a pub car park and a few motorbikes are parked up, sports bikes and adventure bikes, and a row of expensive looking racing cycles leaning against the pub wall. We take off our helmets, cross the quiet road to the café and by now both of us are laughing at Tony's near-miss. I know that's the end of it. Tony doesn't like analysing mishaps. He just gets on with it. Or that's what he likes you to think.

The café is full and we have to sit on the wall outside in the cool air. The clouds are low and I can feel the remoteness of the town and the altitude. The cyclists chatter and clatter out of the café, clumsy on their heels, and slowly ride off down the narrow street, shoes clicking into pedals.

Tony lights up and blows smoke into the air. I check my mobile.

'We should be over the border by two o'clock if this weather holds out,' I say.

'What's the plan? Up the M74, get past Glasgow before it gets dark, then pull in somewhere for the night?'

'I reckon so. That'll give us a good start for tomorrow.'

'I'll go and get the map,' Tony says and he hobbles and groans across the road to the pub car park. I don't know how he rides that sports bike at his age. He comes back and spreads the map out on top of the wall for us both to see, smoke from the cigarette in his mouth making him squint.

'I fancy riding Fort William to Inverness. It looks a great run,' Tony says flattening the creases. 'Alongside Loch Linnhe, Loch Lochy, and Loch Ness.'

I follow his finger along the route and waft the smoke away from my face.

'And then across country to Ullapool via Loch Lol,' I say. I'm sure Tony looks for a Loch Lol but then he stubs out his cigarette and smiles.

'We've more chance of seeing the Loch Ness Monster than we have of finding Lol,' he says.

We turn and watch a couple of motorbikes appear over the hill and stop outside the café. They park up and inspect the new wear on the outer edge of their tyres. We get a nod from them as they enter the café and Tony lights up another cigarette. He must still be thinking about the bend he miscalculated. A post office van pulls into the pub car park and the driver delivers a bunch of mail.

'When you think back, Tony. All the air mail we must have sent and received when we were on the road.'

'I know. Dozens and dozens. I bet we kept the post office in business. Funny. I don't remember Lol sending or getting many letters.'

'I don't think he did,' I say. 'I think the few letters he got were from his little sister. "Our nip" he used to call her. She must have meant a lot to him.' I shake my head. 'Old Lol.'

'Those letters from home kept me going. I don't know how Lol coped.'

'I know. I feel guilty looking back. We used to spend hours spreading them out on the bed, and then more hours writing back home.'

'We did,' Tony says. 'Hours and hours.'

'Lol must have thought we were showing off. We used to give him some right stick about him not getting many letters. I never thought about the effect it must have been having on him.'

4

Bread, Education, Freedom: Greece

8 December1973 – 7 January 1974

It was nearly three in the morning when we arrived at the Greek border. Each of us was searched and we had to let the officers into the back of the van and go through our stuff. I think they wanted something to do. Either that or we looked suspicious turning up at that time in the morning. The border office was a sleepy little building and the officers were tired but friendly. There was no place to exchange a traveller's cheque and tomorrow is Sunday. We would have to manage on what we had.

After driving all that way under the beautiful blue moon, it was a bit depressing to park up in a small, dark, lifeless village. It was going to be a cold night. I lit the pipe Lol had loaned me and tried to write a letter to Jean. It was hard. Our relationship wasn't designed for correspondence.

We found a hotel-garage next morning and exchanged our last few dinars into Greek money. The old lady in charge gave us thirty drachmas for twenty dinars. We trusted her, having no idea what the exchange rate was, and bought bread from her. The little village turned out to be better than it looked when we arrived in the early hours of the morning and everyone was cheerful and friendly. As we set off, youngsters began scrawling something in the dirt on the sides of the van.

Lol said, 'Look well if they've written piss off back to Barnsley.'

I thought, he's definitely getting funnier.

We stopped in a layby and ate beans and eggs and the sun came out. What a transformation it was. The light was brilliant and we took off our shirts and played soccer in the snow. Passing motorists must have assumed we were mad Englishmen and they pipped their horns and waved.

There were many little villages on the road to Kozani, spaced out and isolated, with religious icons and symbols on the approaching roadside and dogs running wild. One of the villages was overshadowed by a coal mine and it reminded me of Barnsley. Men in old suits were playing cards and drinking coffee in full view behind big windows. Packed single decker buses swayed along the road and pedestrians dodged each other on the busy pavements. Everything was covered in snow except for the road we were on which had solid ridges of ice running from right to left, as rough as a crocodile's back. Hooded crows and magpies scavenged for food.

We were all feeling tired and road sore and when Tony suggested we stop for a break I pulled into a space outside a cafe. The food looked good and we spent two hundred dinars on coffee, ouzo, ham sandwiches, and chocolate cake. Most of the men in the café were fiddling with their beads and I started doing the same with the van keys. It didn't relax me and I got the cigarettes out. I'd smoked more than Tony today and he can be a heavy smoker sometimes. Lol only ever smokes ten a day, no matter where he is or what mood he's in. If you offer him a cigarette outside of his regular time slots, he'll say no thanks.

Three Greek lads sitting at a table opposite came over and joined us. They could speak good English and we told them about our adventure. They were impressed and wanted to know everything about our journey. We felt like brothers and when they left, they paid for our coffees. They were good guys.

Side by side in bed. All is calm. Had daft little arguments today. Got over them quickly, though. Going to try to be more mature. Going to try damn hard. Didn't like the idea of being alone tonight. Unusual for me. Feel a little sad. Could be homesick. Could be the coal mine we passed. Wonder how they are getting on back home. Lol's pipe has made me feel ill.

Up early the next day and off to Larissa past Mount Olympus. Tony read out some interesting facts noted in our AA itinerary. Mount Olympus is the highest mountain in Greece and the legendary home of the Greek gods. It is also a national park. Lol, with a straight face, wondered if any gods lived in Locke Park in Barnsley. Tony looked at me as if to say, is he kidding us? I hadn't got used to Lol's humour yet and I was thinking the same.

As we skirted the mountain, we picked up a weird looking hitch-hiker. He was a tall, big hippie, balding at the front with long straight blonde hair down to his shoulders, and a ginger curly beard and round nose. He wore dark glasses and carried a rucksack that sat high above his broad shoulders, its pockets packed with maps. When he climbed into the back the van's suspension sank an inch.

Tony said, 'How long have you been at the roadside?'

'Four hours,' he said without any hint of frustration or anger.

He was a Canadian, cool and friendly and he spoke in a low and sure manner. We pulled into a layby and made tea and Lol got out the biscuits. The guy had his own cup.

I said, 'Where are you bound for?'

'I'm on my way to Crete,' he said. 'I have a key to a house on a hill owned by a teacher friend of mine from England.'

He was a decent guy and I liked him. Tony joined him in the back and they talked easily and I thought nice one Tony.

We dropped the hitchhiker off in Amfissa and he said he was staying there for a couple of days then catching the bus to Delphi. It started raining and although he didn't look put out, I felt a little sorry for him. I could sense Tony and Lol felt the same way.

I said, 'You can stay with us in the van tonight, if you want.'

'Thanks, guys. But I'm okay. Ride on.'

We parked up in Amfissa and Tony made a dinner of pork, beans, egg and bread followed by biscuits, bread and marmalade. It was another good feast. Tony stayed in the van writing a letter home and I went with Lol for a walk around. It began to rain heavily so we nipped into a bar and had ouzo and a bun. It was cheap and we didn't think Tony would mind.

I'd not spent much time on my own with Lol since setting off and I tried to start up a conversation to find out what he was thinking.

'Considering all the miles we drive every day,' I said, 'I'm not a bit fed up. It's as good as I thought it would be. The scenery changes so much. How about you, Lol?'

'Me arse gets a bit sore,' he said and that was the end of that.

We turned in early as usual, too tired to do anything, and had a talk and a good laugh in the warm bed. The rain sounded like pigeons walking on the van roof.

We woke up late again, still tired from the distance covered yesterday. The rain had stopped and the temperature had dropped. We drove to Itea, a seaside town on the Gulf of Itea, intending to book into the campsite shown on our map but when we got there it was shut for the season. It was disappointing because the little town looked a friendly place with a beautiful beach unaffected by tourism. We drove ten miles around the coast to the next town, Galaxidi, hoping to find a campsite, despite none being shown on our map. The map turned out to be accurate. It was looking like another long afternoon and night in the van on our own in the middle of nowhere and none of us fancied that. We parked up overlooking the deserted bay and ate our eggs and beans in silence.

Lol lit a cigarette and said, 'I'd still rather be sitting here than gas fitting,' and that cheered us up.

We had made up our minds to stay in Greece over Christmas, find somewhere to settle down and write cards home to family and friends. Delphi, about an hour's drive from Galaxidi, looked like a good location and it had a post-restante. After spending so much time in the van we thought we deserved a bit of luxury in Delphi and we tried to book into the Youth Hostel. Unfortunately, with Christmas being so close, the place was full. We were told rooms might become available over the next few days so we settled in a layby nearby and put the washing line out.

We were all feeling a bit home-sick. I'd never been further than London and Lol had only been to the Isle of Man so it seemed reasonable that England felt a long way off to us two. Even Tony, with his childhood holidays abroad and the three months' working experience in Spain, said he felt a bit lonely as well.

On the second day of camping by the roadside we visited the amphitheatre and the temple of Apollo, were caught sneaking under the fence and got kicked out. Outside the gates we met an Australian girl on her own called Heather. She was about twenty-two years old, confident and decent looking even though her front teeth were a bit off-colour. Heather must have had a bit of money because she had flown from England to Italy, hitchhiked all the way to Greece and was planning to fly back to Australia. She tagged on without any concern and joined us in a café in the town centre. Tony and Lol were a bit quiet and I found myself doing most of the talking. I thought well done, lad. It was good to be talking to a girl again. I think she could tell we were counting our drachmas because she shared a piece of appetising cake with us and paid for her own food and coffee.

Heather went back to the youth hostel where she was staying, saying she would come back to the café later. When she'd gone, we talked about her for an hour and a half. Lol fantasised about the three of us having sex with her, Tony said she was okay and he would have talked more to her if he'd not been thinking about Gloria, and I went on about how easy she was to get on with.

Heather came back an hour later with an Australian guy called Ray and we talked about Australia, England, Europe, ouzo and coffee. There was loud Greek music playing in the background and a man was standing on the table behind us singing his heart out. Thankfully, he had a fine voice. The waitress was good-looking, about forty, bulging and sexy. We played cards for a while and talked about life outside our planet. Tony can get a bit serious if you let him – too serious for Heather and Ray by the look on their faces. I came in with a glorious crowning statement regurgitated from the lecturer who took us for General Studies at the building college in Sheffield. I had no idea what it meant but all agreed I was right.

We moved on to the reasons for being on the road and I tried to explain mine. They all thought it was too complicated and I felt a little rocked. Ray said he didn't really know why he was on the road and he didn't think he needed to know. Heather said she was travelling around Europe to visit the countries where her parents and grandparents were born. She said a lot of students in Australia take a year out to travel around Europe before settling down.

'And it's not just students,' Ray said. 'Because Australia's so bloody remote, heaps of teachers and other workers with good jobs take sabbatical leave, sometimes for up to a year. And a lot of them head off into Europe.'

'Do ordinary workers get a chance to take a sabbatical?' I said.

'Providing they've put in the years with the same company, then yes, mate. Anybody can,' he said.

'Although not everybody wants to take time off on reduced pay,' Heather said.

'Now that's what I call a civilised approach to work,' Tony said. 'We ought to have that back in England.'

I said, 'Imagine how much more settled you would be if you knew you could take some time off work for a while to do something different with your life?'

It was good to be talking about travelling and Australia with two Australians and I wished Lol would get more involved. He never said a word.

Back in the van Tony and Lol fought each other through their sleeping bags after Lol said he was no pansy and Tony said he wanted proof. They went for each other hard enough to rip Tony's bag.

Over breakfast, Lol said he would like to go to Athens and see a bit of life. Tony consulted the map and although the city was off our chosen route, we agreed it was near enough to visit for a couple of days. It was raining and miserable when we set off. Tony and Lol shared the driving and I caught up on some sleep in the back to the mournful sound of Neil Young and Leonard Cohen.

Athens' main streets reminded me of London – all retail, food stores, street markets, voices, lights, buildings, faces, clothes, girls, cars. We drove to within a few hundred yards of the Acropolis and parked up for the night. It had been a long drive and we wanted a quiet drink. The bar we picked was perfect and we settled in a corner. Lol took out his pack of cards but as soon as he started dealing, the staff waved their hands and said we weren't allowed to play. They didn't say why and we didn't ask. They were a bit stern but it didn't stop them selling us an expensive bottle of ouzo. The aniseed flavoured spirit warmed us through and with no cards to distract or hide behind we opened up a little.

I said, 'I think I must have been feeling a bit homesick yesterday. I don't know why because I'm really enjoying all this travelling.'

'I felt homesick a few times when I was in Spain,' Tony said. 'but it soon passed. When you know those back home are thinking about you as much as you're thinking about them, it comes through the air somehow.'

Lol said, 'The only thing I'm missing is our nip, my little sister.'

I was going to ask him about his ex-fiancée but he had that look on his face that said don't come any nearer, and I didn't want to spoil the mood.

'What about the lads back at the gas depot, Lol?' I said. 'Aren't you missing meeting up with them in the café on a morning?'

Lol said, 'What gas depot?'

'Exactly. Here's to Athens,' I said and raised my glass. 'I can't believe we're sitting here within spitting distance of the Acropolis.'

We chinked our little ouzo glasses and emptied them in one go.

When it was Tony's turn to raise a toast, he said, 'Here's to getting on with each other. Brothers in arms.'

And we finished off the bottle.

We splashed out on three kebabs with chips and strolled back to the van through the beautiful white streets. Lol said it was just like being at the seaside. It was comforting being in a big city, thankfully only for a short while, knowing what to expect, after all the unknowns in the tiny villages and quiet towns we'd driven through. We carried on talking in bed, enjoying the effect of the ouzo in our blood. Tony said he was still thinking of Gloria. Somebody bumped into the van while we were half-asleep. No damage.

The next morning, we discovered we were parked in the middle of a busy shopping area with hundreds of people walking around. If any of them had sneaked a look through the windscreen they would have had a shock seeing the three of us snuggled up in bed together. And if they'd sniffed the air inside, they wouldn't have been too impressed. We smelt like tramps. There was a tiny lavatory close by and we took turns to get washed all over.

The entrance fee into the Acropolis was high and we jumped over the fence like we had at the ruins in Delphi but a little spy saw us and we got kicked out. Even though we caught a glimpse of the Parthenon, I didn't get a feel for the historical site. It might have been something to do with the ice-cream van parked right in front of the entrance. The view, however, down on to the city of Athens was worth the climb. White buildings, tightly packed, beautiful and biblical, its orderly streets of right angles and straight lines mirroring the structure of the Parthenon. I wished we had a guide and plenty of time.

We had an ice cool beer in a bar after walking through the busy, warm streets and I noticed a good-looking oriental girl sitting opposite talking to a too-smooth Greek barman. Both were about twenty-six years old. The girl kept looking at me. I don't think Lol or Tony noticed. When she stood up to answer the phone, I saw she had callipers on her leg and for some strange reason I liked her even more.

Our two days in Athens was up and I drove out of the city like I did it every day. The roads were busy and

Tony, checking his map, said we would never make Delphi in the day so we pulled up at Dafini camp site and booked in for the night. The place was empty except for four VW camper vans and a few tents. Lol was in a bad mood. I had no idea why and it was no use asking him. It could have been because we were running short of cash and good food.

I was reading a novel about the cold war called Fail-Safe and I ended up arguing with Lol when he started reading it before I'd finished. Then, on top of falling out with Lol, I had an argument with Tony when he said he had thrown the tax disc away while cleaning and tidying the van.

'There was still six months left on that,' I said.

'We don't need it, now.'

'We might do'

'I'll buy another one if we do.'

'That's not the point.'

I was nasty and Tony was upset and I apologised five minutes later. It was the first time the two of us had argued. It wasn't a good day for me. Lol, who had kept out of the argument, put his pyjamas on and within minutes he was snoring. Tony turned over and went to sleep without speaking.

The next day nobody said anything about yesterday's little arguments and it looked like the tension between us had gone. It was mid-morning when we set off back to Delphi, calling at various hotels in an attempt to cash a traveller's cheque but without success because everything was closed on Saturday. No money, no eggs, no fruit, no meat, and worst of all, no fuel. Our petrol tank was on reserve and we cursed ourselves for not filling up earlier or refilling the jerry cans on the roof rack. Now we had to park up in a remote village for two days and wait until everything opened on Monday.

Depressed at the thought of being stuck in the van with no money or food. Two loaves left, a tin of sardines and not much imagination. Bed by nine, tired, nothing to do. Smoking again. Trying beard again. Wished that ice-cream van hadn't been parked in front of the Acropolis. A beautiful site spoilt for the sake of a 99 Flake and a rocket lolly. Must learn to look beyond the commercialisation.

Tony spread the AA leaflets and itinerary on the little table in the back of the van and Lol lit a candle. We hadn't studied the information in detail and we were a bit sickened when we looked at it more closely. According to the AA, the roads are very bad all the way through Iran to India, especially in Afghanistan. After a serious discussion about the route, our money situation, the weather, and the need to succeed, we decided to try to get to Australia in ten weeks. Tony put the papers away, blew out the candle, and we were in bed by half past seven.

On Monday morning the sun was extra brilliant and the people extra friendly. I think it was because we were on the road again. At a garage, while we were waiting for our van to be filled up with fuel, a white VW beetle stopped at the adjacent pump and three Greek students got out, clowning around like the Marx brothers. They looked like guerrillas in their identical khaki uniforms and black berets. All three jogged over in step to admire our van. They told us they had driven up from Athens and were from the same college where the fatal shootings had taken place. We said we didn't know what they were talking about.

'Haven't you heard about the riots?'

We shook our heads.

The three guerrillas raised their fists and together said, 'Bread-Education-Freedom.'

The one laughing the most said, 'We resisted the military junta. We barricaded ourselves in our college. Many of our brothers and sisters were assassinated by the junta snipers.'

Fists were raised again. 'Bread-Education-Freedom.'

We laughed along with them, not knowing whether they were having us on or not. We pulled off the forecourt and they invited themselves into our van for a cup of coffee.

I said, 'When was all this trouble, then?'

In unison they said, 'The sixteenth of November.'

The smallest of the trio said, 'They crashed a tank through the gates of our college and we threw petrol bombs at them.'

It all seemed a bit far-fetched and harmless until they started writing letters to some student friends of theirs in England saying they had planted bombs in Athens.

We followed them to Delphi and although they were entertaining, we were relieved when, later that afternoon, they set off back to Athens.

That night in the van there was nothing to do and Lol went straight to bed. Tony and I sat in the front and talked about our philosophies, money and Gloria. Tony said he needed money to feel secure and confident with women, which surprised me because he always seems so self-assured.

I said, 'If somebody said, I'll give you a million pounds and all you have to do is press a button and an insignificant little man somewhere deep in China will die, would you do it?'

Tony looked to be thinking about it and then he said, 'Would you?'

'I hope I wouldn't. If somebody gave me a million pounds, I think I'd give it all away before I got used to it.'

Tony shook his head and said, 'Mmm. Not sure about that.'

I was up first and it was a beautiful, hot morning. Eggs and beans again and then off to the Poste Restante to see if there was any post. Our families know we are staying in Delphi for a few days and we were hoping there would be mail waiting for us. Nothing.

Back outside the office we met four Americans and a Canadian on their way to Nairobi. They had been to the amphitheatre that morning and were planning to go again in the afternoon to investigate a mysterious hole they had discovered deep in the rocks. We told them they could borrow our torch and suggested they follow us over the fence rather than pay to get in. We were almost at the mysterious hole in the rocks when the same guard caught us again. I held up the torch and spun a story about climbing over the fence to collect the torch which we'd left behind when we visited the other day. He kicked us all out.

We said goodbye and good luck to the rock hunters and drove the forty minutes to Itea again and its beautiful little beach. Tony is a faster driver than me and Lol and I began to worry about the screeching tyres and the hot engine but I didn't want to say anything. Not after the argument about the tax disc.

The beach was peaceful and quiet and Tony pulled on to the soft, white sands and parked up. I got the ball out and we played football with some young kids. It was warm, it must have been above sixty degrees, and we stripped to our Y-fronts and ran into the sea for a swim. We came out a lot faster. The water was freezing cold and I hoped nobody was watching.

When the sun went down dragging the temperature with it, we found ourselves looking up at the sky. None of us had ever seen so many stars. We decided to spend the night camped on the beach and I slid the door shut on a silent night.

Must get up early tomorrow. Maybe sunrise. Watch the world. Hope that mail from home comes tomorrow. Didn't think I'd miss my mam and dad as much as I do. Wonder if the Marx Brothers detonated their bombs?

We all had a great sleep and woke up to the sun shining through the window. Lol made wonderful egg and tomatoes and we dined on the beach. The sea was still too cold for swimming and we settled down to sunbathe. Being fair skinned, I couldn't sit for long in the sun and I went for a paddle. The water was clear and the light strong. Lol shouted to me to dive in. When I turned round to tell him to get stuffed, I saw my own shadow shimmering on the sea bed and nearly ran out, thinking it was a shark. The shallow water was alive with pulsating blue jelly fish, minute red crabs, and little iridescent fish flashing and changing colour as they turned in the sunlight. Two good-looking girls came on to the beach and I motioned for them to come in and join me but they just waved and walked on.

In the afternoon, I went into Itea town with Lol and bought some potatoes for roasting on tonight's campfire. Around four o'clock we were settling down for tea in the van and I had a fierce argument with Lol, accusing him of stealing my bread. He told me he was sick of me getting at him and we nearly got to blows. I apologised and shook hands. I thought what a twat I am lately.

As it got dark, we gathered driftwood and made a fire in the sand close enough to the van to be able to hear the 8-track. I pushed the potatoes into the burning wood, the way I'd seen in films, and we sat around for an hour, chatting, the fire flickering to the backdrop of a calm sea and shimmering lights in the distance. A fishing boat lit by a single lamp rowed slowly and silently by. A larger boat, its deck illuminated by a string of coloured lights, sailed almost as silently the other way and they crossed. Two, one, two.

Our fronts were hot, our backs were cool. It was magical and we became philosophical. Flames devouring wood like years devouring life. Lol smoking his pipe, staring out to sea, his mind somewhere else. Tony playing a few chords on his guitar, singing to himself. All lazily poking and prodding the beach fire recalling our childhood. The magic of fire is so powerful. So is the heat. Almost every one of the potatoes was burnt to a cinder. I took the blame and we laughed and enjoyed the charred remains with mixed veg and bread.

It was raining when we woke up the next day and the beach looked miserable. Some young lads had gathered around the van as we were having breakfast and they started pestering us. We were expecting mail today so after throwing our cold tea dregs on the youngsters we drove back up to Delphi. Still no mail. We couldn't believe it and we were all a bit down. We went to our usual café intending to play cards for an hour or two but the barman seemed to have forgotten us and he was in a bad mood. We mooched around and ended up at the only pub-like building in Delphi. It had a clean toilet and we bought a coke and watched an hour of mind-numbing TV at the bar. Everyone around us was eating well and we promised ourselves we would dine like that on Christmas day.

Inevitably we traipsed back to the van and Lol cooked up a meal of soup and egg on toast yet again. We decided to save the bread pudding as a treat for supper.

Been more tolerant today. No arguments so far. Atmosphere is good. Smooth as Tony's chin. Hope the mail comes tomorrow. Can't afford to stay too long in Delphi. How did my dad manage to bake spuds on the fire on bonfire night without incinerating them? Dads can do anything.

*

Mail was on our minds when we got up and we ambled to the Post Restante before breakfast, not feeling optimistic. We were right not to. All three of us were a little sick again but there was still a chance the letters might come tomorrow. The van was beginning to feel like a prison cell. When the rain stopped, we played football on the mountain side. Lol lost the ball once and had to scramble down the scree and recover it. Thirty minutes later he lost it for good.

Christmas was only days away and we stocked up with food in case the shops were closed over the holiday period. Buses had been pulling into Delphi all day and there were quite a few more tourists around. Sadly, there were hardly any twenty to forty-year-old women among them. The town's old women, identical in black, seemed unaffected by the influx of brightly dressed tourists, and continued to lead their knackered, stick-legged donkeys, down from the hills, the beasts weighed down with firewood and baskets of weak-looking olives.

That evening the moon was a thin crescent and the streets were quiet.

Lol said, 'Do you fancy going out for a walk before tucking in to the bread pudding? Get a bit of fresh air?'

Tony said, 'Sounds like a good idea to me.'

I told them I wouldn't mind being on my own for an hour or so if that was okay. I expect they'll want to do the same before long. I think my mood was triggered by the feeling I got looking over the mountains. I wanted to soar between them like a kite. It was a strange sensation being on my own in complete darkness, wrapped in a sleeping bag in the back of a VW van-come-home, in the middle of a foreign country. A dream I had last night came back to me as I listened to Neil Young with my eyes closed. I was taking an exam on a moving train. I couldn't answer the questions and I couldn't work out whether the test was important or not. The train was speeding over a bridge, far too fast to stay on the rails, and I woke up trying to scream.

I was half way though listening to Melanie, when Lol and Tony returned and I was glad in a way. I was beginning to feel lonely. We ate Tony's bread pudding – best yet – shared a bottle of coke and smoked a Greek cigarette each. It was a fitting end to the day.

We all rushed to the Poste Restante early next morning, even Lol was swinging his arms, but there was still nothing. That was our last hope before the building closed for Christmas. Outside the office we met a middle-aged man from Bristol who had been living in Delphi for five years. He told us that Britain was in dire straits due to the oil crisis and to prove it he opened the Greek newspaper he was carrying and tapped a page showing photographs of an unlit street in London and long queues outside a bread shop in a village. The man translated the accompanying text, saying measures had been introduced by the British government to conserve electricity generation which had been severely restricted owing to the effects of the oil crises on transportation and inflation. There was a possibility of further restrictions over the next few days leading up to Christmas. The man folded his newspaper and said the lights were going out all over Britain.

Tony said, 'If things are shutting down, maybe the post office has been affected and that's why we've not received any letters.'

Whatever the reason for no mail, it sounded like it was going to be a grim time for those back home and a lonely Christmas for the three of us. The man from Bristol wished us good luck and we waved him goodbye as though he was a distant relative.

Later that morning, we met an Aussie who was travelling through Europe in a VW van. He was hairy and scruffy, typical of the Aussies we had met on the road. The guy was from Sydney and told us we would have no problem getting a flat there. He made it sound as though Australia was just down the road and we felt good.

In the afternoon a telegram arrived for Tony. He went pale and his hands started shaking. The telegram was from his mom and dad and it said, 'All OK. Ring Thursday six o'clock. G will be here. Letters on their way.' Lol and I were almost as happy as Tony even though it confirmed we had to stay in Delphi now for a few more days over Christmas until the Poste Restante reopened. We tried to think of things to do to pass the time. I fancied cross country running. Tony thought he might find somewhere quiet up in the mountains and practice the guitar. Lol wanted to learn to stand on his hands.

Sounds bad back home. Three-day week. Wonder how my mam and dad and my little brother, Jonathan, are coping. And Sandra, Anne and David and their young kids. Hope they've all got plenty of food, coal and candles.

Another bus full of tourists landed in the Delphi Hotel car park but it turned out they were mainly pensioners on their way to Athens. We were getting bored again in the van and Tony offered to take us to the café for a coffee (instant) and chocolate cake out of the money the kitty owed him. We hadn't cooked any supper because we were trying to conserve the bottled gas. A stray cat was in the habit of sitting under the van and we fed it with bits left over in a sardine tin.

The next day we met an old man in our usual café. He told us he used to be a mechanic and had done his training in England. He was a happy family man and the café was full of his children and grand-children. His eldest son, Theodore, who ran the family garage in Delphi, sat at the old man's side. Listening to them talk to each other with respect made me realise how unappreciative I'd been towards my own family.

The old man's granddaughters were attractive and one in particular, she was about fourteen, knew how sexy she was. Lol asked Theodore why no girls came out on their own.

'Everyone is related,' he said.

The old man and Theodore offered to buy us wine and we promised to meet them both in a restaurant next to the cafe for dinner on Christmas Eve.

By the time Christmas Eve came round we were almost out of gas for the cooker. We hunted around Delphi trying to find a bottle but no one sold gas. The old man advised us to go down to Lavardia. As Lol took the wheel, the sun came out. We were on the move, something to do, at last. The scenery was magnificent and we drove through craggy mountains and snow-capped high peaks like kids off to the seaside for the first time.

The atmosphere was bustling in the town and there were lots of girls around. Lol was going mad. After being sent from one shop to another by helpful assistants we finally found a store selling camping gas. Able to relax now, we sat at a table outside a bar drinking ice cold beer and smoking Greek cigarettes. Christmas Eve had been the hottest day of our journey so far. Even so, the friendly Greeks were dressed for the cold, and there were lots of handshaking and bead fiddling.

We decided to return to Delphi and search for a good sun-bathing spot. Less than a hundred yards into the journey the ignition light came on and then the indicators and petrol gauge stopped working. We pulled up in the middle of a shopping area, lifted the engine cover and scratched our heads.

'It's the ignition switch,' Tony said.

'It's the voltage regulator,' Lol said.

'I think we've short-circuited something with the home-made alarm,' I said.

We checked and rechecked the VW manual, eventually replacing a fuse and everything was fine again. It was getting hot inside the van and half way back to Delphi we pulled into a layby to sunbathe and have tea. I indicated and the fuse blew again. I was panicking a bit at the thought of breaking down so far from a garage. Tony, calm as always, noticed the new camping gas bottle in the back of the van had rolled against the rear light cluster. He reckoned it could have caused a short when I put the indicator on. We moved the bottle, replaced the same fuse and it never blew again.

When we got back to Delphi we parked up in a layby and washed our clothes in the open. They were beginning to honk a bit. We made tea and Tony and Lol had a smoke. I had stopped smoking yet again and it was agreed that every time they bought twenty cigarettes, I could take six drachmas out of the kitty. The money was enough to buy a baklava from our favourite cafe. I don't know which was the unhealthiest, the tar or the honey.

Our clothes were almost dry when the local police knocked on the van window and told us to move along. I must admit we didn't add to the beauty and mystery of the ancient town with our underpants and socks hanging from a line between the van and a telegraph pole. We found a piece of spare ground on the edge of town, well away from street lights with a good view of the ruins, and we put the washing line back up. We opened the Christmas cards we had brought from home and I pushed Beethoven's 1812 overture into the 8-track. It was the nearest thing we had to a carol song.

When we arrived at the restaurant on Christmas Eve, the old man and Theodore were already there and we shared two bottles of ouzo with them over dinner. At the table opposite, a large family of about twenty people, young and old, were singing and making a lot of happy noise. We joined in the best we could, miming and making up our own words most of the way through.

During the celebration we talked about how Tony's phone call home on Thursday would be the deciding point. Tony had finally accepted that he might end his travels with us before much longer and return home. I felt really helpless and sorry for him. I suggested Gloria coming out to India and taking it from there but it didn't live.

We cheated the bill by about sixty drachmas and walked out talking and mixing with the large family from the next table. The head of the family told me he had played nine years for a Greek football team in the first division, which would explain his bandy legs. I fancied one of the women in the group, she was about forty-years old, and I kept smiling at her but I think she was a little guarded. Maybe her husband was an ex-boxer.

I went for a walk on my own, slightly drunk, and I prayed out loud to God to safeguard my family. There were even more stars in the sky than we'd seen from the beach in Itea and it was comforting to know those same stars were in the sky over Yorkshire.

In the morning we hung the Christmas cards over the dashboard and Lol put an orange inside his sock and pinned it to the back window but it still didn't feel like Christmas Day. No snow. No family. No lights. No trimmings. No carols. No pudding. Noel.

The next day, Lol and I were talking about the meaning of Boxing Day. Lol said it was the day when traditionally all the blokes who had had enough of Christmas went out to the local pub looking for a fight. I suspected he knew it was about the rich giving to the poor but I suppose his version was more believable. We were laughing at each other and Tony was busy playing his guitar when a strange character, a Greek youth about twenty-four, moustache, shortish hair and dressed like a clown, poked a flute through the side window and started playing along with Tony. Then he pulled open the sliding door, jumped into the van, snatched the guitar off Tony and proceeded to play and sing Greek songs. His guitar playing wasn't bad but his voice was terrible. Tony thought the guy was cool. I didn't. Lol continued to read his book as though nothing had happened. I could imagine this guy selling dope to Tony. Eventually something must have clicked in his head and he picked up his flute and jumped out of the side door without saying a word.

We were still talking about the intrusion when Lol, whose turn it was to do the washing up, dropped my tea cup breaking it in two. It was a good luck gift from my mother and I couldn't hide my disappointment. Lol picked up the two pieces and laughed.

'Tha only drinks afe a cup of tea anyway,' he said and I had to laugh. I thought sometimes it's a better outcome when the other person doesn't apologise.

Great news this morning. The Poste Restante had opened and both Lol and I received mail. Lol's letter was from his little sister, and I had a letter from my dad and a separate one from my mother. We were both chuffed and Lol looked happier than I'd ever seen him. He even said good morning to the bread man.

I laughed and cried when I read the two letters from home. In my dad's, written in red biro and full of spelling mistakes, he said our David, my younger brother, had no respect and was making life a misery, causing friction between him (my dad) and my mother and he didn't know what to do about it. He also said he had built a conservatory between the back door and the combined outside toilet and coal house and he thought it looked smashing. In my mother's letter, my dad was causing friction between her and our David because he wouldn't listen and he thought more about his pigeons than he did about our David. She didn't mention the conservatory. Neither said anything about the three-day week. I knew they wouldn't.

Tony phoned Gloria at six o'clock from a booth in the telephone building. We kept out of the way and when he came out, we could see his eyes were moist. Gloria was going to Switzerland to start work in a hotel on 12 January. That gave us the answer. It looked as though Tony would be leaving before long to meet up with her in Europe.

On the way back to the van Lol's financial grip on our spending loosened and he bought half a dozen sausages for supper. He fried them perfectly and they were delicious. We were all happy, talking of school days and listening to the Rolling Stones belt out (I Can't Get No) Satisfaction.

That evening we drank ouzo in the café with the old man and Theodore and got drunk. They wanted to settle our bill, I think it must be a Greek custom, but we wouldn't let them. Yorkshire men have a reputation for being tight but we don't freeload.

When we got back to the van, stumbling along the back lane in the dark, Lol pulled a glass out of his pocket.

'I've nicked this. Fancy a seance while we're parked under the ruins?'

'It's fine by me,' Tony said. 'I'm open-minded. I'm prepared to believe anything.'

'It'll be spooky,' Lol said. 'Sitting in candlelight in complete silence right next to the ancient seat of prophecy.'

'I think it's all a load of bull,' I said. 'But I'll give it a go if you two want to.'

Lol drew some letters and numbers on a paper bag and Tony and I cut them out, which was a pretty impressive team effort considering all the ouzo we'd drunk. Lol spaced the letters out on the table in a circle and placed the upturned glass in the centre.

We each put a finger on the glass and when it went deathly quiet, I couldn't help whispering, 'Is anybody there?'

Lol asked the home-made spirit board in a slow, low voice what the future held for us. I thought I saw something move in the blackness outside but it could have been the flicker of the candlelight. The temperature in the van seemed to drop and I gave a little shiver. The glass didn't move and Lol repeated the question. Still nothing. He asked the question a third time. Still no movement apart from a little tremor which I put down to the cold.

Lol said, 'Thee ask it, Tony.'

Still nothing.

'Let me have a go,' I said.

Not a thing.

We all shivered and after a few minutes of cold silence Lol took his finger off the glass and sat up.

'Fucking spirits.'

The next day we met a couple of Americans, about our age, who, like us, were travelling east in a VW van. J was a cool cat, bearded, clumsily dressed with a devil look about him. D, good-looking enough to be a fashion model, had long fair hair and wore tight faded denims.

We parked the two vans close together, side door to side door, and D prepared a pizza. Lol and I played soccer and J tried to show Tony how to throw an American football ball. When Theodore, unshaven, his shaggy black hair a mess, rode up on his push bike and chatted, it felt like we were in a hippy commune.

After the pizza appetiser, we went to the restaurant at the side of the café for dinner, sitting together at one big table. I talked to D about her life on the road and she seemed very complex and hard, the total opposite of my girlfriend, Jean. Theodore suggested we go to a nightclub in Arachova, about four miles up the slope of Mount Parnassus. Everyone climbed into our van and started singing and stamping. The road was steep and as I changed down to tackle the climb, the engine spluttered and cut out. That morning I had cleaned the points so it was the first thing I checked. I reset the gap and the engine fired up and ran as smooth as ever. I thought that'll teach me to service the engine when it's running fine. But at least I didn't panic this time. Tony's calmness must be catching.

I wasn't looking forward to the club, it's not my idea of fun, but as soon as James Brown and the Rolling Stones came on, I couldn't stand still. When the DJ played a Greek record, we tried to dance like Theodore but kept losing our balance and falling off the stage. Theodore ended up dancing on his own under the spotlight, smashing plates on the floor to the cheers of the crowd. He told us later it was the custom to break plates and he would be sent the bill.

It was just after midnight when we got back to our parking spot and Lol said he wanted to go for a walk on his own. He came back an hour later and even under the candlelight we could see he'd been crying. He didn't say anything, just fell asleep on the bed. Tony lit a cigarette and said he too was going for a walk in the night air. The contrast between the silence of the van under the stars and the lively dancing and singing must have put us in a reflective mood.

The old man had invited us to his house to celebrate New Year's Eve and when we arrived, it felt like we were part of one big happy family. Lol, Tony, me, J and D, the old man and Theodore sitting around the table, chatting and laughing. I couldn't take my eyes off D and she kept smiling back at me. The more wine I drank the more attractive she became. Thankfully, J was too busy telling everybody how cool he was to notice our looks and smiles.

We ate well and drank even better, the Greek custom being for each person in turn to stand up and say Yassou followed by everyone around the table taking a drink. I was getting to like the taste of ouzo and the evening was building up to a grand crescendo. At ten to midnight, I felt a bit dizzy and I just made it to the toilet where I remained spewing and cursing despite J banging on the door and flicking the light switch on and off. At five past twelve I felt fit enough to make it back to the table. The climax to the meal and the celebration of the New Year had passed and I felt a fool.

I made it back to the van and lay as still as I could until the sickness subsided. Just as I was dozing off, Tony came in and we talked again about Lol's quirks. Not just his metronomic foot rubbing and cigarette discipline but other things we had discovered like how he always knows exactly how much money he has in his pockets. An hour later, Lol came in slurring and making a racket when his foot got caught in the passenger door.

'God, I'm missin chuffin shex,' he said and he flopped across the front seats.

I turned to Tony.

'We'd better make sure our sleeping bags are fastened up tight tonight, then.'

So, Tony might be going back. Hope he finds a way to carry on with us. I'll miss his calmness. If he does go back, I wonder how me and Lol will get on. It's a long way to Australia. Maybe we should have asked the Oracle. Maybe not.

I woke up at six o'clock and Lol had left the van's interior light on. He had not made it into bed and was asleep in his clothes on top of his sleeping bag. When I disturbed him, he leaned over and pulled Tony's ear.

Tony woke up startled and hurled abuse at him. What a laugh, I thought. Happy New Year.

Tony had a pain attack in his stomach during the night. He had appendicitis a few years ago and was a bit worried it might be connected and something serious. He had toothache as well, poor kid. I hoped his mail from Gloria would arrive tomorrow, not so much so we could finally set off for Turkey, more because he looked as though he badly needed the letters.

J and D came round to our van the next morning and said they were getting ready to leave. J offered us all a pipeful of smoke and Lol and Tony took a drag but I resisted. J became a bit sarcastic, asking me when did I intend to do my own thing in life. I told him I didn't need drugs to find stimulation. I didn't say anything about my liking for Tetley bitter and Embassy Regal. As we were saying goodbye, he took me to one side and said he could never stay faithful to D because he loved women too much. I suspected he'd seen me and D looking at each other on New Year's Eve. I wondered what D thought of infidelity.

Tony's toothache got worse and the old man told us there was a good dentist in Itea. Walking into the dental surgery was like walking into a barber's shop. All the equipment was on view and the dentist talked to us about her holidays while she operated on Tony. Lol and I, sitting only two yards away on a bench, couldn't help laughing at the informality. That was until she started digging into Tony's gum with what looked like a small dagger. It was like watching a joiner lever up a floorboard nail. Later, Tony said being on view made the experience less frightening. Not for us it didn't.

By the time we got back to the post office in Delphi, the feeling in Tony's jaw had returned and he was no longer spitting blood. Ecstasy – there were letters for all three of us. Two for me, three for Tony, and one for Lol. It meant we could set off for Turkey now and we read the letters in the café as a kind of last token of thanks to the owner for letting us hang out there for so long.

Before we left Delphi, we called round to the old man's house and thanked him and his family for making our Christmas and New Year. They have been so kind and helpful. I would like to think my family would treat three Greek lads in a van with the same generosity. When we left, it was almost like setting off from home all over again. On the road. The world to see and meet for the first time. No family. No friends. Just the three of us.

It's been hard being away from home at Christmas. What must it have been like for my dad when he was away from home at Christmas during the war, and for my mother and her family and all the other soldiers and families? Can't get over how generous people have been. They give you food, buy you drinks, swap information, give you their home address. It's humbling. So genuine. And all the amazing scenery. Everything is new. It's like growing up again.

August 2018 - Café near Pitlochry

It's day two of our search for Lol and we stop at a roadside café a few miles out of Pitlochry on the way to Inverness. The cafe is a converted sixties bungalow, its former front garden now a small car park just big enough for half a dozen cars. The tables in the two bay windows are occupied with straight-faced customers. Inside, in what must have been the original kitchen and dining room, the few remaining tables are empty. A hand painted sign in the window says No Coaches and I have to give the owners credit for self-belief. We order tea and coffee and two sausage sandwiches.

The clouds have lifted and we sit outside in the shadow of the Grampian Mountains. It's been a long ride from Glasgow and we sit in the sun with our legs stretched out to get the blood flowing. Tony ruffles his hair and pushes up his sunglasses. He lights a cigarette and we look at our bikes, parked side by side like tethered horses.

'I thought you were packing that game in, Tony.'

'I ought to do. I've tried vaping but it's like driving a steam engine. You've been stopped a while now.'

'I had my last cigarette in nineteen seventy-nine, the year I got married. It's the best thing I've ever done.'

The woman who took our orders brings our sandwiches and Tony takes a last, deep drag of his cigarette.

'Smoking's been a godsend this past year,' he says and he screws the stub into the ashtray and watches the smoke peter out. 'It saved me when my mom passed away. I was in a bad place for a while.'

'You took it bad. I know.'

'It wasn't my mom passing away, as such. I got over that. But it triggered something inside.'

'That we're all mortal?'

'No. I'm not frightened of dying. Not at all. It wouldn't bother me one bit. I can't explain it. I couldn't stop looking back on my life, wondering where it had all gone.'

'I know what you mean. But you've done okay. You've travelled. You've got a wife and two kids. A house. You've always worked.'

Tony shakes his head and I know I'm talking rubbish.

He says, 'It's like that time I was working in the Tate Gallery in London a few years ago when they were refurbishing the place. Did I tell you?'

'No,' I say. He has told me, but he looks like he needs to retell the story.

'The company I worked for at the time got a contract to do the wiring for all the security doors in the building. It was a big job. Twenty doors. I was there for three weeks. One day I was doing a first fix in one of the side-galleries and I saw this guy organising where all the paintings should go on the walls. He was taking photographs of everything, I think he must have been the curator, and I thought I'm sure I know that face. I didn't say anything and then later that day he came up to me and said, "It's Tony from Barnsley, isn't it?" He turned out to be a guy I knew called Luke. We were in the same class at the sixth form art college in Barnsley.'

I nod and try to look surprised.

'He stood there in his jeans and his arty T-shirt with his neat little beard and expensive haircut, looking at me through his designer glasses, and there's me in my overalls and hard hat, covered in dust. He looked me up and down and said, "Where did it go wrong, Tony?"'

'The bastard. I'd have told him to fuck off?' I think I said that last time.

'What's the point? But it didn't make me feel great.'

'At least you were doing something useful. You could argue you were doing more for society than he was. Anybody can hang a few pictures on a wall.'

Tony tries to smile and he says, 'I could have made some money, made a success of something if I'd taken things seriously. But I was more interested in having a good time.'

'Nothing wrong with that.'

'That's what I thought at the time.'

I bite into my sausage sandwich and grin at the pleasure of hot fat in my mouth.

Tony says, 'I thought tha were a vegetarian?'

'Not when I'm hungry.'

Tony manages a weak smile.

'At least we've got our health,' I say. 'Even if this thing is full of fat and sawdust. Not like poor old Lol, by the sounds of it. If it's true what we've heard, and he has had a massive heart attack he'll not be in great shape. But as my dad always used to say, there's always somebody worse off than you.'

'When I'm down, thinking like that doesn't work.'

Tony lights another cigarette and I decide it's best to keep my big mouth shut.

5

Two Loaves: Turkey

7-14 January 1974

Into Turkey at last. The bridge between Europe and the East. This should be the start of things peculiar and fascinating. Tony pushed Melanie into the 8-track and we started singing and swaying, happy again, feeling good to be back on the road. We pulled into a large tourist centre in the middle of Tekirdag, a small city situated on the coast of the Sea of Marmara and the capital of the Tekirdag Provence. There were bright lights, amusements, hotels, buses, noises, and stares and we parked up safely for the night. We had not seen one fez since arriving in the country and Lol was disappointed there had been no sign of Tommy Cooper.

Our heads were cold all night and the cold made the bed feel hard and uncomfortable. Lol, still wrapped tight in his sleeping bag, slid off the bed to check the five-gallon water carrier and reported ice floating on top. Tony and Lol put on every bit of clothing they owned and ventured out to the shopping centre. I reminded them to watch out for pickpockets and bandits. Every traveller we met warned us to be vigilant in Turkey.

I jumped out of my sleeping bag, took a deep breath and dressed faster than I'd ever done. There was a restaurant nearby and I took a wash in their toilet. The place was filthy but I was no better than a beggar and

I couldn't complain. Tony and Lol came back with carrots, bread and oranges. Variety at last.

Outside there was a whiff of tobacco mixed with body odour. The sickly smell reminded me of the brown glue we used to boil up in the woodworking class at school. Tony didn't know what Lol and I were talking about. Apparently, they didn't do woodwork at high school.

Once we reached the outskirts of the city, the wind whipped up off the sea causing the van to shift yards at a time and I struggled to steer a straight course. Magpies were everywhere. And buses. Our fingers were cold, the sea was angry, and we couldn't get away from the stares. All the men looked the same. Darker than I'd imagined. Poor, cold old men with hairy faces, sitting defiantly on top of their horse and carts. Locked up, cheerless tourist attractions gave the place a feeling of desolation. People wrapped in layers of ragged clothes walked the windy streets as though their only purpose was to keep moving. It was like witnessing the aftermath of a disaster where people were in shock. It was the strangest place I had ever seen. We were three Martians driving down the road.

Two and a half hours later we landed in the centre of Istanbul. We parked up in a quiet backstreet and with everyone staring at us it was difficult to feel at ease. Istanbul is a big city. It looked both ancient and modern. Mosques reached into the sky, some overshadowed by blocks of flats. There were fifties American motors zooming along, dodging through carts, trams and old ladies and the stares were full frontal. There were some attractive women and some dirty buildings. Every shop had a pot belly stove with a dog-leg flue and no rain cap. The rainfall must be low, I thought, otherwise the stoves would drown. Fruit stalls skilfully and artistically displayed their produce. Dripping raw meat hung from hooks. Roast chickens turned on spits inside hot glass cabinets. Sacks of seeds, grains and nuts sat heavily on the pavement their tops rolled down level with the content. Best of all there were no tourists.

It was half past six. Time to try out the night life. We saw an underground bar that looked like it might be lively. Inside, it was a dirty little hole and we ordered bottled beer to be safe. The men's toilet was overflowing with foul water so we sneaked into the women's toilet and that was just as filthy. The bar area was full of shifty characters and we felt uneasy despite there being three of us. We left the beer half drunk and were glad to leave.

We walked around the main streets eating pancakes to keep warm. My eyes were running and my hands felt as though they didn't belong to me. Car horns blared non-stop and lights were shifting and reflecting. People banged into us every few steps and we held our pockets tight. Cold barrow boys, little ice men, tried to sell their remaining, end of the day wares, wheeling their goods up to pedestrians and being ignored.

Back in the van, Lol made another superb rice pudding and we felt fat and warm. As we were clearing up ready for bed, two Turkish men knocked on the van window and warned us that we were parked in a shady district.

'Bandits break in,' they said. 'Take cassettes. Take spare wheels. Take petrol cans from roof.'

We didn't understand every word but we got the message by the frightened look in their eyes and the cut throat sign they made to their necks. We thanked them for the tip off, shook their hands, and moved to a brighter area. The warning had unsettled us and before we slipped into our sleeping bags, we fastened the tow rope to the sliding door handle and secured the other end to the cooker in case someone tried to break in. I wasn't sure whether it was the cultural shock of being in the west in the morning and the east in the afternoon but the Turks had frightened us a bit. I wondered how bad it would be when we got to Iran and beyond. We shared an orange and went to bed with one eye open.

It was a quiet night apart from Lol waking me up at half past six to tell me someone was on the roof. It turned out to be a garbage collector ten yards away.

The bank we called in to change money was so warm and cosy that we were tempted to curl up in their comfy chairs and go to sleep. There were no foul Turkish tobacco smells in the building and the staff were helpful and efficient. We came out wondering why we had been so worried about sleeping in the van last night.

Tony had been reading up on Istanbul and suggested our itinerary for the morning. First, he wanted us to visit the Sultan Ahmed Mosque and then the nearby Topkapi Palace. I could see why the mosque was number one on his list. The domed exterior with its six minarets, built of white smooth stone and roofed in faultless leadwork, dominated the skyline. I looked at the craftsmanship, the quality of construction, the free-flowing eastern architecture, and I shook my head in admiration. As a newly qualified tradesman, at the end of a five-year apprenticeship learning about gas and the art of pipe bending and lead jointing, I felt humbled. But it was the interior that took my breath away. The

Sultan Ahmed Mosque is also known as the Blue Mosque and it is an understated name.

A service was taking place and there was silence under the huge dome. The air was so full of respect we removed our shoes without thinking and quietly declined the offer of help from a guide. There were a hundred shades of tiles, mainly blue and red, and a red, blue and yellow carpet covered the whole floor. There was barely a mark on the walls, not even a sign of a shoulder ever having brushed against the fluted stone pillars. Blue light from the stained-glass windows blended with the light from the huge chandeliers suspended way up high. Worshippers seemed oblivious to the movement and noise of tourists. We watched the ritual of stooping, kneeling and touching the floor with the forehead. A guide told us Muslims prayed five times every day. He said worshipping Allah was the purpose of existence.

We left the vastness of the mosque to visit the Topkapi Seraglio museum a short walk away. It was modern and busy. There were tiles, jewels, pottery, historical religious relics, and armoury displayed in a straightforward order. We saw the preserved hand part of St John the Baptist and two blood-stained garments worn at his death.

The experience was enlightening and even in the less fascinating rooms we lingered to keep warm. Most of the food looked delicious but it was too expensive for us. We made do with black English tea, a goat's cheese sandwich to share and a square of honey layer cake each. Even so, by the time we tipped the over-eager waiter, we had spent thirty shillings. That meant we couldn't afford to visit the harem. Tony thought there might be real girls there. Lol was already feeling bad about our over-spending and now he felt even worse.

There was so much more to see but we were tired and cold and we returned to the van, thankfully still where we had left it, feeling a lot wiser for Tony's cultural tour.

When we set off for Izmit, we looked back on our few hours in Istanbul and vowed to return one day. The way out of the city entailed crossing the Bosporus over the new bridge, its modern clean lines sitting beautifully under the mosque skyline. It was only when we were on the other side and looked back that we saw the wonder of the construction.

I said, 'Look at that for a piece of engineering.'

'And a piece of art,' Tony said. 'It's beautiful,' and he read out a few facts from one of his brochures.

'The bridge was opened on 30 October 1973. Bridging the Bosporus Strait will connect Europe and Asia for the first time since 512 BC.'

I said, 'Wow. How lucky are we? Only completed a few weeks ago. We're one of the first people to cross it.'

Lol said, 'I bet we're the first three lads from Barnsley to cross it in a camper van.'

We kept looking back in awe and I couldn't take it all in. The engineering, the history, the beauty, the setting.

The road to Izmit was poorly lit and we drove slowly, barely able to see more than thirty yards of road ahead. That increased to fifty yards when Lol suggested we clean the headlights. I liked the town of Izmit. People walked the streets with a light step and a smile on their face. The staring increased but it seemed friendlier. We parked in the middle of the town and settled down to chips, egg and carrots. Our stay in Istanbul had been educational and enjoyable and we agreed to take things more slowly from now on, starting with a detour to the Goreme Valley later in the week. We sat in the front seats smoking and staring out of the steamy windows with the rain hitting the roof. The streets were dark and wet and we were on edge because a gang of young Turks kept staring at us.

Can't stop thinking about the mosques, and the Muslims praying five times a day. I couldn't get out of Sunday school fast enough when I was a kid. The only reason I go inside a church now is to attend a wedding or a funeral. It felt different in the mosque. You could feel the devotion. I think it was the way the worshippers were able to ignore the sightseers without putting anybody down. Somehow it was a privilege to be in their presence. Can't remember seeing many women praying. Wonder what they do?

What a great sleep. We didn't wake until half past ten. Lol was the first to rise and he went in search of bread, rice, cheese and candles. Half an hour later he came back with just the rice so I got up and went looking for the rest.

It was sunny and cold. The market was busy and the tradesmen looked happy in their work. There were a few beggars around asking for bread to put in their sacks. I imagined them going home to a shack or a tarpaulin somewhere and feeding the family. Smiling shoe-shiners worked methodically. Occasionally, a business man would come strutting by, apparently oblivious to the dirt and poverty. Dolmuses drove up and down the streets, packed with people. The flats, built of wood and plaster were painted dirty pink and blue, and outside the market, horns blared and people shouted and whistled.

I bought the bread, cheese and candles and everyone stared and this time I stared back. The head scarves on the women shoppers didn't prevent them from bartering. It must be in the eyes, I thought. All the men had moustaches, and their shoes were caked in mud from the sludgy roads and paths. Bun shops glistened with chocolate cakes, treacle tarts and sweet bread. It was endless and I wondered who bought it all. More stares.

It was nearly noon when we ate breakfast and then we were on our way to Ankara. The roads were straight and the lorries and buses were going fast, too fast, and we advised Lol to take it easy. The traffic thinned out as the light faded and I took over from a tense Lol and lit a cigarette. The roads were quiet. We were quiet. I thought about how lonely it can get and told myself not to look back. Sometimes I think I may never look forward to returning home.

Ankara by night could be any city in the world – blocks of flats, cars, illuminated shop windows, bars and restaurants, people crossing roads at traffic lights. We parked up under a big tree in the deserted grounds of a large building and Lol used his culinary skills to make a stew without meat. It tasted great and reminded me of home.

We woke up with iced heads and shoulders. The sleeping bags were too cold to touch and there were ice nodules on the ceiling lining again like the time we were in Baden-Baden. We heard car doors slamming and brisk footsteps but no voices. It was as though the cold had muted everyone. We walked briskly into the city with our heads down, blue hands in pockets, to buy bread and milk. There were some good-looking girls at the information centre where Lol was changing a hundred Turkish lira note into smaller change. I tried to look cool but it wasn't easy with matted hair, crusted eyes and a week's growth on the chin.

There wasn't as much staring that morning. Perhaps three would-be hippies didn't stand out in a big city like Ankara. We set off for Goreme Valley, escaping the centre without trouble, and then got held up in a line of crawling traffic. Right in front of us a bread van stopped and its back doors flung open. The two men in the back guarding the bread looked like hardened convicts with their shaved heads and broad shoulders. We tried not to look at them but were drawn to their fierceness and wondered what else they might be guarding. After a few minutes, the traffic began to inch forward and one of the men leaped out of the van and jogged towards us.

'Watch out,' I said and I felt for the knife under the driver's seat.

The guy came to the passenger window and people in the queue started laughing at the scared expression on our faces. I expected him to ask why we were staring at him but instead he handed Lol two warm loaves. Tony, agile as ever, grabbed four cigarettes from the dashboard.

'Here, Lol. Give him these.'

The guy took the cigarettes, jumped back up to his mate, and the van pulled away with everyone in the queue laughing at us.

*

The sun began to burn through the windscreen making us squint as we drove alongside Tuz Golu, a massive, white, salt water lake.

'It is the second largest lake in Turkey,' Tony said looking at his brochures, 'and one of the biggest salt lakes in the world.'

I said, 'Bloody hell. I bet tha could get a few little blue bags for thi packet of crisps out of that lake, Lol.'

Lol said, 'Tha could work it out if tha knew t'volume of t'water in t'lake. All tha'd need to do is teck a gallon of t'water and boil it darn until all thy had left wa t'salt. A gallon of unsalted water weighs ten pounds so, if say tha were left with three pounds of salt then that's thirty percent salt. Multiply t'total volume of water in t'lake by thirty-three and tha's got it.'

'Thirty-three point three,' I said. 'Come on, Lol. If tha're going to show off, be accurate.'

Tony said, 'Or you could just look in here and it tells you.'

'Go on then,' Lol said. 'How much?'

Tony lifted the brochure to the light and folded back the page.

'Thirty-three-point-three percent recurring divided by Pi r multiplied by the square on the hypotenuse.'

Tony doesn't laugh out loud that often but when he does it's like the sun coming out.

The road changed dramatically when we arrived in Nevsehir. Compared to the main route from Ankara, it seemed medieval, all sludge and packed ice. The stares were intense again. The craggy faces of the men were darker here and the women covered their heads with scarves and had fat bellies and bowed legs. The young boys were scruffy with crew cut hair and were dressed in rags. The rendered walls of every building were sprayed with mud from passing vehicles and a lack of guttering. Horse and carts rattled by and taxis sounded their horns.

We ate dinner by the light of our last candle and then went off in search of a candle shop. Three quarters of an hour later we still hadn't found one even though we kept repeating the word 'mum', the Turkish word for candle. Maybe our pronunciation was bad. Or maybe it should have been 'mam'.

It was too cold to go back to the van and Tony suggested we visit a museum to keep warm. We had to knock the attendant up at his house next door to the museum and ask him to show us around. I thought he would have been angry but he looked delighted to see us. We must have been the only visitors that day. Unfortunately, the interior of the museum with its bare stone floors and walls, was only a degree up on the outside. The displays weren't particularly interesting but we listened attentively to the attendant's broken English and he looked pleased.

We moved on a few miles and parked in Uchisar, a small town just inside the Goreme Valley. A young boy, about thirteen, came up to the van within minutes of me pulling on the handbrake and introduced himself as the town's guide. He was a scruffy, cheeky, little chap dressed in rags and he spoke good English and French. He sat down with us in a coffee shop and we bought him a coke. He was a likeable lad and he promised to take us around Uchisar tomorrow.

The van was freezing when we got back. It was only seven o'clock and Tony and I cautiously slid into bed while poor old Lol, it was his turn in the kitchen, made rice pudding. The temperature was even lower than the night in Ankara and I went to bed with a scarf around my head like a boy with toothache. I must have looked like my grandmother.

I had eaten too much and felt sick. I kept waking up, my mind all over the place.

What will I do in the future? What will I be? Will Australia hold the answer? Don't sweat. In no rush. Am I avoiding or wisely taking my time? No sense of time. Blackness. Tomorrow could be yesterday. Turn slowly so as not to disturb the others or the coats on top of the sleeping bags. Turn again. Drift off to sleep somewhere.

The next morning, I poked my head out of the sleeping bag, the knot in the scarf still holding tight under my chin. It was half past six and Lol was having a cigarette in the front under candlelight. He said he had been up half an hour writing a letter. I drifted off again and woke at half past eight. It didn't feel as cold as it had during the night but the inside of the van had iced up again and I got dressed inside the sleeping bag. Lol was still in the front, writing.

'Where's Tony?' I said.

'He's gone to that cafe across the road.'

'Are tha coming?'

'In a minute.'

Tony was enjoying a pot of tea at a table in the window.

'Where's Lol? Is he still writing?'

'I think so. He said he wanted a bit of peace and quiet.'

'I wonder if he's been writing to his mom and dad.'

The waiter came over to our table and I ordered a tea.

'More likely to be to his little sister, their nip.'

'Or maybe it's to his ex,' Tony said.

'What? A poison pen letter?'

'He doesn't talk about her much, does he? Do you think he's got over her?'

'I'm not sure,' I said. 'You can never tell with Lol. He still looks a bit teary whenever he's had too much to drink.'

'It's not put him off fancying other women.'

'I know. He's like a ram in a trailer at the side of a field full of sheep.'

Lol came into the café with his blue aerogramme held tight against his jacket. I couldn't see the address and didn't like asking who he was writing to. We had another tea and Lol and I put a few daft words on a picture postcard for the lads and the staff back at the gas depot to pin to their world map.

'Hello to everybody working hard in the office and fitting shop (that reduces the number to a handful!). We're in Turkey and it's freezing but it's better than cutting and screwing pipes on a building site!! Turkey is great and we're loving every minute. Hope everyone is keeping well and getting plenty of overtime in. Wish you were here?! Next stop IRAN.'

Mehmet, the cheeky young guide we met yesterday, greeted us at ten o'clock along with a dozen of his little friends. Once his gang had finished staring, laughing and taking the micky out of us, Mehmet led us off through the cold, shaded backstreets to Nevsehir Castle, carved out of the soft volcanic rock that covers the entire Goreme Valley. He was fit and we struggled to stick close to him as he climbed the scary hill up to the castle. Compared to our heavy scrambling, Mehmet was as sure-footed as a mountain goat. The castle was closed but the view from the top over the whole valley was breathtaking – literally for Lol who had to sit down to recover.

Mehmet said, 'Would you like to smoke hash today?' He could have been asking us if we fancied a cup of tea.

Lol said, 'It's oxygen I need. Not hash.'

'Yes. That would be good,' I said trying to put Mehmet off. 'Maybe later.'

On the way back down the hillside, Mehmet advised us to visit some of the churches, which were also carved out of rock. He led us to a small church and sat on the wall outside to wait. It was expensive. The entrance fee was six Turkish lira each and Tony got caught smuggling in his camera. The place of worship was nothing exceptional, just a few crucifixes on the stone wall and a few wooden seats. Outside, we stood back and marvelled at the large number of churches, obelisks and cone-shaped structures carved out of the valley stretching out in front of us. Mehmet never stopped talking, feeding us lots of interesting general information. He told us one of the valleys was called Pigeon Valley which took me right home to my dad and the pigeon paddock.

Mehmet wanted us to continue the tour of the whole area but we had seen enough and decided to move on to Kayseri. He seemed a little disappointed. We asked him how much we owed him for his guidance. At first, he said fifteen Turkish lira but after a bit of haggling he reduced it to ten. The way he kept the upper hand reminded me of the Artful Dodger. Eventually he settled for a twenty pack of JPS then totally out of character he gave us a crude hand-made vase as a leaving present. That made us feel bad. We shook his little mucky hand and gave him another ten cigarettes.

There was a light flurry of snow as we left Nevsehir and headed for Kayseri. Within half an hour I could hardly see the road due to the blinding reflection off the snow. The road was in good condition but I had to keep my speed down and it was late afternoon when we pulled into Kayseri. The town looked okay and I wanted to stay the night but after consultation we decided to drive the 120 miles to Sivas. The strong wind stopped the snow from settling on the road and as the light faded the bright reflection eased.

It was exciting driving against the clock, like a rally, and I drove as fast as I could without letting the others know I was racing. When darkness fell, all I could see were the red and white road markers flashing past the van and I felt like a pilot in a plane about to land. I was hypnotised by the endless sparks of flying colour. Speed and distance became distorted. Now we were in a submarine deep below the ocean, enclosed, totally remote. I told myself to snap out of it. Talk. Smoke. Anything. The road surface worsened and the van began to bounce and shudder, shaking me back into the real world.

In Sivas we parked up in the first space we saw and enjoyed chips and egg. Lol slipped into his sleeping bag, and Tony and I found our own little private space and began to write home. I was in the mood and I wrote a quick air mail letter to Jean, another to Ken, and I was half way through a letter to Trev when I heard yet another moan from Tony. He had been fidgeting since we settled down to write, chewing his pen and staring out of the van window.

'What's wrong, Tony? Struggling?'

'Just a bit. I can't find the right words.'

'Is it to Gloria?'

'No. It's to a mate of mine. George. We went to art college together.'

I leaned over and all he had written in the half hour we had been writing was Dear George and he had spelled George, G o r g e.

We laughed so loud we woke Lol up.

I hadn't noticed how cold it had become in the van and when I tried to seal my letters, I could barely bend my fingers. My feet were even colder than my fingers but not cold enough to stop me from chasing three cheeky kids around the railway station after they threw freezing water over the windscreen.

Lol and Tony were already up when I peered out of my sleeping bag and both of them looked frozen. We realised that in our rush to settle down last night we had parked in a railway yard and now there were hundreds of busy commuters swirling around us. I didn't know whether they were trying to keep warm or were in a hurry. I thought we must stop this careless parking. One day we will pay for it.

We ate breakfast on the move, partly to keep good time, and partly to make sure the struggling heater kept on top of the ice trying to cling to the windows. It was too cold to stop anywhere for a break or to have a look round. Tony was driving fast and it looked like we would make Erzurum that night, our final stop before the Iran border. Our bottled gas was low again and we searched around a remote village for a shop. We ended up buying two bottles and a new tap because Tony broke the governor trying to replace the old bottle. The mishap cost us a few lira and Lol wasn't happy.

The light had faded so I took over the driving with my cat's eyes. Despite what we said about taking in more places of interest, it was becoming a round the world rally instead of a sightseeing tour. The windows had iced up again and I was driving too fast. The roads were bumpy, I was tired, and my back was aching. I thought why do I insist on driving at night? Is it because I want to be in control?

There were so few vehicles on the road we wondered if there had been an accident or a closure somewhere. It was unsettling. It was lonely. A breakdown out here would finish us off. When we finally arrived in Erzurum it was like driving into a typical English town with its red brick buildings and traffic lights at every junction. We parked up and searched for the beautiful Chinese girl Tony had seen as we entered the town. No luck.

It was too cold to sleep in the van and we pulled our collars up and went in search of a cheap hotel. We looked at three, each costing ten lira per person, each with brown, bare, filthy and no doubt cockroach-infested rooms. We weakened and booked into a class hotel, at a cost of thirty lira per person. I had to admire the English-speaking woman on the front desk who appeared to be up for the receptionist of the year award. If I hadn't been so tired, I could have sat up all night looking around our gorgeous, heated bedroom. There was a shower, toilet, proper beds, warm lighting, radiators, tables and chairs. It was so good we walked around naked.

The sound of running water entered my sweet dream. Lol was in the shower and Tony was already up and getting dressed. There were plenty of soft pillows on the bed and I plumped them up around me, making a sort of throne, and I felt like a king.

Tony and Lol set off to find a bank and I took a long shower. I left the hotel wearing my worn flying jacket and with my shabby travel bag under my arm, and the king had turned into a tramp. As I was waiting for Lol and Tony, I was accosted by two people trying to sell me snow chains and Iranian money. Turks are friendly people but they seem to be forever trying to make money.

The battery was flat and Tony and I had to push the van to get it started. Lol drove for a hundred yards with the two of us hanging on to the back of the van like binmen. Young and crazy.

The road to the Iran border was slippery and the battle between the van's heater and the icy windows had resumed. When we stopped at noon for dinner and a stretch, we tried to identify the hundreds of tiny animal footprints in the fresh snow all around us. Busy little lives.

Tony checked the map and itinerary and told us there were worse roads ahead. Lol was enjoying driving through the snow and the van slid and spun occasionally, but he skilfully managed to keep going forward. We passed two articulated lorries with GB stickers on their big bumpers and we flashed headlights at each other and for a few minutes felt nostalgic.

It was another long drive, and we only stopped for petrol and food. No one felt like talking and the 8-track was silent. In the peaceful atmosphere it came to me why the lonely feeling I occasionally experience doesn't always feel painful. Sometimes it's seclusion and I enjoy it. Once I understood, I relaxed and began to wallow in the isolated feeling.

The border appeared out of nowhere and we passed through the friendly Turkish side in under an hour. Things looked more serious at the Iran side. Pairs of unsmiling soldiers in heavy uniforms, armed with rifles, fingers on triggers, feet planted, watched every move made by the lorry drivers and travellers.

'Jesus. Just think,' I said. 'If I accidentally tripped over and fell on to a soldier, I'd probably get shot dead.'

Lol said, 'Make sure thi shoe laces are fastened up, then.'

Our passports were stamped without a problem and we bowed our heads to the border guard in gratitude. As we turned towards the van the guard held up his hand.

'Carnet de Passage.'

My name was on the vehicle documents and he looked directly at me for an answer.

I said, 'I didn't know we needed a carnet.'

'You must have a Carnet de Passage to enter Iran.'

A soldier casually stepped in front of the van, rifle in hand. I checked my shoelaces.

I said, 'Can't we get one from you, from here, now?'

'Not possible.'

We knew we might have needed a carnet. Our AA itinerary had warned us it was best to apply for one while still in England. The itinerary said it provided a guarantee to countries such as Iran that we would not sell the van in that country. But it wasn't cheap and we decided not to bother.

I looked at the soldier, hoping he might soften. He shrugged his shoulders, stepped back and motioned for me to do a three-point turn.

Tony said, 'Damn and double damn.'

That was the nearest I'd ever heard him come to swearing.

I parked the van and said, 'This could be the end of our journey, lads.'

Lol said, 'If they don't let us in, we'll have to find a different route to India and Nepal.'

'Or do we turn round and find somewhere else to aim for?' Tony said. 'Maybe go back into Europe.'

'That means we've failed,' I said.

I didn't need to say that. We all knew the implications of turning back. But it made me feel stronger.

I put the kettle on. As they say, if in doubt, brew up.

'I suppose we could change our plans and go to Africa,' I said. 'I wouldn't feel as though we'd failed, then.'

Nobody said anything and we drunk our tea in silence.

Lol said, 'Let's gi' it another go. See if we can get 'em to change their minds.'

'You mean bribe them?' I said hoping he didn't. The idea of spending a few months behind bars didn't appeal to me.

'No. Just ask 'em how much it'd cost to let us through and wink at 'em.' I was relieved when he added, 'Only kidding.'

I noticed Tony was looking through the AA itinerary.

'It only says it's advisable to have a Carnet in here,' he said. 'It doesn't say anything about it being compulsory.'

Lol said, 'Come on. Drink up. Let's gi' it another go.'

What he meant was I should give it another go and they would back me up.

I showed the border guards the guidance notes in the AA itinerary, smiling as though there had been some silly little mistake somewhere, and told them proudly we were heading all the way to Australia. I even told them how much we were looking forward to seeing Isfahan and the rest of their beautiful country. Tony smiled his most innocent, harmless smile and Lol endorsed everything I said. The guards didn't smile back and we spent three hours walking up and down the muddy, cold compound, watching for any sign of hope in their faces as they continually checked with someone higher up. Each time they returned from their supposed consultation, they shook their heads and looked surprised that we hadn't turned round and gone back.

We were beginning to talk more seriously about adjusting our plans and travelling to Africa when one of the guards came over and almost snatched my passport and log book off me. We stayed as quiet as school boys lined up for a caning outside the headmaster's office. The guard began to fill in a huge form. It took him twenty minutes. I timed him. I didn't know whether it was a Carnet de Passage or a visa or something else and I didn't care. He checked the van over in silence and without eye-contact, then he waved us into Iran.

August 2018 - Inverness to Atlandu

The first spots of rain hit my visor as we leave Inverness. I flash my headlight at Tony and we pull into a layby and put on our waterproofs. We can do without the rain. There is still plenty of daylight left for riding. At least the midges will retreat until the sun comes back out. I follow Tony across the Moray Firth, gripping my handlebars and steering into the wind, which is gusting from the east, and we pick up the A835 towards Ullapool.

Thirty miles later the showers are heavier and the rain has penetrated my sleeves and the collar around my neck. I take the lead and we keep to the A835 and ride through Ullapool. It looks a pretty little place set on the side of a Loch that leads straight out into the sea. The town is small and quiet and for once I manage not to lose Tony.

We ride along a flat coastal road, looking for signs of log cabins to rent, then turn inland heading north. We approach a little settlement called Drumrunie and then turn left on to a single-track road.

My feet and fingers are wet and cold and I have to exercise them to retain some feeling. We ride alongside three lochs in between craggy, low mountains and the smell of pine is in the air. Tony pulls up at a tiny village called Altandhu, a few white buildings scattered around a rocky outcrop. There is nowhere to shelter, not even a tree, so we pull up outside a building signposted general store and Tony gets the map out again.

'Whose idea was this?' he says. 'I told you we should have gone to look for him in Spain first.'

We read the map with our backs to the rain.

'This general store looks like it's the centre of the village,' I say.

'It must be. I can't see a post office or a newsagent's anywhere,' Tony says, looking around the sparse hamlet. 'What are we going to do? Just walk in and ask them if there's a log cabin round here being rented by an old mate of ours called Lol?'

'See if they sell megaphones,' I say. 'And we'll ride round every village shouting, 'Has anybody seen Lol?''

We laugh at the absurdity of the situation, walk into the store and nod to the storekeeper, dapper in his brown apron.

'Afternoon,' I say. 'I wonder if you can help.'

'I'll try,' he says, a bit too quick.

'We're looking for an old friend of ours. His name's Lol. We think he's staying in a log cabin somewhere round here.'

The storeman looks at us, waiting for the punchline.

Tony says, 'All we know is that it's somewhere on the coast north of Ullapool.'

The storeman laughs so loud I'm sure the tins on his shelves rattle.

'North of Ullapool,' he says. 'That's a heck of a lot of coast, laddie. You've heard of a needle in a haystack?'

We get back on the bikes and set off for Achiltibuie. It looks bigger than Altandhu and it might have more than a general store. It's about three miles away.

6

Stones: Iran
14-26 January 1974

We didn't stop singing until the hunger and fatigue hit us. I drove steadily along a barren road, eyes fixed in a stare, and after an hour we landed out of nowhere in a town called Mako. We saw a hotel. It was one in the morning and we had to knock the owner up. We had doubts about the quality of the room but the three beds drew us in and we couldn't say no after disturbing the man. Lol wanted to eat.

'No way,' I said. 'I'm too tired to bother. I just need sleep, sleep, sleep.'

The kind owner lit the oil stove in our bedroom. He had no trousers on, just a shirt tied around his waist, poor man, and we bowed as he left the room. We slipped into bed. No words were spoken and the day ended.

The sound of hammering woke me up at half past ten. There were men at work outside the hotel. I hoped we hadn't missed breakfast and I woke up the others and in fifteen minutes we were ready to eat and leave. The dining area was warm and friendly and a log fire burned in the middle of the room, its flue pipe disappearing through the timbered ceiling. People came in and stamped the snow off their feet, leaving little puddles of water by the door. We ate boiled eggs, some strange dark bread, and drank Nescafe. It was heaven. We posted letters home and drove off into the snow.

The light was blinding again. Our hands looked orange and my eyes were aching. It was warm in the van once we got moving. We were skidding and sliding and couldn't go beyond forty miles an hour. A fox ran across the road and bounded over a field of fresh snow, disappearing and reappearing.

Tony sat up and said, 'Look. Camels.'

We counted three in a corner of a field half a mile away and cheered. Thirty minutes later, camels were as common as cows back home. The throttle started sticking making driving hell. I had a look underneath and the cable linkage running from the accelerator pedal to the engine at the rear had iced up. We carried on.

I pushed Joe Cocker into the 8-track and we listened to the former gas fitter from Sheffield sing 'With A Little Help From My Friends'. We were heading towards Tabriz and with each mile the scene became more eastern, all flowing robes and head scarves. The windows were beginning to freeze up again and the roads were getting worse. Darkness was falling when we arrived in Tabriz and we knew it was too late to travel any further. We booked into Hotel Morvarid, the first decent hotel we saw. The place was warm, clean and friendly. I read Jules Verne 'Around the World in Eighty Days', for a while in an armchair under the window, my technical college knowledge coming in handy.

Could stay up all night but it's a pity to waste a good bed. My feet are swollen with all the driving. Can't be rheumatic fever again, surely? Have a thought - spend three months in Australia then head back home through America. Round the world in twelve months, never mind Jules Verne and his eighty days. Wonder what the

*others will think. What time is it? One in the morning.
Others asleep. Look out on to the snow-covered
deserted streets of Tabriz, many miles from home.
Carrying my own little world with me. Sleep.*

I was up at half past nine, my mouth hot and dry. We
showered, ordered coffee and sat around the dining
table discussing our future. Christmas, Australia,
America. I couldn't remember the last time we'd talked
in depth about the future since leaving home. We paid
the bill and left without tipping. Outside there was a bit
of hassle with a lad about paying for the overnight
carparking. Nobody had told us about the extra charge
and we thought we were being conned. The young lad
looked genuine but we'd seen it all before and we left
without paying. Straightaway, I felt guilty. The small
amount would have fed him and his family for a day.
And if there genuinely was an extra charge for parking,
I hoped he wouldn't get a rollicking off the owner.

The snow was brilliant again. In a layby up the
road, well away from the hotel, I attached the new
governor to the replacement gas bottle that Tony had
snapped off. I felt good when it worked. So did Tony
and Lol. We set off again, three travellers in our own
little world.

We passed through white, mountainous country,
occasionally coming across remote villages standing out
against the snow. The buildings were no more than huts
enclosed by brown stone walls. The scene reminded me
of the drawings in the little blue bibles we were given
when we were kids at Sunday school. We saw camels,
donkeys, and cold human figures in black staring as
though we were a spaceship from the outer limits. Or

Heaven. We drove on and darkness slowly replaced the whiteness all around. Two extremes.

My body was tired through lack of exercise. The accelerator was still sticking and driving was becoming dangerous. I rigged up a make-shift blowlamp to de-ice the throttle cable under the van, using the gas bottle and a tube spanner to draw in air and increase the temperature. I felt like a mad professor. The flame burned well but it wasn't effective and I ended up hammering away chunks of ice to free the mechanism.

It was Tony's turn to drive. I smoked a cigarette to the sound of Neil Young singing Don't Let It Bring You Down. The moon sent out a strange light like the glow from a gas mantle. We were travelling fast and it was warm in the van. Jean was on my mind and I wanted to be with her. There was no outside world. Like the seconds just before sleep. Life was so clear. There was no difference between hope and achievement. I could have shaved off my hair and become a monk.

The main road through Zanjan was full of narrow-fronted shops, each crammed with colourful wares and decorated with posters of healthy families in the sun eating bright oranges and other glistening fruit, all watched over by the silent shopkeeper fiddling with his rosary, patiently sitting in the shadows at the back. We drove alongside pavements packed with dark-skinned men, full of purpose, getting on with their business, and not a beggar in sight.

Lol pulled off the road on the way out of the city for a break. I shook off my reflective mood and enjoyed tea, bread and marmalade. Tony was feeling lovesick for Gloria and Lol stared out of the window, quiet except for his clicking pen.

We were tired but keen to push on and I took over the driving. The weather conditions had changed. Fog had descended coating the road with ice, stiffening the grass in the verges and turning them white. I stayed in second and third gear counting off the kilometres. Hamadan to be made tonight. The fog was spooky and I couldn't see more than twenty yards. My neck was aching, and I had to force my eyes wide open, frightened of blinking in case they stayed shut.

We got lost driving around Hamadan searching for the bright lights and security of the city centre. It was late and we were too tired to keep on searching so we parked under a street lamp opposite a row of shops. The inside of the van quickly dropped cold. Tony kept his gloves on and prepared soup and boiled egg followed by rice. I hoped the meal would keep us warm until morning. Boy, it was cold.

I woke up four or five times during the night with a cold head and an aching back. For once I was up first and I left the others asleep in bed and shopped around for bread and jam. We were finishing our breakfast when a man in a suit knocked on the van window and introduced himself as a commissioner of the city's agricultural department. He had noticed the GB licence plates and our pale skin and said he wanted to get to know us. He invited us to his little office on a backstreet and we sat around chatting and drinking tea.

'Are you students?' he said.

'Yes,' I said.

'What are you studying?'

'Lol and me are studying Heating and Ventilation Utilisation.'

That convincing white lie made Tony sit up and he said, 'I'm studying electronics and art.'

'What is the education system like in England?'

That floored us and we looked at each other.

Tony, brave as ever, said, 'We go to nursery until the age of five. Then to junior school until the age of eleven. Then we take an examination and that determines which type of school we attend for the next five or six years.'

The commissioner said, 'Ah. Very interesting. And then do you go to university?'

Tony said, 'Yes. If you're bright and motivated.'

I laughed and said, 'But not if you're poor.'

He smiled and said, 'I have heard about the class system in Britain. We have our own class divide in Iran. Much of Iran relies on agriculture. Trade with the West has created an economic boom but it has widened the gap between the wealthy and the poor, especially in the rural population. And the poor, especially women, are excluded from university.'

It was hard to tell from the commissioner's tone whether he was criticising the country or just stating the position as he saw it. He looked contented and the two women in his office looked happy enough typing and filing. I wondered if they had gone to university.

The kind man offered to show us around the city but we declined his good offer, preferring to keep control of our time and plans.

It was cold walking the streets in the snow and we were getting bored of looking at shops and bazaars. The chat about education with the commissioner had inspired us and we decided to devote all of our time and attention to the monument of the tomb of lbn-e Sina.

He was known as Avesina in the west, a Persian philosopher and physician, well known throughout the world of medicine and held in high regard in Iran. His tomb was in a modern building which also housed a library and paintings. It was a history lesson and an art lesson, far removed from the boredom of Longcar Central School. We signed the visitors' book and felt proud of ourselves for taking the time and effort to learn about the great man. Things were improving.

When the cold became too painful, we decided to set off for Isfahan and stop at Borujerd for the night. Borujerd was plain and unremarkable with none of the tree lined boulevards, modern lighting and monuments we had seen in Hamadan. We booked into a shabby but clean hotel, rearranged the beds and seating in the room to give ourselves a feeling of space after being on top of each other for so long in the van, ate a banana sandwich and opened a bottle of coke. We were so tired we stubbed out our cigarettes half-smoked and turned in.

None of us felt like getting up but we needed to make an early start if we were to make Isfahan that day. Up, dressed and out of the room in thirty minutes. Nine inches of snow had fallen overnight and the van had got its hat on. We paid the bill to an uninterested manager who seemed glad to get rid of us. Outside, a man helped us reverse out of the covered garage. We weren't sure why we needed assistance as there was plenty of space to turn round. Then he put his hand out and asked for an extra payment for parking. We didn't look at him and drove off past his arm-waving and shouting. This time we didn't feel guilty.

Tony took up the driving. The main road was covered in ice and when we got to a steep hill, the wheels were spinning for longer than they were gripping. We zigzagged our way past a line of stationary lorries and buses held up behind a broken-down lorry. As we got closer, we saw the lorry had shed its load of steel bars across the icy road. Tony skilfully steered a path through the obstacles and a clear hill of untouched snow stretched out in front of us. Then we got stuck. As much as Tony tried, the wheels kept spinning and we started to slip backwards. Lol and I jumped out and pushed our backs against the van but the slope was too great and our shoes wouldn't grip. I grabbed the hammer out of our tool box, wedged the rubber handle under the rear wheel and the tyre gripped enough to send the van forward a few inches. We jumped on to the rear bumper to add weight to the back end and keep the van moving. We must have looked like shotgun riders, and drivers started hooting and laughing as the tyres gripped the fresh white snow and powered us forward. We were the only vehicle to make the summit and we shook hands and slapped Tony's back.

'It's all the rally driving I've been to,' he said. 'I've watched the drivers. It's all about confidence. Just steer into the skid and keep calm.'

I looked as far ahead as I could into the whiteness and said, 'I hope there aren't any more climbs as bad as that to come. Have a look at the map, Lol. See if it shows you the gradients.'

Lol opened the map.

'Bollocks,' he said.

I said, 'What's wrong? Don't tell us they're getting worse?'

'We've taken the wrong road. We should have gone straight on at the bottom of that climb instead of coming up it.'

We turned around and went all the way back down the hill, waving at the drivers we had passed earlier still stuck behind the scattered steel bars.

When we found the right road, we had to keep to the two parallel wheel tracks in the deep snow and hope oncoming traffic stuck to its own twin set of tracks. Everywhere else was unblemished whiteness and it was blinding. The drive was bumpy and stop-go and every time there was a break in the traffic, hundreds of starlings and crows descended on the slushy brown tracks to scavenge the uncovered ground for food. The birds must have been desperate to survive the snow, searching until the last second, and we hit a few, leaving them flapping helplessly on the ground.

We pulled into a village to buy bread and were immediately pestered by nosey, noisy kids opening the van doors, throwing snow at us and tapping on the windows. It was as though the circus had come to town. We cursed them and after a few minutes they moved on and we ate in peace at the roadside. An old man came up to the van and tried to sell us a sheep. He was a poor, pathetic man, very gentle and I thought about the starving starlings and crows and the lesson on class divide we had been given by the agriculture commissioner.

When we set off again, we passed many industrial buildings, the first time we had come across that type of industry in rural Iran. Workers streamed out of the factories like the steelworkers in Sheffield at the end of their shift. The roads were improving and we were going faster and feeling better the nearer we got to Isfahan.

From what we had read, we expected Isfahan to be an unspoilt ancient city but when we pulled into the centre it looked a bright, clean, modern place. We were tired and hungry and booked into the first hotel we tried. A fat chicken sandwich satisfied the hunger pains and we laughed at the way Lol was wolfing it down. He seems to be more relaxed these days.

What will life be like in Australia? Got to get a good job. No idea what kind. Something manual, outdoors in the sunshine. Maybe working in the fields. Living in a commune. Prospecting for gold up north. Living in a shack. Or working in a city. The three of us in a flat. A fridge, tele, music, beds, women, books.

At half past nine we were up and ready for breakfast. Through the dining room window, we saw the snow had almost melted and water was running down the edge of the road into the gutters. The temperature was only a degree or two above freezing, yet people were walking about in open shirts and thin coats.

Lol and Tony went to the bank to change money and when an hour later they hadn't returned I went looking for them. I found them in a café next to the bank enjoying a coffee and I was a bit angry at first until I realised I was being childish again.

We ate a snack back at the van and read for a couple of hours. At around two o'clock the sun began to shine through the windscreen and Isfahan beckoned us to come out and play. It was warm and fresh walking the streets. Lol bought a pair of sunglasses and I pinched a pair from the same shop. I tried them on outside and they looked pretty ugly so I took them back. Tony picked up some information from the Tourist Centre and we set off sightseeing, eyes and ears alert.

There were pokey, dark workshops on every side street and the workers were smiling and covered in dirt. The bazaar was like a dreamland. There were hundreds of people going up and down the many passageways, which were lit by naked bulbs and filtered sunlight, and the smell of nutmeg, lemons and kerosene filled the air. Hundreds of open-fronted shops displayed everything from soft discoloured oranges to huge bowls of take-away stew, from necklaces to Afghan coats, from leather bags to bathroom fittings.

At the front of each shop, small, dark, busy old men sat cross-legged as though paralysed, working their particular craft, the air and their heads warmed by oil heaters and red-hot cokes. The life, the brightness and the colour of the stalls contrasted with the corroding, grey building housing the bazaar itself.

We finally left the dreamland and came out into the cold, clear blue sky, looking for any sign of young women although we knew it was unlikely. Two good-looking girls, one in a bright yellow dress, the other in red trousers, noticed us and I asked them where all the girls went. They were slightly aloof and said they didn't know. I felt uncomfortable and happy at the same time. I took a few photographs of them both, standing and shooting as though I was a professional. Afterwards, I wondered if I could have been arrested for showing a lack of respect.

On the way back to the hotel we passed dozens of mosques and one in particular captivated us with its beauty. The blue tiled dome of the Shah Mosque looked like a single glistening turquoise gem against the light blue sky. We learned how travellers following the Silk Road through Persia would have seen the dome from miles away. The mosaic tiles in the entrance portal used seven colours – dark Persian blue, light Turkish blue, white, black, yellow, green and biscuit. The inside of the massive dome was just as blue and wonderful as the outside and although I'm not religious I thought if there was a heaven it would look like the Shah Mosque.

Next morning, it was sunny again and we were desperate to walk around the streets, hoping to find girls.

We loved the city. I could see why Isfahan is half the world according to the Persian proverb. But it was time to move on and we decided to make for Tehran. I checked the van over, put a pint of oil in the engine and reminded myself to keep an eye on the level. The landscape was semi-desert on the way to Qom with mountains surfacing abruptly out of the desert, getting higher towards the horizon. The clean blue of the sky and the sharp white of the mountain peaks matched the intensity of the colours we had seen in Isfahan.

A helicopter appeared out of nowhere and I took a photograph of it as it flew over the van. We were close to some kind of military base. The barbed wire enclosures ahead looked like concentration camps with their watchtowers built high on top of metal lattice frameworks. The soldiers looked hard and lonely. I hoped they didn't mind us photographing their helicopters. I didn't fancy the idea of being locked up in one of their camps on a charge of spying. Thankfully, nobody stopped us or followed us and we drove in peace to Tehran, smoking Craven A's to the sound of the Beatles, the Stones and Joe Cocker.

It was dark and my driving eyes were hurting when we eventually landed in the city centre. The place was a let-down. Blocks of flats and high commercial buildings were fenced off and lit up by harsh security lights. The roads were scruffy and sludgy, and I almost crashed into another vehicle. We found a passable hotel after searching for an hour and a half. Externally it looked fair but internally it was dirty. The first room we entered was filthy and we discovered dozens of cockroaches scuttling in the wardrobe and under the sink.

'They're only bugs,' Tony said.' They'll not kill us.'

'I don't care,' I said. 'I'm not sleeping with cockroaches running around.'

'You can catch beriberi off them,' Lol said. I think he was exaggerating.

We strode down to reception and demanded our passports back. The receptionist looked frightened and he offered us another room. We expected this to be a lot cleaner but it was virtually the same. We almost left but the thought of sleeping in the freezing van made us stay.

It took us a while to relax. We smoked and talked about health, and about the danger of falling ill on the road. We got on to the subject of hospitals and I told them for the first time about having rheumatic fever when I was fourteen. I told them how I was moved from one bed to another and ended up next to the door.

Tony said, 'The bad cases are usually moved next to the door.' I went red with fear at the implications. I started to sweat and my thoughts went back to the hospital. Had I been close to death? I knew my reaction was showing which made it worse. But I didn't want them to know the truth. I didn't want them to know that I still hadn't got over the trauma.

'It's not that I haven't got over it. It's just that when I talk about being in hospital I can't stop thinking about my mother. How she kept crying with worry.'

It wasn't quite a lie.

I was feeling really tired, my headache made worse by the buzzing of electricity in the room. The bed clothes looked as though they had been slept in so we kept all our clothes on and slept on top.

Miraculously we woke up with no itches or bites. Even Tony hadn't been attacked and bugs love him. In the dim daylight the room looked worse than it had last night. We were all in need of a shower but none of us was going to risk taking one in the creepy, damp, windowless washroom.

When we got to the foot of the Albortz mountain on the way to Mashhad, we saw lorry drivers parked by the roadside wagging their fingers at us, signalling for us to put snow chains on. We shrugged and nodded and kept going. They didn't know about our secret weapon – the rubber handled hammer. Taking turns behind the wheel, we climbed the steep, snow packed, winding mountain road as though we were driving up Harborough Hill Road in Barnsley, only losing control once and that was on a flat section when I was driving.

'I'm losing it,' I said as the van slewed from one side of the empty road to the other. I kept steering into the skid as Tony had done but I was going from full lock to full lock and the slewing was getting worse.

'Tha're over-steering,' Lol said, sitting calmly in the middle seat. 'Just steer into the skid gently. It'll straighten up.'

I did as Lol instructed and the van miraculously came back under control.

There were no more steep climbs, just the occasional short, sharp kick, and the road levelled out then became a fast descent through rugged, bare mountains. It was hairpin bend after hairpin bend and we shared the thrill of driving. Tony drove fast and he couldn't stop smiling. The curves were hypnotic and as I waited for my turn, I tried to imagine being on my motorbike. When I took over, I think I frightened Tony and Lol with the lines I took, almost clipping the rocks on one side and the barriers on the other as I cut the corners like I do on my bike. Lol couldn't wait for his turn. Unluckily, within half a mile of him taking over, the descent bottomed out and we came into flat, green, boring forest land.

*

Our food store was low and we stopped off at Babol to top up. The town had a friendly feel, clean, happy and well-lit with coloured light bulbs suspended across the roads, shops and bridges. It was bright and youthful and we almost stayed there for the night. Lol complained of stomach ache so I took over the driving and we soon arrived in Sari, the former capital of Iran. It was fairly modern, set in a beautiful location just off the southern coast of the Caspian Sea. The streets were quiet and there were no signs of nightlife or young people. It was still early, only eight o'clock, and the air was warm. We decided to carry on towards Mashhad and pull in somewhere before it got too late to park up and bed down for the night in the van.

Two hours later, we stopped in a well-lit layby in the city of Gorgan. Tony cooked up our staple meal of rice pudding and banana, which Lol had to leave because of his bad guts. We fed a lonely white Labrador-type dog with our old bread and I checked the VW manual with a view to changing the oil seals on the push rod covers. It looked straightforward.

The next morning when I woke up, the sides of the van were burning. It was an unbelievable change in the weather. Tony had already gone off to find the tourist centre and he came back with more leaflets to add to our library.

'Gorgan has four universities and a world-famous Turkmen rug and carpet making industry,' he said, reading from the literature and drinking the tea I had brewed for him.

'Sounds good,' I said looking at Lol. 'Have we got time to look round?'

Lol glanced at the leaflets and said, 'Not really. We ought to be makin' tracks while t'weather's so good.'

A bit of relaxed sight-seeing would have been enjoyable but we agreed to move on and Tony filed away the information for another day, month, year. We tidied the van, snubbed a tramp, waved to passing drivers and set off to Mashhad with our sunglasses on. The countryside was flat and barren and the sparse villages were built of mud. Women in veils and men in turbans washed themselves and their clothes in shallow, pebble-bottomed streams, looking up for a moment as we drove past, neither happy nor sad.

Tony slowed down as we entered a wildlife park in a deep valley, its craggy, dark hillsides sharp against a brilliant blue sky. The sign at the entrance told us we were entering Golestan National Park, Iran's oldest national park and one of the oldest in the world. Goats surveyed the crags and occasionally a loose rock would slip from under their hooves and crash down the rocky face. A family of wild boar trotted through a gap in the trees, and hooded crows circled, landed and took off again. There were deep snow drifts in the dips and up against the rocks. On a short stretch of straight road, a few trees had been felled to create a layby and we stopped for a walk and a stretch looking like trappers in our logger shirts. The dense wood was silent. The light from the fallen snow created no shadows and the trees looked weightless. The air was still and it felt like we were being watched. We went in deeper, disturbing snow as we stepped over fallen branches. Lol, who had been lagging behind, stopped and called out.

'Over here, lads.'

'What?'

'Bear footprints.'

We looked down at the markings in the snow.

'It might be a dog,' Tony said.

'It must be a chuffing big dog,' I said. 'Look at the size of its paws. They're like my dad's hands.'

Lol said, 'They're too big for me. I'm off.'

We followed Lol out of the wood, keeping close together, jumped in the van and continued our journey to Mashhad, wild-eyed and refreshed.

In Mashhad we saw a huge luxury hotel and just for a bit of fun went in to see how much it would cost to stay one night. We looked like tramps in comparison to the guests lounging around the hotel and I expected the manager to ask us to leave but he didn't and told us it would cost £14 for the room. Lol shrugged his shoulders so we booked in. Too embarrassed to employ the eager porter, we carried our own belongings, which consisted of blue plastic carrier bags stuffed with bananas, dirty underwear, socks and shirts. As we went up the silent lift to room 409, I kept my head down conscious of being stared at by the other guests. The porter had to assemble an extra bed for us, the norm being two beds per room. It took him almost ten minutes and he never smiled. I think he had already worked out from the state of our belongings that the chances of a tip were zero. When he left, we laughed at the luxury and sat in every chair and looked inside every drawer and cupboard.

'Now this is what I call living,' I said bouncing on the bed beside the window.

'Are you sure we can afford this, Lol?' Tony said as he back-flopped on to his bed, grinning.

'This is the kind of flat I'd like to live in when we get to Australia,' Lol said.

'We'd have to do a few years fruit picking to earn this kind of luxury,' I said.

'Unless we did a bit of prospecting for gold in Western Australia and struck rich,' Lol said.

'I'd buy myself a Ferrari, if we did,' Tony said and he put his hands behind his head and was lost for a few seconds.

We spent ten minutes each in the shower, drank milky coffee and felt like lords. Our faces were still glowing as we took the silent lift down to the bar. The main sitting area was empty apart from the barman, and a couple of customers drinking quietly in a corner. In the entertainment lounge there were only four customers, all men, sitting at the same table, serious and well-dressed, looking like actors on stage.

After an hour of whisky and Winston cigarettes we glided up the four floors to our room and took turns to wash our jeans, underpants and socks in the bathroom basin. Fresh linen over a soft mattress sent me into a deep, expensive sleep.

Obviously, we had breakfast in bed. The ham and eggs followed by cheese, jam and coffee were worth the

£14 alone. As the brochure would surely have said, the view from the veranda was splendid, taking in the expansive hotel grounds and waterfall and the distant snow-capped mountains. We strolled around the ground floor of the hotel gazing at the variety of shops selling luxury items. The hotel even had its own bank. It was a world within a world. We paid the hefty bill, leaving behind a blocked toilet in Room 409 thanks to the evacuation of Lol's bad guts.

We left the hotel and parked on a quiet backstreet in the city, wound down the windows and smiled at any good-looking young Iranian woman who played her eyes at us. Lol made the teas and Tony got out the map and we went over our travelling plans again. Our intention was to look around Mashhad for a couple of hours then press on to Afghanistan, get through that dangerous country as quickly as we could, drive across Pakistan into India, up to Nepal, and then find a way to work our passage to Australia before selling the van. Lol worked out how much it would cost. I had just enough money in traveller's cheques to get to Nepal. But it was tight.

We put the map away, feeling satisfied with our review, and there was a tap-tap on the window. That's when we met Magic Mohammed, the guy with the perfect white teeth, and were invited to his brother Ali's house with the offer of tea, accommodation and something unspoken that might help us in India.

At Ali's we played cards, drank tea and ate oranges, and I was enjoying the sight of Ali's pretty wife as she slipped gracefully in and out of the room carrying her silver tray when Mohammed offered to show us around Mashhad. He grabbed his expensive-looking leather jacket, jumped into the back of our van and directed us around the city.

We viewed the Imam Reza shrine, the largest mosque in the world. The two imposing domes, one gold and one turquoise, were stunning. I'd only ever seen colours as pure as that once before and that was in a sunset over the moors in Sheffield. Mohammed told us the complex of mosques, courtyards, madrassa and museum was the second holiest site in the holiest city in Iran. Tony asked Mohammad what a madrassa was. When he said it was an educational institution, Lol and I nodded as though we already knew. Then he took us to a Persian carpet factory so big it had its own sales outlet on site. The building consisted of cramped shops stacked high with damaged and part-finished carpets. Skilled craftsmen, their skinny crossed legs flat to the floor, worked non-stop and smiled at us as though we were their captors, which I suppose we were in a way. It was late afternoon by the time we had been shown every corner of the factory and I was glad when Mohammed offered to take us back to Ali's apartment with the promise of music, drink and good smoke.

Tony had a go on one of the African guys' Tom-Tom drums and he wasn't bad and then we shared a smoke with Mohammed and Ali. I inhaled, remembering J's sarcastic comment in Delphi asking when was I going to do my own thing in life for once. I waited for a kick but nothing happened. It was different for Lol. He took a big drag and that's when he said his legs felt heavy and he ended up in the toilet, crying again.

There was only one window in the room in Ali's flat and it was blacked out by a heavy blanket but I could sense it was dark outside. We sat around the edge of the

Persian carpet, everyone cross-legged except me, my footballing legs too big to bend beyond ninety degrees. All night we kept the music spinning, the vodka bottle moving and the smoke drifting. Someone passed around a plate of nuts and we played cards until I couldn't sit upright any longer. Before long I was horizontal.

Eyes half-closed. Watery. Focussed in mid-air. Quiet people. Noisy people. Peaceful. Together. Loud hypnotic music. Cigarette stubs. Open bottles. Nut shells scattered over the floor. Bare feet. Beards. Heavy atmosphere. Room hot and smoky. Rock hard floor.

I woke up and checked my watch. Six hours had slipped by, mouth dry, back aching. The three African guys were flat out asleep, snoring. Mohammad and Ali were resting on their sides in a corner of the room, talking quietly to each other. The music was softer and the smoky air had cleared. The clutter on the floor was just as it was when I'd fallen asleep yet somehow the mess looked older than a single night. I was desperate to get some fresh air, to get a drink from somewhere, afraid to touch the tap water.

Ali and Lol went to the market and returned with bread, cheese, butter and milk, and we sat on the Persian carpet, picking food and chatting about life.

The breakfast revived Tony and me but Lol wasn't quite with us yet, his eyes ringed red. It was just after ten, still early, and we decided it was time to leave for Afghanistan.

Tony said, 'Mohammed. Before we go. What was that you said to us yesterday about having something that might help us in India?'

I had been wondering the same thing but I wasn't as curious as Tony and would have been quite happy to leave without knowing. I suspected it was bullshit.

Mohammed nodded and said, 'Ah yes. There is a good way to make a lot of money in India by buying and selling turquoise stones.'

Ali nodded and said, 'Yes indeed. A very good way.'

'You can buy a precious stone here in Mashhad,' Mohammed said, 'and sell it at three hundred per cent profit in India.'

We'd heard about this trade from almost every western traveller we'd come across in Iran and it still sounded like bullshit to me. But we listened and asked a few questions, and Lol, normally the cautious saver thought it was a risk worth taking. Tony agreed but I wasn't sure so that was that. Our decision-making process was simple. All three had to agree. Mohammed and Ali didn't seem too disappointed, which made me doubt my judgement, and we shook hands and exchanged addresses.

On the way to the Iran/Afghanistan border we smoked a joint given to us by Ali. Once again, the drug had no apparent effect on me and Tony and Lol laughed at my sceptical expression. At least, I think that's why they were laughing.

We drove through fog and drizzle as miserable as in England and arrived at the border where we found a dozen people waiting to cross into Afghanistan. There were Indians in robes and turbans, hikers dressed in anything that fitted, and a good-looking guy wearing a fur coat, earrings, rings, bracelets, a beard and eye-make-up.

We got through the Iranian side of the border without any major hold up but were told by the officials there that we would need visas to enter Afghanistan, obtainable from the Afghanistan Consul back in Mashhad. Having been told a similar story about the need for a Carnet de Passage on entering Iran I was sure that with a bit of pleading and obstinacy we could get the appropriate documents at the border. Lol and Tony said it was worth a try seeing as we had come this far.

As soon as we drove up to the Afghanistan side of the border, we knew we had made a mistake. There were only two guards on duty, a hut and the wreck of a VW van in the muddy parking area. And that was it. There was no one in authority and that meant there was little room for anyone to show initiative. Sure enough, the two guards told us the same story – return to Mashhad for the correct documents.

Back at the Iran border I felt like apologising to the officials for not believing them. They smiled and shrugged. It must happen regularly I thought. We set off back to Mashhad retracing the hundred and fifty long miles we had just completed. The fog returned with the darkness and it seemed to sum up our misery.

By the time we reached the city our optimistic selves had returned. The lack of a visa and carnet meant we had to wait just one more day, that's all. What did sicken me, though, was the oil light flickering on and off. I had to fill up with oil again and it was obvious we would have to get the leak fixed urgently even if we had to do it ourselves.

We came across another two friendly Iranians in the centre of Mashhad and they directed us to a cheap, bare hotel but it sufficed. None of us fancied another late, noisy night at Ali's apartment.

We didn't rise until twelve noon the next day. There was no reason to get up any earlier. It was Friday and the hotel manager had told us that all the shops would be shut, including the Afghanistan Consul. It was snowing and gradually the sick feeling we had experienced at the Afghanistan border returned.

Lol cooked chips and eggs in the van and I had a little argument with Tony over where to eat. He wanted to stay in the van and I wanted to sneak back into the hotel and eat there. We didn't lose our tempers and the conflict soon smoothed over. It was obvious we were both in an angry mood because of yesterday.

We sneaked upstairs to our room hiding our hot dinner and cutlery in our coat pockets. The food was fine but we didn't enjoy it. We were down. It was only one o'clock. There was nothing to do except lie on the bed and read. Tony broke off to wash a few clothes which livened things up for half an hour. The book I was reading transported me to a happy place, deadening Lol's snoring, and it was seven o'clock by the time I checked my watch. Lol's book was on his chest and he had slept for the last two hours. He seems to have lost some of his drive lately and is getting a bit weary.

The day was wasting away and we lounged around waiting for tomorrow to arrive. I ordered what turned out to be three lousy cups of tea and just as we were thinking of what to do next, there was a knock on the door. It was Magic Mohammed, looking cool in his expensive leather jacket and his Levi jeans tucked into his boots. He said he had been skiing and his friends had told him we were staying in the hotel. When he asked us why we hadn't gone to Ali's apartment, we told him we didn't know the way. It was impressive to see the three of us lie so effortlessly as a unit. I don't think he was fooled and we arranged to meet up the next day. We felt even worse now for having offended Mohammed.

Mohammed turned up again the next morning and took us to the Afghanistan Consul to get our visas. The Consul was a scruffy place, cold and bare, and looked like a condemned building. I was surprised to see people already waiting for documents. We filled in a form and left our passports with the official and were told to report back at eleven o'clock. Mohammed took us to a VW garage and we arranged for the van to have two new rocker cover gaskets fitted. He tried to show us a bit more of the city but today was the King's anniversary and most of the streets were blocked by processions of proud Iranians singing and banner waving.

We finished up at Ali's business address. The place was cold but we soon warmed up after drinking chai and talking. Mohammed and Ali asked us again if we wanted to buy turquoise stones. They showed us photograph albums full of pictures of the two of them posing with groups of western travellers holding up packs of neatly cut small stones, everyone smiling, thumbs up. We read the testimonials from travellers who had made a good profit. Lol and Tony were even more convinced that it was an opportunity to make money and this time I felt under pressure. We went for a walk and Lol did a quick calculation of our finances.

'We can afford to spend a hundred and twenty-five quid,' he said. 'Just over forty quid each.'

I said, 'Forty bloody quid. That's a week and half's wage for a gas fitter.'

Tony smiled, slightly embarrassed, and said, 'It's only a week's wage for an electrician.'

'Look on it like borrowing money to invest,' Lol said. 'When we sell them in India, we'll be quids in.'

After a careful inspection of the goods – what we were looking for I don't know – we bought the stones, which were all carefully laid out and beautifully displayed in cardboard packs, together with six turquoise rings.

Mohammed told us he lived with his father in New Delhi for half the year and he gave us his address. He said he hoped to be there in a few weeks' time and asked us to offer the stones to his father first before trying to sell them to anyone else. Lol reckoned it was a duty-free way for Mohammed's family to import turquoise into India. We'll see, I thought.

We gave Ali a pair of old jeans and he gave us a piece of smoke. I really liked Ali. He was a happy guy, sometimes serious, fumbling, good-looking, cool and sure and he didn't have the salesman streak of his brother. We said goodbye after picking up the van from the garage where the two new rocker cover gaskets had been fitted at a good price. Mohammed and Ali have been really helpful, I thought. No denying it.

Ten minutes after driving out of Mashhad, Lol clambered into the back of the van for his cigarettes.

'Hey up,' he said.' Look what I've fon. It's Mohammed's leather jacket. He's forgotten it.'

'Brilliant,' I said. 'If this stone thing turns out to be a con and we lose our money, at least we've got an expensive leather jacket we can sell.'

We punched the air and I was so happy I played a tune on the horn and waved at startled motorists. Tony felt the quality of the leather and tried on the jacket.

'Does it suit me?'

'Fits you like a glove,' I said.

Lol said, 'Are tha sure tha didn't nick it, Tony?'

One hundred and twenty miles and almost four hours of driving later, we parked up in a small town near the Iran-Afghan border for the night and prepared a dinner of bananas and soup. Half way through the meal, there was a tap-tap on the van window. It was Mohammed. He was laughing and shaking his head and he told us that when he realised he had left his jacket in the van he caught a bus and instructed the driver to keep an eye out for a red VW van with GB plates. We handed him his jacket and he departed as quickly as he had come.

We were too downhearted to speak. Five minutes later, still in a state of disbelief, a German guy carrying a heavy rucksack peered through the driver's window and said he was looking for a lift to Turkey. When we said we were on our way to India and Nepal, driving through Afghanistan as quickly as we could, he screwed up his face.

'You've not heard about the Pakistan border?'

We shook our heads.

'Pakistan is hosting an Islamic conference. The border is closed now to all foreign travellers until 28 February.'

I said, 'What? That's a whole month from now.'

'That's life, guys. Enjoy,' he said, and he went off in search of a lift.

We looked at each other. If what he said was true then we were in trouble.

'Looks like bread and water every day,' Lol said. 'We can't afford to hang around for a month. Money's tight.'

'I don't fancy killing all that time here in Iran,' Tony said.

Lol said. 'Me neither. But I don't fancy killing time in Afghanistan, neither. I want to get to Australia with my arms and legs in one piece.'

'We'll just have to keep going and see if we can get through the Pakistan border somehow,' I said. 'He might have been having us on.'

Within the space of a few minutes our flimsy guarantee of Mohammed's honesty had evaporated, and our optimistic plan to get through Afghanistan and into Pakistan as quickly as possible had been put in serious doubt.

We spent the night in a cheap hotel, too downhearted to sleep in the cold van. Early next morning, we arrived at the Iran customs. We knew the place well. There was a long line of lorries top-heavy with goods, and a separate queue of about twenty or thirty travellers. They were mainly Germans and Americans and a few Indians and Pakistanis and we heard more tales from them about the situation in Pakistan. Our optimism had returned a little following a good night's sleep and we weren't totally put off by the bad news. We thought there may be a chance that British passport holders would be allowed through.

While we waited in the queue, half a dozen guards began to torment an Iranian foot passenger. He was clearly struggling to understand what was going on around him. One guard in particular was enjoying the bullying and he kept telling the unfortunate passenger to strip to his pants then get dressed then strip again then get dressed again. The hapless man did as he was told quickly and without question or protest. The guards were laughing at his distress although some looked uneasy. What is it about uniforms and authority? I thought. Why are we so obedient? I was angry but what could we do? Their cold rifles and heavy boots were real.

We passed through the Iran side of the border and pulled up at the Afghan barrier. The hut with its two guards and the solitary wrecked VW van we had seen the other night looked just as bare in the daylight. When our turn finally came, we presented our new visas and the friendly guards let us through. The whole procedure through both sides of the borders took less than two hours.

'Well, that was easy enough,' Lol said.

Half a mile down the deserted road leading away from the hut and its two guards we were flagged down at a barrier by three men in military uniforms carrying guns. I was feeling tired but seeing those characters woke me up sharp.

'Uh-ho,' I said reaching down for the knife under the seat. 'I don't like the look of this. I hope these aren't bandits.'

I stopped at the barrier and wound down the window, fast enough not to look suspicious, slow enough to be able to make a run for it if needed. One of the men took off his peaked cap and shoved his head through the window to check the inside of the van. I could smell the oil flattening his black hair. We said nothing and he put his cap back on.

'You must fill out two forms,' he said. 'One for the driver and passengers and another one for the vehicle.

You must also have your vaccination certificates and passports stamped. And you must take out an insurance policy.'

We were so relieved to find that this was the official border control and not a hold-up that we almost welcomed the prospect of a delay. Each check had to be completed separately which meant going back and forth to the custom office each time to get approval from the solitary official working there. The whole area where vehicles were parked and inspected was a mud bath and the customs office itself was cold, bare and muddy. The Medical Centre was no better. On a table in one corner there was a tray of syringes and other medical accessories sitting in what looked like bread crumbs. I thought I hope to God none of us gets sick.

After three hours, we had everything signed, stamped and approved. We were wise enough not to show our frustration and by the time we were allowed through, the guard on duty at the barrier waived us through with a smile as though we were old friends.

August 2018 - Café at Achiltibui

We ask the same question at the village post office and the newsagents and get the same answer – they haven't heard of anybody called Lol renting a log cabin, either. There is a cedar clad café opposite the post office and we go in and order tea and scones. I spread out the damp map on the table and put my glasses on.

'I don't think this is going to work, Tony.'

'I was thinking the same. There's dozens of these little hamlets along this coast.'

'Is it worth trying Facebook again or one of those other social networky things you've got on your fancy phone? See if he's on there?'

'I've tried everything I can think of. Why on earth would anybody want to rent a log cabin somewhere as deserted as the west coast of Scotland?' Tony says.

'Maybe he feels more at home in Scotland. He was always canny with his money when we were travelling.'

'He did a good job looking after our budget. I'll give him that,' Tony says.

'Maybe he's become a recluse in his old age. Or what about this for a theory? He is married, like we were told. He spends most of his time with his wife in Spain and Barnsley, and then in August he sneaks up here out of the way, pretending to be going fishing, and he has an assignation with his secret lover.'

'You've got a wild imagination. Can you imagine if it turned out to be his ex-fiancée?'

'Now that would be a story,' I say.

'Had he been going out with his fiancée for a long time before she up and left him?'

'I think they'd known each other since they were at school.'

'That's why he took it so bad, then,' Tony says.

'He once told me they used to go the Youth Club together when they were fourteen or fifteen. Nothing serious. Just messing about. And his dad used to follow them around like a private detective. He used to appear on street corners and shop doorways. Lol said he could never take her anywhere near his house because he was too frightened of his dad. They had to say goodbye to each other at the Youth Club, a mile away.'

'Weird.'

We finish our tea and scones and watch the rain flow over the gutters on the houses and shops. There's hardly anyone on the streets. Houses have their lights on and the buildings in the distance are beginning to fade in the mist.

'What do you want to do?' I say and I look at Tony's face to see his reaction before he answers. I'll carry on if he wants to carry on. It's taken us over forty years to get here. We've come a long way.

Tony says, 'Why don't we keep looking for another hour before it gets too dark and then find somewhere to stay for the night? Then see how we feel tomorrow.'

'That sounds like a sensible idea,' I say.

7

No Need for the Knife: Afghanistan
26 January – 26 February 1974

We were elated at finally getting across the border but we weren't looking forward to travelling through Afghanistan. Almost immediately we came upon the much-reported rough surface that forms the major road network circulating inside Afghanistan. Our AA guide had warned us about the condition of the ring road and the likelihood of roadside bandits. Their advice was to get through the country as quickly as possible. I felt under the seat to make sure the knife was still there.

Mud swilled across the surface at every dip in the undulating, broken road and in places we crawled through deep fords, occasionally on the more deserted sections getting out and wading in to test the depth of water. At one stage we nearly lost the van on a particularly atrocious stretch where the mud was eighteen inches deep. Crashed lorries and buses, abandoned where they had fallen, were a constant reminder of the danger we faced. Thankfully we arrived in Herat without sinking or turning over and we never saw a bandit.

Herat was rough. I thought some of the towns and cities in Iran were dirty. If I'd laid down in the gutter and died, I'm sure no one would have blinked an eye. There was a skinned look to the place. Muddy, bare concrete steps and walls. Earth pavements compacted under straw, soggy oranges, stones, phlegm and slurry from the gutters. Men in long, baggy pale coats, and loose scarves around their heads, women completely covered in black shawls with mesh face pieces. Scruffy, scar-faced beggars of all ages. Horse and carts and a few mud-splattered old cars and bikes. A meat shop with the head and skin of a bull thrown on to the dirt pavement, the various select pieces of the poor animal strung up on bent nails on plaster-peeling, blood-stained, muck-daubed walls. Welcome to Afghanistan.

We had only been parked up a few minutes when an Afghan guy aged about forty came over and started pestering us to follow him to his hotel. He was persistent, not aggressive, and we were too tired to ignore him. The hotel was really a hostel and to say our room was bare was being kind to the man. The wood stove was cold and dusty. The smiling owner switched on the light and the naked bulb couldn't have been more than ten watts. But it was better than staying in the van in this weather and at just over ten shillings we didn't think we were losing out. I wrote home and mentioned the possible delay at the Pakistan border, probably more for my sake than my mother and dad's. It was rice pudding again, washed down with mint tea for a change and I drifted off wondering about Afghanistan.

Sunday 27 January

The unnerving sound of a cockerel woke me up at half past six and an hour later I opened my eyes trying to shake off a dream about a prostitute and blood. Tony had already lit the wood fire and we ate two fried eggs and bread and jam in a warm room.

We heard more rumours about the Pakistan border being closed from three American guys staying at the same hotel. Like us, they were on their way to Nepal, and said they'd decided to spend the dead time in Herat because it was such a 'trippy' place. The owner of the hotel was as bright and friendly as he had been last night and when we tipped him his kind face lit up.

As we drove out of Herat on the road to Kandahar, we passed dozens of men leading their camels into the city from the fertile valley with stacks of firewood strapped to the beasts. Wood seemed to be the key industry. The smiling, friendly, open faces in Herat stood out against the raw backdrop of the streets and I could understand why the three Americans wanted to stay there.

The long, straight, grey concrete road stretched out over the semi-desert. In between the scattered mountains, their peaks hidden in mist, the landscape was barren and flat. Tony pulled off the road and the tyres sank a few inches into the hot sand. We drank tea, spellbound by the isolation and listened to the tick and crack of the engine as it contracted. There was no breeze and it was painful to look at the sky despite the haze. I lifted the tailgate to take some heat away from the engine but it made little difference. We knew we could die out here if we became stranded. Lol took over the driving and Tony and I rode on the rear bumper for a laugh. We clung on for over a dry, dusty mile and all around the landscape was lifeless. It was a silly thing to do. Maybe the heat had got to us.

We smoked and drank tea on the move to the sound of Crosby, Stills, Nash and Young. The straight road in front of us seemed endless. The sun was high and so were we. On the road again.

Isolated communities would appear out of nowhere, black people in black tents in brown sand, and we didn't hang around, fearing bandits. We were passing one of these settlements when four figures on horseback galloped towards the road ahead of us, on course to cut us off in a hundred yards. I grabbed the knife from under the driver's seat and we wound up the windows. We were doing close to thirty miles an hour, as fast as I dared on the rough road. As the horses closed in on us, we could see the bare-back riders were young kids, hardly ten years old, and they were enjoying the race. I slowed down to twenty miles an hour and wound down the window. They came alongside, laughing and striking imaginary matches. They were so close we could hear the horses pounding the earth and we applauded their horse-riding skills and cheeky mimicry. Tony leaned out of the window and handed the closest rider a full box of Swan Vestas. They peeled off still laughing and I put away the knife.

The light was fading when we got to Kandahar and we weren't sure we had arrived in the city. It wasn't a big place and there were no name plates to guide us. We tried one hotel but it was poorly lit and too expensive. Hotel-hunting in the dark is hard work and just as it looked as though we would have to spend another night in the cold van, a gang of kids pestered us to try a hotel they knew. We followed them to a hostel-type building on a back street. It wasn't bad and only cost twenty-five Afghanis (Afs) each, which was less than five shillings.

There were some friendly young girls staying there on their way home to Germany and three loud American lads on their way to Greece. It was like being in a youth camp. We kept our coats on in our room and I collected an armful of logs from a stack round the back of the hotel. Tony lit the log fire and within half an hour we were in jumpers and jeans, walking bare-foot on the well-worn Afghan rugs covering the packed-earth floor.

Monday 28 January

Impossible. Lol was up before me and Tony. It was half past six and he was shouting at us.

'Come on, lazy sods. It's time to ger up,' he said and we scrambled out of our sleeping bags in shock. It was a new day. We had new miles to eat up and new things to find out.

Our plan for today was ambitious. Drive the three hundred and ten miles to Kabul and then call at the British Embassy before it closed at half past three to see if there was a way we could get into Pakistan. We met a British couple outside the hotel who had just arrived in Kandahar from Kabul and they warned us that the road we were about to take was very bad.

It sure was. There were foot square blocks of ice hiding in the slush and snow. On top of that the throttle was sticking again due to the icy conditions and there was a strong side wind. I lost control and skidded into a hedge. It was my fault. I was going too fast and we were all a bit shaken. Within half an hour I was back driving faster than it was safe to do so.

The roads got worse. We were making poor time and the plan to reach the embassy before it closed for the day looked more and more doubtful with each sapping mile. Decorated trucks and buses made up the bulk of the traffic with just the occasional foreign traveller, usually a bearded hippie behind the wheel of a VW van.

Lorries were parked by the side of the road, small fires burning under their diesel tanks to thaw the fuel.

Light turned grey and grey became coal black. There were no cats' eyes or street lamps to indicate where the road was. Lorries and buses only had full beam headlights and they waited until oncoming traffic approached before switching off their blinding lights, allowing everybody a few seconds to see where they were going before switching them back on again.

We were tired and hungry. The throttle was still sticking. The windows were icing over. We arrived in Kabul having driven for nine hours, only stopping to change driver, in an attempt to make the British Embassy and we failed.

Tuesday 29 January

Compared to Herat and Kandahar, Kabul is a big city but the buildings, the people and the commerce appeared to reflect the character of the two smaller cities. When we parked up, Tony, reading from our guide book, told us to look out for the slight variations in the turbans worn by Afghan men to distinguish their ethnic group and status. Simple colours are chosen so as not to draw attention. The women's full body and head covering is known as a chederee. Lol and I were too tired to ask questions and eventually Tony gave up and put the guide book away.

We bought bread, the best I'd ever eaten, freshly made in one of those rough concrete domed ovens to be found on every street, and waited in the van like experienced travellers for someone to knock on the window and show us to a hotel. No one did and we eventually ended up at the Ansari Guest House, recommended to us last night by one of the loud Americans staying at our hotel in Kandahar. Our room was a wooden shack at the back of the guest house, similar to yesterday's place.

The tea room was full of travellers lounging around on rickety cane chairs and old settees. The roof was supported by rustic wooden poles which were covered in hanging flowers and creeping plants, and the floor and walls were decorated with Afghan rugs. Only the high ceiling with its forty-watt naked bulb hanging from a single flex escaped decoration. Staying there were two British guys, Kev and Rod, two German guys, a Swiss guy and a Japanese couple. We found three spare chairs and chatted around the hot, wood stove, drinking tea out of brown earthenware tea pots. The travellers were friendly and as interested in our adventures as we were in theirs. We got to know the ins and outs of the guest house and learned, most importantly, that Mali, an Afghan guy who ran the guest house, was the unofficial information bureau and knew everything and everybody in Kabul.

Mali must have heard us talking and he came into the tea room and introduced himself to the three of us. We complimented him on his English, which was far better than ours, and he told us he had been privately educated in England. He even corrected me when I said, 'further down the road,' instead of 'farther down the road'.

Over a cup of tea and brownie, Mali, in his immaculate western suit and tie, confirmed that the Pakistan border was indeed closed for four weeks. We explained our predicament, slowly and in the clearest English we could manage.

'We haven't got enough money to stay in Kabul for four weeks waiting for the Pakistan border to reopen,' I said.

'And we can't drive north to China,' Tony said, 'and skirt around Pakistan into India that way. It would take us a month to get the paperwork sorted out.'

'And we definitely don't want to turn round and travel back to Europe,' Lol said. 'We were planning to drive to India. Maybe Nepal. Then sell the van there and use the money to sail to Australia.'

'But now we might have to sell the van here,' I said, 'and fly over Pakistan to India.'

Mali listened carefully, nodding sympathetically, and then told us what was and was not possible.

'Unfortunately, you cannot sell your vehicle in Afghanistan. Neither are you allowed to sell your vehicle in Iran, Pakistan or India. It is against the law. If you enter one of these countries with a foreign vehicle you must take that same vehicle out of the country with you when you leave.'

Mali let us think about that for a few seconds. He could see it was something we weren't aware of.

He said, 'In the past, many hippies and travellers arrived in these countries and sold or abandoned their vehicles without paying tax and this was adversely affecting the local economy. Therefore, the governments introduced regulation and put an end to the practice.'

We looked at each other and grimaced.

I said, 'That's that, then. We're stuffed.'

The other travellers had been listening in to the conversation while drinking their tea, and they nodded at my conclusion. Maybe the vehicle situation was something they weren't aware of either.

Lol joked that because the van was in my name, he and Tony could fly to India and leave me here in Kabul to stew. The other travellers laughed. So did I but it was a nervous laugh.

Mali said, 'There is another option. You could pay to leave your van in storage at the Afghanistan Consul here in Kabul. That way you would be free to fly over Pakistan into India, travel on to Nepal or Australia or wherever you wished, then return to collect your van at a later date.'

Before we had time to discuss the option Lol said, 'How much would that cost?'

'It all depends on the value of your vehicle and the length of time in storage.'

Mali must have seen our faces drop.

'If you needed to raise cash, you could sell your van spares and surplus equipment from here in my guest house. I could help you with that.'

I did a quick mental calculation of the value of spares and equipment and it didn't amount to much.

'There is one more option.'

We sat up. I had to give Mali top marks for drama and sales technique.

'I may be able to help you sell your van. I know a French guy at the French Embassy who may be interested in buying your vehicle.'

Tony was quicker than me and Lol and he said, 'How can we do that, Mali? You have just told us we are not allowed to sell the van in Afghanistan.'

Mali nodded. 'That is correct. You would have to travel to Iran with the French guy in order to complete the transaction and then come back into Afghanistan.'

'Iran?' the three of us said in unison.

I said, 'But I thought you said we weren't allowed to sell the van in Iran, neither?'

'You are allowed, providing the buyer is a foreign person working in a foreign embassy.'

'You mean like the French guy you know?' I said trying both to keep up and not sound sceptical.

'That's correct. It is what you might call a legal loophole.'

The thought of returning to Mashhad, an almost eighteen hundred miles round trip, made the three of us slump in our creaky chairs. But at least it was an option and it would give us the money we needed to get to Australia. If Mali was telling the truth, then we were lucky to have an eligible, potential buyer, willing to go through such a convoluted sale. This French guy must want the van badly, I thought and I began to work out in my head how much the van was worth. I could see from the studious look on Lol's face that he was already ahead of me.

We smiled and nodded and I took a big sup of tea. It tasted better with each mouthful. We thanked Mali for his help and offer of assistance. As he stood up to get on with his guest house duties, two cops strode into the tea room and demanded to see everybody's passport. They seemed to enjoy their power over us, taking their time inspecting the passports as though the documents belonged to them. They kept the long-haired Swiss guy's passport and left without comment. Mali said all the local police were the same.

Towards the end of a long day, the two British guys, Kev and Rod, invited us back to their cool, as in stylish, room. It was small with low beds and in the corner, there was a wood stove with its door open to reveal a crackling fire. Kev and Rod looked like brothers with their identical clogs, Levi jeans, and fur coats. They shared their bubble pipe with us and whatever was in it had no effect on me. Lol smoked a joint and was bad again. Tony, strangely, wasn't bothered about either pipe or joint. Tapes played all night long, Roger Daltry, Leo Sayer and others I hadn't heard before. As the night went on Rod looked increasingly blocked and Kev began to gabble. The guys were leaving early in the morning so around midnight we said goodbye and they gave us a box of tea bags as a parting gift.

Kev said, 'Good luck with the van, guys. Hope you sell it.'

'Yeah', Rod said. 'Mali's a cool cat.'

Feeling good. Wood fire hypnotic. Beatles coming through the wall from Rod and Kev's room. Good ending to the day.

Wednesday 30 January

Lol woke up with an idea.

'Hey,' he said sitting up in bed. 'I've been thinking. I wonder if we could put the van on a plane here and fly it to Australia?'

It was like lighting a firework and we charged off to the BOAC offices (British Overseas Airways Corporation) to see how much it would cost to transport the van and the three of us by air. The guy behind the counter told us the cost would be extortionate and anyway, he said, there were no freight lines to Australia from Afghanistan. He advised us to go to Iran, to one of the ports on the Persian Gulf such as Bandar Abbas, and ship the van from there to Australia. He could probably see from our faces what we thought about that notion. He had no idea how much it would cost to transport the van by sea but he told us it wouldn't be cheap. We were up one minute, down the next.

By then it was nearly lunch time. We'd not eaten since breakfast and it wasn't helping our judgement. We had a bowl of rice at Siggy's Restaurant on Chicken Street, an eating house recommended to us by Mali. The restaurant was a freaky place, with its spicy smells, colourful rugs, smouldering log fire and good music. There were lots of guys wearing silver and turquoise stones. Sadly, there were no women.

When we got back to the Ansari Guest House, everyone was laughing except us. A German guy told us he was leaving his car in customs while he flew to India for a month and he thought the cost was reasonable. We went to our room feeling better. Pen and paper out. Suggestions, alternatives, doubts, problems. Finally, after raising everything we could think of, we came up with a decision. Forget selling the van to the French guy from the French Embassy. Send home for £260, the maximum available within forty-eight hours (my contribution of £75 meant my bank account was now zero). Sell every van spare and piece of equipment we could. Put the van into customs. Fly to New Delhi. Sell the turquoise stones and rings. Find a merchant ship heading for Australia and work our passage. Return and pick the van up after five or six months in Australia. Then travel back overland to England. It meant we would have failed to travel all the way around the world as planned but it had a good feel to it.

The decision was easy in the end and it didn't need writing down. But we weren't overjoyed at the thought of leaving the van in customs. We envisaged coming back in a few months' time and finding the engine had been swapped.

All in all, I had been up and down more times that day than I had been for weeks if not months, but by the time I slipped into bed I was feeling relaxed about it all.

'It's only a van,' I said.

'It is,' Tony said. 'I'm cool about it.'

Lol said, 'The only thing I'm bothered over is that we mek a profit from the stones and rings we've bought. Or at least get our money back.'

*

Thursday 31 January

They say before making a big decision it is best to sleep on it. I know what they mean. I had been awake since the sun came up trying to convince myself we had made the right decision. I wasn't sure and I kept quiet the next morning over breakfast. Lol and Tony didn't mention it either.

As the morning progressed, the thought of being carefree travellers on foot with no van to worry about began to excite us and we were in high spirits. After a bowl of rice at Siggy's Restaurant to the sound of Deep Purple and Free we went back to the Ansari Guest House, unloaded the van of all saleable spares and accessories and stacked them neatly in our room, lined up ready to sell. Mali and his assistant, Charman, came to our room to barter for some of the stuff. We got a reasonable deal and should be able to sell the whole lot at a pretty fair price. It was time to celebrate with a shish-kebab in the guest house tea room, which was superb, finished off with a cup of delicious tea, a tasty brownie and a K2 plain cigarette.

Our morning's accomplishments had put us in a great mood and we sat in the cosy tea room for the rest of the afternoon chatting to the Germans and the Japanese travellers, reading through English and American newspapers and commenting on the coverage of the troubles in Afghanistan, Ireland, Vietnam and the rest of the world.

'It doesn't feel like a dangerous world, sitting here,' I said, pouring my third cup of tea.

Lol lit his second cigarette of the day and said, 'I can't understand what all the fuss is about.'

Tony raised his cup and said 'Here's to travel and as far as we can go.' We couldn't have put it better.

Later in the tea room, while I was writing a letter home on my own by the side of the wood fire, Mali and Charman came in and we talked about Afghanistan. Mali said Afghanistan was a poor country, a backward country where women and men were not treated as equals and wives were bought. I asked him what it was like living in a poor country.

'Afghanistan,' he said,' has been badly affected by drought for the past three years with many poor people dying of starvation. Last year, the long-reigning King Zahir Shah, was overthrown in a bloodless coup and the Republic of Afghanistan was formed. Life improved initially but now things are beginning to deteriorate. Who knows what the future holds?'

Lol and Tony joined us and we drank tea made in our favourite little brown tea pots. The atmosphere was warm and we were making good friends with Mali and Charman. Charman is from the north of Afghanistan and has that striking Mongol look. He wears the traditional Afghan knee length dress and baggy trousers known as shalwar kameez. He always looks to be standing to attention, arms straight by his side, back straight, good eye contact. With Mali's help, Charman told us that once a year he leaves Kabul and travels to northern Afghanistan on the border with China to take part in Buzkashi. He explained that Buzkashi is the national sport, a very dangerous sport, where players on horseback try to drag a goat's carcass into a goal. Charman had a habit of ending each sentence with 'Perhaps, maybe.' It came out as 'Furhaps, baby' and we laughed good-naturedly as he tried to correct it. We couldn't speak more than two words in Farsi – chituresti and obestine is how we pronounced what we understood to be a form of greeting – and we admired him for having a go.

Friday 1 February

Snow was falling when I woke and it was warm in our room. Tony had lit the fire while Lol and I were still asleep and by the frightened look on his face he must have nearly set the hut ablaze. Today was going to be a lazing about day. Everything was closed on Friday and here, too, in the guest house tea room it was quiet. There were only two German travellers, both photographers, and us three. Everyone else had disappeared.

Tony took the stereo out of the van and stacked it on the 'For Sale' bed. Charman bought some bottles of Boots shampoo off us and we think he did us and that was okay. I showed Mali a card trick and he laughed and laughed until I wondered if he was taking the mickey. I played chess and cards with Lol and Tony all day, winning and losing. If it wasn't for the physical inactivity of chess, I could get into that game. Lol and Tony smoked as they played and I watched the ash tray fill with butts. I wanted a cigarette but I've stopped again.

Late in the afternoon, we struggled to light the fire in our room. Even Tony the fire-maker couldn't get it going and we ended up asking one of Charman's assistants to help us. The man couldn't speak a word of English but he took control and he knew how to light a stove. We watched him prepare the fire, each finger working delicately and independently, building a lattice of small sticks over a handful of wood shavings and dried orange peel, playing his lighted match under the kindling, fanning the little flames, adjusting the door to create a draught until the fire was powerful enough to ignite two small logs. We shook his hand and put our thumbs up to show we appreciated not only his time and effort but also his skill. The air in the room gradually warmed as it passed over the hot cast iron and I fetched more logs from the stack round the back. It had started snowing again.

Through the thin partition wall, we could hear our Japanese neighbours chopping wood and chattering. Lol was restless – sleeping, waking, rubbing his feet together for five minutes, walking around the room, sleeping again. Tony was feverish and thought he might be suffering from dysentery. I was hungry and tired and had the feeling I was going to drift into a mood before falling asleep. I didn't know whether it would be a good mood or a bad mood.

Feel isolated. Not lonely. Might have a smoke. No. Yes. See out the day in front of the crackling fire.

Saturday 2 February

Saturday and up early. We have to visit the British Embassy this morning and start the process of putting the van into storage. It must have been snowing all night, about five inches worth, and we had to clear a path leading from the rear of the guest house to the van. All was quiet and Kabul was stunning in its white robes.

There were a few other Brits in the embassy enquiring about various things with typical British politeness and certainty. They came across as unfriendly and I didn't even feel like saying hello. Being the official owner of the vehicle, I had four forms to complete and as I worked through the sections I noticed how clean my hands were. They were like my dad's hands at the end of feast week before he went back to the pit. While I filled in the forms, Tony and Lol read the Times newspaper and flipped unhurriedly through a pile of British magazines. I half expected a waiter to appear with a tray and serve them cigars and brandy.

For a bit of excitement, we drove to Kabul airport to see what the place was like. As we walked through the entrance, a Swiss traveller, just having arrived from India, told us there had been a few crashes at Delhi airport recently. One involving a plane from Kabul.

'I hope the rubber band on the plane we get is in good nick,' Lol said with his usual straight face.

I'd never flown before and couldn't understand why Tony wasn't laughing with us.

'Just wait,' he said. 'You'll see.'

It was still busy on Chicken Street when we got back, despite the holiday, and numerous traders were haggling, selling knives, rings, Jews harps and the like. The clothes and jewellery were good quality and cheap. There were some freaks lounging around on rugs in the window seats in Siggy's Restaurant trying to look like freaks lounging around. We had a beef steak and it was gorgeous and I had to loosen my belt. I was getting fatter and poorer.

Sunday 3 February

After an early rise we made a late start. At eleven o'clock we checked the bank to see if our money had arrived. The paper system at the bank seemed chaotic. We chased around different departments and eventually were told the money hadn't arrived. We weren't too worried. Not yet.

One of the bank assistants put us in a taxi and kindly directed the driver to our second port of call – the Ministry of Foreign Affairs. We got a letter of authorisation to leave the van in customs stamped and signed for a fee of 400 Afs, around £4, which just about emptied our pockets, then it was off to the Ministry of Finance for another stamp. We were surprised when everything was completed by half past twelve bar delivering the van itself to the customs depot. We called at the BOAC office and booked our flight to New Delhi and a really helpful Afghan man working there offered to take us to the airport on our departure day. I love Kabul.

Back at the Ansari Guest House we enjoyed a tasty Shashlik Kebab. That was until someone said a dog had been reported missing that morning. Lol went back to the room for a lie down and Tony and I prepared a letter to the *Barnsley Chronicle*. We were seriously thinking of offering to do a set of articles for the paper based on our adventure. The German freelance photographers had impressed us with their collection of shots taken in Africa and America and we thought we could liven up our articles with a few photographs of our own. Half an hour later our enthusiasm had faded and we put the sketchy letter away for another day.

We ordered more tea and Mali told us the French guy from the French Embassy wanted to buy the van for one thousand dollars. Mali said his name was Pascal and he had left his work address and said to call round tomorrow afternoon if we were interested. We rushed into our room, woke up Lol, and told him the news. He was unmoved.

'I don't want to go back to Mashhad if I can help it,' he said. 'I'd rather we stick to the plan and put the van in customs.'

Tony and I went quiet. We knew Lol was right. Still, it was an option and we agreed it would do no harm to call at the French Embassy the following day and discuss it more fully with the French guy.

Our room had turned into a shop and we sold all but a few things to Charman at a giveaway price. He deserved first pick and we didn't mind if he robbed us a bit. A friend of Mali's kept picking up the 8-track and the tapes but eventually he walked away without making an offer. One of the German photographers came in to have a look around the items. I wished he hadn't because he told us the French Embassy man was 'full of shit.' Thanks very much, I thought. We'll see.

We lay on our beds and Lol and I discussed the ins and outs of selling the van without coming to a conclusion. It left me unsettled and I didn't want to switch the light off. Tony woke up and told us he had just had a dream where he and Lol had their heads kicked in on a backstreet somewhere. It reminded me of a dream I had last night. In the dream, my seventeen-year-old brother, David, was a toddler. He had cracked open his head, and my mother was on the settee rocking him in her arms. Behind her, a huge aeroplane, packed with faces of every colour, slowly taxied past the front room window pulling a train of endless railway carriages.

Monday 4 February

Lots to do today so up at half past seven. Lol had a lie-in again and joined us for breakfast at ten. Off to the bank. It was cold, frosty and sunny and the mountains were hard edged against the blue sky. We employed a cheeky, harmless-looking lad working in a cobbler's shop to wash our van while we went inside the bank. The bank clerk flipped through the files, smiled and told us our money had arrived.

Outside on the street our van looked stunning, better than the day we picked it up from Sheffield, its red paintwork gleaming in the sun. The lad had done a great job, even so we only gave him a third of what he asked for which was still expensive. I wondered if he would be allowed to keep the money or have to pass it on to the cobbler. Anyway, he seemed happy and we were happy. Our bartering skills were improving.

It was one o'clock. Just in time to call round to see Pascal in his office at the French Embassy. The official on reception was expecting us, which was a nice touch, and he called Pascal on the desk phone. The interior of the embassy was grand with mahogany and red leather furniture and big portraits of important-looking people on the walls.

Pascal wore a casual checked jacket, slightly too small for him, and his tie was off centre. He introduced himself and took us to his office. The name plate on the door read Attache Commercial Adjoint, Ambassade de France. We sat down on shiny leather chairs and Pascal confirmed that a foreign diplomat, like him, was allowed to buy a foreign registered vehicle but that it was complicated. He seemed uneasy and acted as though he didn't really want to buy the van.

'Why do you want to buy our van, Pascal?' I said, trying not to put him off any further.

'For leisure. I will keep it here in Kabul and then when my military service is finished, I will drive it home to France. It is for camping.'

'Cool,' Tony said. 'Would you convert it to left hand drive?'

I felt like telling Tony not to ask any more questions like that as I could hear the price of the van dropping.

'Perhaps. It depends on the cost to convert it. Okay,' Pascal said, grabbing his overcoat from the hat stand in the corner of his office and almost pulling the thing over. 'Let us go now to the VW garage to test the vehicle.'

The mechanics took the van for a short, bumpy ride, checked the suspension and steering and reported that they couldn't find anything wrong. I felt proud of the old girl. Pascal didn't seem pleased or disappointed with the news and he said if the cost of converting it to left hand drive wasn't too much (he spoke as though he was hoping it would be) he would buy the van. He arranged to see us at six o'clock that evening at the Ansari Guest House to discuss the deal further.

Over a pot of tea, Lol came round to the idea of selling the van, mainly because he didn't think we would see the French guy again. But at six o'clock sharp Pascal turned up and we quickly agreed a price of a thousand dollars. Then we listened very carefully to what he had to say about the procedure for changing ownership. His English wasn't that good and we didn't want to misunderstand him.

'We have to go to Iran to make the sale. Who is the owner of the vehicle?'

'I am,' I said.

'Both of us must go to Mashhad and sign the correct paperwork at the Afghanistan Consul there. We must do this together. Then we must drive back to the border and the van is mine when we enter no-man's-land between the two borders.'

The three of us nodded, even though I could tell Tony and Lol didn't quite understand the procedure, either. I could also see, like me, they felt a little sickened. We had a faint hope that a man in Pascal's position might know of a way to exchange the van here in Kabul.

'No. Impossible,' he said. 'We have to go to Iran.'

We ordered tea to slow things down and after a brief confab decided to ditch the idea of putting the van into customs and instead drive back to Iran with Pascal and do the deal there.

'Excellent,' Pascal said. 'Now I consult my colleagues at the embassy to see if the plan is possible. Please come round tomorrow morning at ten o'clock.'

Tuesday 5 February

A cold shoulder and a painful bladder forced me out of bed at half past eight on an icy, freezing morning. I was beginning to be the first riser every morning now. It was quite enjoyable sitting alone for a few minutes before the day began. There was not much time to lounge around, though. We had an appointment with Pascal.

He was a different man this morning.

'Everything is fine,' he said. 'A cheque is being sent to my bank and I have a letter of authority from the French Embassy to take to the Iranian Embassy to be signed. Shall we go now?'

He was full of positive words and we began to feel optimistic. All four of us climbed into the van and took a short drive across Kabul to the Iranian Embassy. I went inside with Pascal to see the General. The good-looking secretary at the desk asked us to take a seat and after half an hour we saw the main man. Everything was so straightforward it was unbelievable. Charming man. I liked him. He gave us a special road pass to enter Iran and assured us we would be exempt from paying any taxes. Back to the van and we were on top of the world. All we needed now was authority from the Afghanistan General. According to Pascal that wouldn't be too difficult. He was a good friend, he said, and they would meet tomorrow. Things were looking up and we arranged to meet Pascal on Thursday at noon. We called at the BOAC office and cancelled our flight to New

Delhi. The likeable man was there again. Shame about his cold fish handshake.

Back at the Ansari Guest House we changed most of our remaining Afs into dollars and finally got down to enjoying a shashlik kebab in the busy tea room, a meal that tasted better than anything we had eaten in weeks. Charman introduced us to Algy, the tea room cook, and we thanked him personally. He smiled and bowed his head with pride and we shook his hand.

Tony and Lol went to the bazaar to look for gifts while I stayed in the tea room and read. I ordered tea and a brownie and sat back with my hands behind my head as though I owned the place. While I was relaxing, three new faces arrived. A young German couple, he was tall and blond and she wasn't bad looking, and a guy from New Zealand. I acted very cool and I think I caught the eye of the pretty German girl.

Hope the van sale goes ahead. Hope everything works out. Don't fancy trailing all the way back to Mashhad only for it to fall through.

Thursday 7 February

There was frost on the inside of the room window when we got up. We played chess all morning with our flying jackets zipped up to our necks until it was time to visit Pascal. He was all smiles and handshakes. It was good news. The letters he needed had been signed by the General and he was keen to set off to Mashhad tomorrow afternoon.

'Tomorrow afternoon!' we said in unison.

It was time to kit ourselves out ready for life on the road without our own transport. On the way back to the guest house we called at the leather shop and bought three passport wallets, a pair of cowboy boots each, and three travelling holdalls. The holdalls were the last in the shop and I ended up with the runt.

At the guest house tea room we filled our bellies with a big rice dish and lounged around all afternoon. The tea room was quiet and I tried to make an impression on a German girl travelling alone. I think I did okay. I was surprised at how self-conscious Tony was.

In our room I ripped my new leather holdall stuffing in all my gear. Of course, Lol and Tony laughed. As well as my few clothes and passport, I had to pack the rubber-handled hammer – the one that stopped us skidding in the snow in Iran – which I thought might come in handy if I got a job in Australia, a small knife stolen from a shop in Greece, a bundle of letters from home, a fist-sized marble statue of the Buddha bought in India, and half a dozen film canisters. Each of us had more stuff than we thought and we may need to buy another bag.

Charman knocked on our door and told us Pascal was on the phone. I thought what now? and trudged across the yard to take the call. Pascal sounded anxious and asked us to come over to his office straightaway. He always sounds as though he is panicking over something but I think it's just his manner. When we got there the anxiety in his voice had gone. He wanted us to get some snow chains for the van and he would pay. I wondered why he couldn't get them himself but I didn't say anything. He introduced us to an Afghan guy called Abdula who was to come with us and barter.

Abdula directed us to the bazaar and what an amazing experience it was. I never realised we'd missed so much. Abdula wasn't happy with the price of snow chains in the bazaar and he directed us through the backstreets from one shop to another. I was behind the wheel and just beginning to enjoy zipping in and out of the traffic when I clipped the massive bumper of a lorry at a roundabout as I tried to sneak in front of a tuk-tuk. It was my fault. The lorry stopped on the roundabout, blocking the traffic, and we got out and inspected the damage. There was a small hole in the rear wheel arch the size of a penny as though a bullet had gone through. It was nothing really, but it looked like a write-off to my guilty eyes. I felt a real fool and I looked at the lorry driver and motioned to him that I was sorry, expecting him to make a big fuss at my careless driving. But he just shrugged and drove off with no expression on his face. Lol and Tony kept their opinions to themselves and I admired them for it. I would probably have gone off my head. We decided to pay for the chains because of the damage.

Back at the Ansari Guest House we spent an hour saying goodbye to Charman, Mali and Algy.

'We'll see you all again when we get back from Iran,' Tony said.

'Keep that kettle boiling, Algy,' I said.

Algy smiled and said, 'Of course,' and he handed us three parcels of food. 'Please. For you.'

He is so caring, I thought. All the staff are.

Friday 8 February

We were invited to Pascal's house before setting off to Mashhad and over lunch he introduced us to his two friends, Jacques, a medical doctor, and Francois, a doctor of psychology. Jacques and Francois, like Pascal, were doing their military service in Afghanistan. Jacques was dark, untidy, balding, and confident. When he smoked, which was most of the time, he left his cigarette hanging loose in his mouth and didn't take it out until it was time to swap it for another one. Francois had long fair hair and a beard, and looked intelligent, preferring to listen rather than talk.

We drank wine and ate a meal of meat, a fish we couldn't identify, and cake. It felt strange and good to be sitting with two French doctors, eating dinner at the home of the French Commercial Attache, in the capital of Afghanistan. Not bad I thought for two gas fitters and an electrician from Yorkshire.

Over coffee, real coffee, Pascal said, 'Jacques and Francois are coming with us to Mashhad. The three of us will lead the way in Jacques' car.'

Jacques turned to us and said, 'I will go with you as far as Mashhad then I will continue on to France to be with my wife and family. My military service has finished.'

Tony said, 'All the way to France on your own?'

Jacques shrugged and ash fell from his cigarette.

Pascal said, 'Jacques speaks Persian, Pashto and Dari. He will help us through the border and help us with the documentation in Mashhad.'

Francois, who had hardly spoken during the meal except to ask about our travels, lit a cigarette and said, 'I am coming along for the ride.'

Well, well, well. Two French doctors and a Commercial Attache. What would my mam and dad think to me socialising with doctors and the like? My mam would have fretted and told me to mind my manners. She brought us up to be deferential towards doctors and educated people – our betters she would call them. Not my dad. Not a chance. He would have been very suspicious. He didn't trust many experts or people in authority. As I said to Lol and Tony before we turned in, I've had a balanced upbringing.

*

Saturday 9 February

Pascal, Francois and Jacques set off on the road to Kandahar in Jacques little white Fiat 128 and we followed close behind. Unfortunately, the van wasn't running well. Like a dog being taken to the vets, it must have sensed we were up to something and the accelerator linkage had frozen again. At a refreshment stop, I fed a wire through the floor at the side of the accelerator pedal, ran it under the van to the rear engine compartment and fastened it to the carburettor, operating it by hand from the driver's seat.

All the way to Kandahar I tried to keep a safe distance from the Fiat, closing up only as the car slowed on particularly treacherous stretches of ice-covered, rocky roads. The throttle was tricky to control by hand, the wire cutting through my woollen glove, and I nearly crashed into Jacques car going through a ford. We drove past many wrecked lorries and buses, some abandoned for years by the look of the rust and the amount of scavenging, and some more recent with people still inside.

We spent a night in a hotel in Kandahar and pressed on to Herat the next day with the throttle acting up all the way. It was late afternoon when the Fiat pulled up at a remote, cement-rendered hotel a few miles outside Herat. We gathered our overnight gear and followed the three French guys through the heavy wooden door into the reception area. When the hotel manager saw Jacques, he held out his arms and rushed from behind his desk.

'Jacques, Jacques,' he shouted and the two men embraced.

The noise brought three other members of staff into the foyer and they surrounded Jacques and took turns to embrace him and shake his hand.

Francois smiled and said, 'Jacques completed his military service working as a doctor among lepers in a colony very close to here. Up in the mountains. He is treated like a god.'

'Wow. What a man,' I said and we nodded in admiration.

'Jacques also worked among lepers in a village in Iran,' Francois continued, 'near the Black Sea coast. It is because of him and the Iranian doctors who worked with him that the village survived. Now it is a small town with engineers, doctors and agricultural technicians.'

I looked at Jacques, his cigarette wedged in the corner of his mouth, eyes squinting in his own smoke, thinning, untidy black hair in need of a good brush, and I saw a modest, sincere, friendly man. Like the good doctor in the films.

We were hungry and a simple dinner was prepared for us. Jacques must have been the hungriest, scoffing his bread and chips and throwing scraps all over the table. During the meal, Francois told us he was very concerned about the people we had seen walking alone along the remote roads and those stranded in the crashed lorries. His sympathy made me feel selfish and inconsiderate. Francois appeared to be totally at ease with himself. Maybe it was something to do with his psychology background. You could see it in his mannerisms, such as when he blew his nose. It sounded like a trumpet blast and he didn't care. If I had done that as a kid, my parents and teachers would have told me off for drawing attention to myself.

After the meal the three Frenchmen went to the bazaar in Herat to buy glass and silverware and we went to our bedroom. A power cut, apparently common in Herat, sent the room into blackness, penetrated only by the flicker of three red dots as we dragged on our cigarettes.

Our travelling companions returned during the blackness and we drank their rum by the light of a paraffin lamp. Pascal dropped a clock and kept knocking things over, apologising whenever he walked into something, his clumsiness made worse by his relatively poor English. Francois stayed cool, whistling to himself in the dark while Jacques talked to Pascal, the good doctor's rapid flow of words halted occasionally by a slight stutter. When Jacques and Francois started fooling around, doing party tricks and setting fire to the rum, Tony lit another cigarette and asked me if there was any point in him and Lol coming with me to Mashhad.

'I don't suppose there is,' I said. 'It only needs me as the owner.'

Lol said, 'It'd cut out all the faff of us getting visas and jabs and having our passports checked again. Why mek it more complicated?'

'Yes. I suppose so.'

I could tell they'd been discussing it and although it made sense it didn't stop me from feeling slightly abandoned.

Tony said, 'We might as well stay here until you get back.'

In bed I felt ill for half an hour then fancied Shreddies and cream.

Not looking forward to getting up at five o'clock in the morning. Going to be strange driving the van without Lol and Tony at my side. Wonder when they decided not to come with me?

Monday 11 February

The room was dark and quiet at five o'clock and Lol and Tony were still in bed half asleep. I joined the three French guys and we sneaked downstairs like children on Christmas morning. The air outside was cool, but there was no frost on the windscreens. Pascal jumped in the van with me, and Jacques and Francois got in the Fiat. The engines of the two vehicles fired up, shattering the cold silence, and our headlights searched for the road to the border. The main road was concrete, mostly solid down the centre, breaking up badly at the edges, which wasn't a problem at that early time of day.

Early dawn gave the mountains a sharp, black outline against the red sky. I was accelerating hard to keep up with Jacques, hoping with every bump that the wire

I had fitted to the throttle stayed attached. Somehow, Pascal broke my Leonard Cohen tape and he spent half an hour trying to reel in the spool. We finally arrived at the Afghan border at half past eight and had breakfast of rice and omelette in a nearby tea house recommended by Jacques.

I knew the procedure at the border control and I watched patiently as the line of lorries, stacked double their height with fragile cargo, were unloaded roughly by the border guards. Pascal kept biting his lip and rubbing the side of his face, worrying, I suppose, whether we would get through.

Our slow, steady progress towards the check-point was halted for half an hour when the van was searched for drugs. A small team of officers turned everything over, even drilling holes in the interior lining, tapping the hardboard with screwdrivers and light hammers. I assumed the officials were trying to impress the Frenchmen. I was relaxed knowing we'd left the turquoise stones back at the Ansari Guest House but I did begin to worry when the guards fished around the inside of the petrol tank with a long, hooked pole. I tried to recall if we'd ever left Magic Mohammed on his own near the van.

The military chief in charge, battle-weary in his muddy boots and well-worn uniform, seated behind a big wooden desk, was responsible for every individual leaving Afghanistan and he alone controlled the flow. It was finally our turn to have our documents checked and I was expecting the usual two hour-long procedure. Jacques was the first to hand over his passport and vaccination certificate and I heard him say something to the chief in Pashto or Dari that made the official look up. The chief tilted back his braided peaked cap and smiled, his face transformed and after a short, friendly conversation with Jacques, he stamped all of our passports and documents and wished us well on our journey. The whole procedure took ten minutes. As we walked back to our vehicles, I asked Jacques what he had said to the chief.

'I told him I was a doctor and I asked him how he was feeling and he said he had a very, very bad sore throat so I wrote a prescription for him on an envelope for medicine to treat his great pain.'

Our paperwork and Jacques mastery of Persian allowed us to get through the Iran side of the border without the need for a Carnet de Passage and Pascal stopped biting his lip. We arrived in Mashhad a few hours later and our vehicle sale documents were stamped with approval at the Afghanistan Consul. We patted each other on the back and it was time to say goodbye to Jacques. We watched his little white Fiat set off down the road for France and I felt both sad and happy. I thought what a great guy. I was proud to have met him and I hoped we would meet up again sometime.

Pascal joined Francois in the passenger seats of the van, the official change of ownership not taking place until we passed through the border, and I drove with extra caution not wanting any mishaps at this late stage. Pascal started biting his lip again but we passed through the Iranian border without a hitch and I pulled up in no-man's-land.

'It's all yours now Pascal,' I said with a big grin on my face.

We swapped seats and all three of us shook hands. That was it. Lol, Tony and I no longer owned a vehicle.

The van from Sheffield had been a good servant and friend and I was relieved it had found a new home.

The feeling of serenity didn't last long. Pascal was a rough driver. Flat out in each gear, too fast for the conditions and talk about slow reactions. Francois, of course, sitting in the middle seat, stayed cool throughout it all. After what seemed like years we arrived back in Herat and discovered that Pascal had been driving with the handbrake on, ruining the rear brakes. This on top of changing into first at thirty miles an hour and almost crashing half a dozen times.

It was so good to see Lol and Tony again. I had missed them more than I thought I would. All five of us went to a Paulo house for a kebab and rice dinner to celebrate the successful sale and we talked about Jacques and how helpful he had been and how we will miss him.

I told my story to Lol and Tony and they told me theirs. They had been horse riding for the day in the valley. Neither had been on a horse before apart from sitting on a seaside donkey.

'Did you have fun?' I said.

'We did until my horse nipped Lol's horse on the back end and it bolted,' Tony said, laughing.

'I've niver been so terrified in me life,' Lol said. 'I thought I wa' goin to dee.'

'They went off like they were in the Grand National,' Tony said. 'I waited an hour for them to come back but there was no sign so I went back to the hotel. You didn't get back till it was getting dark, did you.'

'Bloody hoss.'

'Did it have the bit between its teeth?' I said, laughing along with Tony.

'I think it had t'saddle between its teeth,' Lol said and he managed a smile.

'And we bought some boots, as well,' Tony said, showing off his new leather footwear. 'What do you think? Cool or what?'

'Very nice.' I said.

Then I saw Lol's.

'What's them tha's bought?'

'What's wrong with 'em?' Lol said, polishing the studs on his white leather cowboy boots.

'They're toppers, them Lol,' I said and we all laughed.

Wednesday 13 February

We arrived at Kandahar at a quarter past eleven in the morning and Pascal decided to have the brakes repaired at a mechanics' training school. We searched the bazaar and found a stall selling brake cylinder rubbers. I reckon with time we could have found enough parts in that one bazaar to build a complete VW van from scratch.

By two o'clock the brakes had been repaired and we were back on the road to Kabul with Pascal behind the wheel, Francois and me in the front, and Lol and Tony tucked into their sleeping bags asleep in the back.

The light was fading as we started to climb through the mountains and the roads became snow-covered. In the headlights we saw an Afghan man walking on the roadside on his own in the freezing night miles from anywhere. Francois asked us to pull up and we offered the man a lift. He lifted up the hood covering his turban and squinted at us through the blizzard of snow. His thick beard was frozen. He said nothing, turned his head, and walked on into the driving cold. No nonsense and proud. He could have been from Yorkshire.

Thursday 14 February

I couldn't suffer Pascal's bad driving any longer and I played the ostrich and climbed into my sleeping bag between Lol and Tony and within minutes I was fast asleep. When I woke it was half past two in the morning and we were parked outside Francois' home. I was tired, hungry and cold. We'd done it. It was all over. Tony had driven all the way through the mountains over the treacherous roads back to Kabul. I shook his hand and told him he was a hero.

Francois' house was a modern villa and what a place it was. He suggested we stayed there until our flight to India. Pascal offered to put one of us up at his house but none of us wanted to. I thought sorry Pascal, we want to stick together and besides, this place is too good to miss. Francois searched through his kitchen cupboards and put together a late-night meal of cheese, bread and a kind of spicy sausage. It wasn't as good as Walls but it went down well and there were no scraps left for Tipp, the house dog. We smoked and relaxed and Francois showed us to our bedroom. Tony and I chose to sleep in the double bed with Tipp separating us and Lol slept on his own on a lumpy mattress on the draughty floor under the window.

Friday 15 February

Francois introduced us to his manservant, Sellick, a proud man, immaculate in an ironed Afghan three-quarter length jacket and loose trousers. Sellick cooked us a wonderful breakfast of fried eggs, bread and jam and coffee.

'I think you've already met Tipp,' he said, patting the dog's head.

Francois, dressed in a dark, striped suit which somehow let his bohemian image down, showed us around his big house. Upstairs on a dresser in his huge bedroom there was a photograph of his girlfriend and she was very pretty. I noticed a book by Freud on the desk in his study, and there were tapes and lots of books and papers scattered around.

Francois took us in his little silver Renault to Pascal's house for lunch. Pascal was more relaxed than yesterday and we chatted over a glass of whisky while the final preparations were being made to our meal. I remembered, as we sat in the sun in the back garden of Pascal's fine house, eating partridge, and banana and rum pudding, that it was a week ago to the hour since we were here having lunch, preparing to drive all the way back to Mashhad to sell the van.

Despite the luxury and finery at Pascal's house I became bored and fidgety and couldn't wait for Tony to finish fitting a new cassette player in the van for Pascal. I thought it's funny how we've detached ourselves from the van in such a short time. Perhaps it's because we're still so close to our old home-on-wheels and Pascal relies on us to keep it in good order. Maybe we'll miss it when we have to leave it behind.

The streets of Kabul were cold and quiet when we left Pascal's to look for a leather shop with Francois. Lol and Tony both bought an Afghan coat before we returned to Francois' for hot chocolate and a Kent cigarette. I picked up one of the books left lying around in the study. It was called 'Electric Kool-Aid Acid Test' by Tom Wolfe, about hippies and drugs and I couldn't tell whether it was fact or fiction.

Francois looked lonely, although it could have been contentment, and we sat around feeling inadequate. When the three of us started talking among ourselves, slipping into pure Barnsley dialect, Francois smiled and shook his head.

'What language are you speaking?' he said.

'Barnsley,' I said. 'It's easy.'

To prove it, we taught him to how say the greeting, 'How are you, my friend?' in Barnsley dialect. He got it straightaway. 'Arta guin on, auld cock,' sounded wonderful spoken with a French accent.

A timely entrance by Pascal and his dog livened up the place. He tried to get his dog to play with Tipp. There were lots of chasing, jumping, growling, snapping and shouting, accompanied by harmless kicking and laughing, and the two dogs remained unfriendly. We drank Cinzano, a drink I'd only ever seen people sipping on TV and billboards. Francois suggested we eat out at a restaurant he knew then go on to Kabul's only disco. The restaurant was European in style and we enjoyed a German dish and also a beautiful Afghan dish sitting opposite. She was gorgeous and she responded to my looks and smiles. It felt good and I ought to have said something to her before leaving, but as usual I just walked away and she went out of my life.

The disco was opposite the restaurant and it was a cool place playing good music. There weren't many people in and we enjoyed a quiet drink. We were just about to leave when a crowd of Afghan men and women bustled in. Francois knew them all, they were the Kabul jet set, and he was soon on the dancefloor, rocking and rolling with them. One of the women he danced with kept smiling at me and when Francois sat back down, I told him how lovely she looked. He said that although she was sophisticated, and was married to the owner of the disco, there was still a chance of me getting off with her. I got the feeling he was extracting the Michael, or should that be Michel. Anyway, she made me feel great.

Saturday 16 February

When Francois drove off to invite some friends of his to a party he was hosting on Wednesday, the three of us went round to Pascal's. As we walked down his drive, we noticed our old van parked outside with the sliding door wide open. Pascal was still in his pyjamas when he answered the door bell.

'Do you know the van door is wide open?' Tony said.

Pascal rushed outside to check, still in his pyjamas, and he came back panting.

'Someone must have broken it open last night,' he said.

'Is there anything missing?' I said.

'No. Everything is okay. It is the local police. He tries to teach me a lesson because I leave the van in the open air.'

Pascal said he couldn't get the VW into his secure compound because it was too high to go under the gate with the roof rack fitted. We laughed. Poor Pascal. It took me and Tony ten minutes to remove the rack and when we got back in the house, he poured us all a cognac, put Santana on the tape-deck and told us to help ourselves to the pile of magazines on his coffee table. I was first to get hold of Playboy.

After coffee, we left for the Ansari Guest House to see Charman and the rest of the staff again and it felt good to be walking the streets of Kabul without a single worry. There was a homely, familiar feeling as we entered the tea room and Charman, Mali and Algy joined us at our favourite table and we drank tea and ate rice and told stories and laughed and got looks from guests who probably thought we were noisy Americans. Lol and Mali exchanged their almost identical Afghan coats, Mali's being slightly too small for him and Lol's being slightly too big. Both were happy with the swap and Mali told us the drinks and rice were on the house. Just before we left, I pulled Charman to one side and showed him one of the turquoise stones we'd bought from Magic Mohammed.

'We got a few of these in Mashhad,' I said 'And a few rings as well. We are going to sell them in India.'

Charman turned the stone over in his hand a few times and then held it up to the light bulb.

'Plastic.'

On the way back to Francois' we bought eight packs of cigarettes, pinched three post cards, and remembered to buy some honey and milk for Sellick. Pascal came round later with a windscreen wiper in his hand and said someone had tried to rip it off when he was parked outside his office. Luckily, neither the blade nor the windscreen was damaged and Tony and I refitted it for him in minutes.

We sat down to a huge four course dinner and when we told Sellick how good it was, he smiled and lowered his head politely and with pride. After drinking a full bottle of red wine, Pascal felt brave enough to admit that as well as someone ripping off his windscreen wiper, they had also stolen his wing mirrors. He still thought the local police had it in for him.

The main room was lovely and warm thanks to Sellick having lit the fire an hour before. Pascal left around midnight and Francois poured himself a cognac and went to bed. Tony wasn't tired and he settled into Francois' study, put on some soft romantic music, and wrote to Gloria. Lol went to sleep on the mattress on the floor and I fed Tipp, did thirty press ups and read until I was tired.

Need a woman beside me, tonight. Soft hair. Gentle words. Can't get over that beautiful Afghan woman at the disco and how she kept smiling at me.

Monday 18 February

On our way to the leather shop where Tony's old boots were being repaired, Lol and I posted a card to the gas depot. The sun was shining and there were lots of people on the streets and I felt wide awake. For the first time since leaving home, I had money to spend and there were many fascinating shops to visit.

Back at Francois' we were lounging around drinking real coffee when Lol tried to get one of Francois' gloves out of Tipp's jaws. Without warning, Tipp jumped up and snapped at Lol's face. Lol looked terrified and turned white even before the blood surfaced at the bite marks. Francois tapped naughty Tipp on the nose and treated Lol's wound with pure alcohol. Lol was quite friendly towards Tipp after that.

Francois had work to do and he disappeared upstairs, the only evidence of his presence being the dull bass boom of his stereo system. Pascal appeared as suddenly as Francois had disappeared and I knew he wanted me to change the oil on the van. It didn't take long and there were lots of good-looking Afghan girls walking by to make the task enjoyable. I smiled and nodded to them and felt good at being so bold.

At eight o'clock, Francois took us to a French movie at the French Embassy cinema. It was a warm, plush place with comfy red seats and atmospheric lighting. There was no smoke or noise from the audience and it wasn't as much fun as being at the pictures on a Saturday morning in Barnsley. The film was about a cavalier and it was daft and poorly produced. When it finished and the lights brightened, we recognised a lot of people in the audience. I thought it's funny how many people we've got to know in such a short time in Kabul.

Lol and Francois went straight to bed. I fed Tipp and listened to Tony complaining about being bored and how he was ready to set off travelling again. He said he kept thinking of Australia. I thought I'm not that desperate to leave just yet. Everybody has been so friendly, both locals and foreigners, and the cold, bare, mountains around Kabul suit my temperament and make me feel strong.

Tuesday 19 February

I had a bad back when I got up, caused, I'm convinced, by all the driving we've done. A hot bath would have helped but there was no water. Sellick thought the pipes were frozen somewhere in the grounds of the house. I didn't tell him that Lol and I were qualified gas fitters and knew a thing or two about pipes in case he asked us to dig up the front garden. I felt a bit guilty for not offering to help as a way of repayment for all the hospitality but the ground was rock hard and our hands had gone soft.

Tony and I had a game of badminton in the back garden and Francois had a knock around with us in between wrapping a bandage around Tony's weak ankle. It was good to be sweating through sport again.

Lol came downstairs after his nap and he seemed a bit edgy. He was probably thinking about dog bites and tetanus. Tony was as happy as I've ever seen him. Francois kept popping in and out of his study and we could hear Joni Mitchell singing Both Sides Now, loud then soft then loud again. When Francois finished his work, we talked about Tipp pissing in the room, tomorrow's party, badminton, and him going home at the end of his military service. He said if he was alone when it was time to go back to France, and we were still around, we could go with him if we wanted. He went quiet again and I tried asking him about his job but he didn't open up.

Time to feed Tipp. Francois and Lol retired and Tony and I began a discussion that lasted for hours covering style, looks, women, everything. We had the music on low and Tony was smoking a lot, every fifteen minutes, right down to the tip. Paul McCartney came on singing 'and the light of the night fell on me.'

Wednesday 20 February

Around eight o'clock, Francois' friends started to arrive at his party. There were two French couples (all four of them were teachers), a man and a woman who worked in the French Embassy, two young English teachers, and a dozen others who we never got round to talking to. Lol got drunk and Tony and I spent most of the time laughing at his clumsy attempts to chat up the women.

'He acts like he's dropped on a hen party in Blackpool,' I said.

'I'd love to hear his chat-up lines,' Tony said.

'Me too. I don't know how he gets away with it. Sometimes I wish I was as uncomplicated as him.'

Tony and I tried to mix but most of the night we were on our own, smoking, although strangely I never felt left out and Tony seemed relaxed. When the first guests began to leave, Tony found a quiet corner and spent an hour on his own listening to Carol King, thinking of Gloria no doubt. By one o'clock everyone had left. Francois looked worn out and he swayed up to bed, stopping for a moment on the stairs to pat the dog.

'Well, Mr Tipp,' he said. 'How's life?'

Thursday 21 February

All this partying had left me feeling tired and I didn't get up until eleven o'clock. Lol was worn out. He'd been in the bathroom most of the night with sickness and diarrhoea and when he pushed the blankets back, I thought it was his dad. So different to Tony, who was full of life.

Over breakfast, Francois asked if we wanted to go hunting and fishing with him and his friends tomorrow. I thought this is great. If only we could have a day off.

The rest of the day was all about meeting more of Pascal and Francois' friends living permanently in

Kabul. I think Francois and Pascal enjoyed showing off 'the three travellers from England'. One of their friends took Lol, Tony and me to another friend's house where two more friends arrived and then three more. When Francois came to pick us up two hours later the place was packed. It was whistle-stop and hard work and I don't know how they keep it up. I wondered if it was the same hectic pace at the British Embassy. Not a bad job, I thought. In the afternoon we took refuge for an hour at the Ansari Guest House and had a good laugh with Charman, Mali and Algy over tea and brownies in front of the wood fire.

Later that night, a slightly wobbly Francois came home and said he was whisky-drunk. Just before he went to bed, we heard a noise from one of the cupboards under the sink in the kitchen. He opened the door and a live quail came running out. The poor bird had escaped from the cage where Sellick kept the meat for the next day. It was funny to see Francois so startled. Drunk, hair and beard ruffled, suit scruffy from a jumping Tipp, and laughing at his own fright. I thought not so cool after all.

Friday 22 February

Done it. Up at eight to go hunting and fishing with Francois and his two friends but that's it. I've had it for the rest of the day. Lol looked shocking again. Even Tony looked older. We packed Francois' Renault with guns, ammunition, dark clothing, fishing tackle, coke and soda water and two apple pies wrapped in foil made for us by Sellick. I sat in the front and as we drove out of the city centre, we passed a large crowd of

Afghan men gathered on a plot of spare land about the size of a football pitch.

'What's going off there?' I said to anybody listening.

'It is the camel market,' Francois said.

It was only then that I saw the dozens of grey camels standing amongst the hundreds of grey traders.

Francois drove fast and safe along the narrow, twisty road and I assumed, and hoped, he knew the route well. He hardly spoke until we came to a rocky gorge. He is the kind of person who doesn't make small talk and that suited us being from Yorkshire. The vast rocky gorge of vertical cliffs hundreds if not thousands of feet above the Kabul River was a beautiful site and I wondered if the word gorgeous came from the word gorge. I thought if not, it ought to.

'Look for crashed vehicles in the bottom,' Francois said.

We did and it was the scariest eye-spy I have ever played.

Francois said, 'Alexander the Great travelled along the river. You know him?'

Lol said, 'Not personally,' and Francois smiled.

'On his way to invade India. It was in the 4th century BC.'

We nodded to each other and stayed dumb. It looked as though history wasn't Lol or Tony's strong point, either. I tried to imagine a massive army on horseback down in the bottom of the gorge, steadily moving towards their enemy in Pakistan and I wondered if there were ancient human and horse bones buried somewhere beneath the wrecked cars and lorries.

Francois said the river started its life in the Hindu Kush mountains and flowed through Kabul all the way to Pakistan, passing close to the famous Khyber Pass. Lol told him there was a fish and chip shop in Whitby called the Khyber Pass and the fish was very good.

The river was a wonderful mix of blue and orange where it crashed and foamed over the rocks. I thought I saw a kingfisher flash between two boulders but by the time I pointed it out it had vanished. Tony said the whole river was like a liquid kingfisher. I turned round and raised my eyebrows at Lol as if to say Oooo. Get him. Then I remembered Tony had been to art college.

Francois threw the Renault around the hairpin bends sending cokes into soda water and Lol into Tony. He pointed to the lake we were heading for and it was big and green. Francois' friends, Pierre and his wife, Michelle, had already gone hunting. Unfortunately, Francois didn't know exactly where, so we spent hours chasing from one end of the lake to the other looking for them. Ahead of us, six mallard had settled on a calm part of the river. Lol and I crept out of the car with our loaded guns and despite getting to within a few yards we missed every one of them. I thought here I am, a member of the Young Ornithologist Club at ten years old and the RSPB since I was old enough to join, and I'm trying to kill half a dozen ducks. I seem to have slipped easily into the fun-loving French way of life.

There was still no sign of Pierre and Michelle so we decided to head back home. When Francois turned the key in the ignition switch it snapped off. He managed to winkle the broken piece out but he had no spare and the steering lock was on. We were stuck. He decided to set off back to Kabul for his spare key, hoping to thumb a lift. Lol volunteered to go with him and Tony and I stayed with the car. It was getting dark and I suppose it was dangerous now, stranded in a broken-down car at the foot of the Hindu Kush mountain range on the road to the Khyber Pass with a boot full of guns and ammunition. Even so, both of us had no problem falling asleep. An hour later we were woken by a tap-tap on the window. In my dream we were surrounded by Afghan bandits in turbans but thankfully it was Pierre and Michelle in bobble caps.

'Here. This will warm you up,' Michelle said in broken English, pouring two steaming hot coffees from her flask.

'That's gorgeous,' Tony said. 'How did you know we were here?'

'Francois phoned us from somewhere,' Pierre said. 'I don't know where he was. He told us what had happened and where you were waiting.'

On the off chance we tried Pierre's car key in the ignition. That would have been a miracle.

We thanked them for their coffee and told them to go back home as there was nothing more they could do. An hour later a set of headlights appeared out of the blackness and Pierre and Michelle returned with a policeman who was to take over guard duties. I felt sorry for the man as we drove off.

We talked slow English for a couple of hours at Pierre and Michelle's house on the outskirts of Kabul, and Michelle's smiling eyes began to draw me towards her. I hoped Pierre hadn't noticed. At last Francois and Lol arrived. Francois was in a hurry. We had another party to go to at one of his friends so off we raced back to Kabul. There were a dozen other people there and all could speak good English. We managed to engage in conversation with every one of them even though they had difficulty understanding our Yorkshire accents and thought we were Scottish. At last, the party was over and we went back to Francois'. Everyone turned in and I fed Tipp. I was dog tired and glad we weren't flying to India tomorrow. It looked like Monday now. Maybe.

Saturday 23 February

I felt fit this morning but that was soon disproved when I tried to do thirty press ups and fell at thirteen. Tony and Lol were eager to move on and we decided to book our flight to New Delhi. There was no room on Monday's flight so the good people at the BOAC office put us on the waiting list. I still thought, and hoped, we would end up staying a little longer at Francois'. It was costing us nothing and he said we could stay at his place until the Pakistan border opened. That way there would be no need for a flight and we could catch the bus from Kabul to New Delhi.

We took a taxi to the music shop in the centre of the city and bought three LP's for Francois – Joe Cocker, Fairport Convention and Fotheringay.

'What about Sellick?' Tony said.

'Good thinking,' I said.

'It's no good getting him an LP,' Lol said. 'I can't see him swinging to Jimi Hendrix.'

'And we can't get him a bottle of wine,' I said. 'I don't think he drinks.'

'What about something from the leather shop?' Tony said.

And we agreed that was a good idea.

It was cold walking back to Francois', even with our jackets zipped up high. It was well below zero, and the snow on the mountains looked harder and whiter than ever. No one was in except Tipp and he gave us a suspicious look before wagging his tail. Tony and I talked about life again. We have become good friends. Lol seems a little more distant with both of us.

Pascal called by and told us someone had stolen his snow chains. When we stopped laughing, he invited us to a party at his house in fifteen days' time. I felt bad for laughing at his misfortune and before Lol or Tony could say anything, I said we would definitely come if we were still around. I could tell Pascal was trying desperately not to be left out.

Monday 25 February

Francois dropped Lol and Tony off at the BOAC office to check if any seats had become free on tomorrow's flight to New Delhi. I hung around the house writing a letter home and reading Playboy hoping a little that there were no seats available. Half an hour later Lol and Tony came back.

'Still no seats to New Delhi,' Lol said looking glum.

I tried not to show my relief.

'But we've got on the flight to Amritsar,' Tony said, flashing the tickets and grinning. 'Nine o'clock tomorrow morning.'

I smiled the best I could.

We went upstairs and started packing our bags. I wasn't in a good mood and had a little argument with Lol over how we should split the stones and who should carry what.

Pascal took the four of us to a restaurant for a farewell meal. It was a strange atmosphere, exchanging addresses, trying to make it obvious we would miss him without saying as much. We get on well with Pascal and Francois and we talked until one in the morning and presented Pascal with a bottle of whisky. When we got back to Francois', we handed over the records we'd bought him. He looked at the sleeves and the songs and smiled and said they were wonderful.

'And we got these for Sellick,' Tony said and he handed over the leather wallet with Sellick's name on, and the leather dog collar with Tipp's name on.

Francois gave us the French double cheek kiss and I knew then that it was going to be hard saying goodbye tomorrow. We shared a last drink downstairs and talked about the good times we'd had and about the future.

Tuesday 26 February

All were up at half past six and Francois drove us to the airport. We sorted the tickets and luggage and it was time to say goodbye. I felt my stomach tighten and Tony looked pale and so did Francois. Lol didn't seem too concerned to be leaving. I didn't know whether he was holding something back. That's Lol. Francois kissed us the French way and said goodbye. It took a while to get through customs and out on to the runway and when we looked up at the window of the viewing area, we saw a smiling, camera-rolling Francois waving to us. I'm going to miss that guy I thought. And I'm going to miss Afghanistan and all the great people we've met. If we hadn't been forced into selling the van, we would have shot through the country in three days, knife sharpened, scared of what might have happened to us, and had nothing but bad to say about the place and the people.

I hardly thought about my first flight until I noticed how quiet Tony had gone. Half an hour into the flight the plane dropped like a big dipper and when I recovered, I looked at Lol and Tony and they weren't laughing either. The pilot announced that the flight would take thirty minutes longer than planned because of congestion around Lahore airport due to the Islamic conference and he said he would take the opportunity to bank the plane a few times to give us a good view of land. He had a sense of humour. It was frightening.

August 2018 – Lochinver to The Traveller's Rest

We double-back through Achnahaird, and head for what looks on our map like a biggish coastal village called Lochinver. We see a few log cabins but they are either empty or the occupants have never heard of anybody called Lol. The rain is still coming down hard as we ride alongside a ragged loch, and where the single-track dips, water is running over the surface. At each dip we slow right down and lift our boots clear. A car comes the other way too fast and the swell almost knocks us over. This could be fun if it wasn't so dangerous.

A few miles from Lochinver, Tony points towards some dim lights ahead and in the rain and gloom I can barely make out whether it's a house or some sort of commercial building. As we get closer, wood smoke fills my helmet, mixing with the smell of pine, and it tastes better than all the cigarettes, pipes and cigars I have ever had. I lift up my visor and see a pub sign hanging above the door. Travellers Rest it says and it is a good name.

In the tap room the oak beams are low enough to touch and there are four or five open doors leading off to small rooms. The light is thin and white like the light from a full moon. Logs are burning and spitting in the grate in the inglenook fireplace and there is a smell of sweet wood and spilt beer in the air. The taproom is empty apart from a man reading a newspaper behind the bar, who I assume to be the landlord, and an old guy with a grey beard slouching on a stool with his hands around his pint glass. A black dog sits quietly at the man's feet and it looks up as we shut the door then settles back into a half-sleep. The landlord closes his newspaper and nods.

'Great evening for surfing, laddies,' he says.

We stay inside the doorway and let the water run off our waterproofs, darkening the already dark red quarry tiles.

'Come on inside,' he says. 'You'll not spoil anything in here.'

The old guy at the bar takes a drink and mutters something but his thick grey beard completely covers his mouth and it is difficult to work out the expression on his face. We smile, hoping what he said was harmless, step out of our waterproofs and leave them by the door.

'There's not many pubs left with gas lighting,' I say, looking up at the chandeliers above the bar.

'Not many at all,' the landlord says. 'Not the original ones, anyrood.'

'Gas gives off a beautiful light,' I say. 'I love it.' I don't tell him it reminds me of when I was a sixteen-year-old apprentice, standing at the foot of the ladders at Penistone railway station while old Gordon Green inspected the mantles and cleaned the glass domes on the gas lights, finishing at twelve o'clock, a pint of beer in the Spread Eagle, and then home by half one. 'Do you have a room for the night, by any chance?'

'I'm sorry, laddies. Can't you see we're full?'

The landlord looks around and then laughs and the old guy on the stool mutters something again, downs his beer and wipes the froth off his moustache. The landlord unhooks a room key from a rack behind the bar.

'Two single beds, is it?'

He looks me in the eye and I know what he's thinking. I deepen my voice without thinking. 'That'll do nicely,' I say.

We pick up our dripping waterproofs and follow the landlord through one of the narrow doorways.

'Watch your heed', he says and we all duck.

The steep steps creak and wind. The landlord asks where we are headed.

'Somewhere north,' Tony says, and laughs.

'We're trying to find an old friend of ours from Barnsley,' I say, blowing a bit. 'We've been told he's renting a log cabin on the coast somewhere above Ullapool. We're not exactly sure where.'

The landlord unlocks the room door and pushes it open.

'That's a lot of coast.'

8

Then There Were Two: India
26 February – 14 March 1974

It took two hours to get a ticket to New Delhi at the railway station in Amritsar and we were done for 15 rupees until I went back and collared the man responsible. Being six-foot tall I towered over the little guy and I felt sorry for him in the end. We finally boarded the train at half past five and it felt like we were on a cattle truck. There was no decoration at all inside and the seats were bone-hard. I thought how are we going to sit on these benches for thirteen long hours? The train was so crowded, unlucky passengers, or maybe ones who hadn't got a ticket, had to hang on to the doors and windows. There was hardly another westerner on the train. The majority of the passengers were Indians, mainly men in turbans, and I wondered how they kept their heads cool in the heat. I asked one of them and he said turbans kept the head warm in winter and cool in summer. I thought same as my dad's flat cap then.

Despite all of us crammed into the carriage, people smiled back when I smiled and the accumulated body odour wasn't too bad. As the train pulled out of the station, Lol got out the cards but we played with little energy. I looked out into the dark night and saw only our reflections. Inside the carriage, passengers were already closing their eyes and mouths. We talked and laughed quietly, remembering the people we'd met in Afghanistan and Iran. Close to ten o'clock, we smoked our final cigarette and drained the dregs of our coke. Lol's eyes closed first, followed by Tony's a few minutes later. I listened to the dying conversations around me trying to guess what was being said. By half past ten, only the occasional cough disturbed the rhythmic click, click-clack of the train, and we leaned against each other and slept until half past six the next morning.

We stepped down from the train on to the busy platform at New Delhi, carrying our few possessions in our new leather bags, all three of us surprised at how refreshed we felt. There were hundreds of people in the station, nobody going in the same direction and nobody in a hurry. Sleeping bodies on the floor were ignored. People weaved their way past each other, belongings balanced on heads, and a good number were just loafing around, staring at us and getting in the way of others.

We found a snack bar in the station and enjoyed a filling breakfast of eggs and rice. The hole in the floor was a bit rank and I pissed in the toilet sink. We put our bags in the left luggage office and set off to find the address given to us by Magic Mohammed, supposedly his father's house, in the hope of selling the turquoise stones. A hundred yards from the train station, an Indian guy stopped us and asked if we wanted to change money then offered to take us to a good hotel. He was persistent and after talking for a while, we ended up returning for our luggage and going to a hotel with him in his cycle rickshaw.

The hotel manager gave us a funny look when we asked him to direct us to the address Magic had given us and it didn't take long to realise it was the equivalent of looking for Number 5, Sheffield, Yorkshire. The humble rickshaw man took the three of us to a huge bazaar and we tramped the labyrinth of passageways trying to find a buyer for the stones. The guy took us from one jewellery shop to another. There were dozens. On each occasion, the shopkeeper inspected the stones, shook his head, and we walked away disappointed. We did get one offer of five hundred rupees for the lot which would have been a loss of around a hundred pounds. As our hopes faded so did the urgency, and after two hours we gave up and went back to the hotel feeling down. We told the rickshaw guy we didn't want a union card, whatever that was, and because he had been so helpful, and we were fed up of bartering, we paid him the full five dollars he asked for.

Tony had been reading about the Taj Mahal and he wanted us to go to Agra for a day's sightseeing. Lol calculated we had just enough money to spend a night there and no more. The plan was to go to Agra on Friday on a local train, stay overnight in a cheap hotel, then catch the express train from there to Madras the following day. Our AA itinerary recommended we end our overland journey at the Port of Madras, one of the largest container ports in India, before sailing on to Australia. We hoped to find a cargo ship in dock destined for Singapore or, even better, direct to Australia, and work our passage.

We knew it would be a long train ride from Agra to Madras, but the alternative would have been to hitchhike in the full heat of the day and not even Tony the sun-worshipper fancied that. According to our itinerary Madras was over twelve hundred miles away and would take two nights by train. Our bones were still aching from the Amritsar-New Delhi train and this time we wanted to travel in relative comfort. The ticket man directed us to a tourist office and we booked a special tourist sleeper carriage for the full journey. I thought the cost was reasonable, so did Tony, but Lol said we should have asked if the price included our own toilet. I think he was kidding.

We got a lift back to the hotel in a tuk-tuk driven at speed by a madman. The driving conditions were the worst I'd ever experienced. Cycles, tricycles, scooters, mopeds, tuk-tuks, taxis, horse and bull drawn carts packed the road and the pavements, and the three of us spent the whole time swerving in our seats yet we never saw one accident.

In the afternoon, after we had rested from the heat and the crowds, we tried again to find a buyer for the stones. We intended keeping the six rings and letting all the stones go for no less than six hundred rupees if possible. The heat was getting to us as we trudged around the streets looking for a buyer. Lol was tired out after an hour and he went back to the hotel for a lie down. Tony and I spent another hour chasing around the shops led by a suspicious-looking Indian guy and we ended up discussing the sale in a house deep down a backstreet with two friendly Indians who made it obvious they were interested in buying the goods. We drank tea with them – it's amazing how the ritual of tea drinking acts as a great relaxer and leveller, a bit like smoking a peace pipe, I suppose – and we bartered hard, hard for us, but the two Indians were masters at negotiating and we finished up keeping three rings, one for each of us, and selling everything else for a measly 475 rupees. I thought the next time I'm involved in bartering and I'm the one doing the buying, I'm going to put the kettle on first.

We weren't going to risk another tuk-tuk ride and instead took a tricycle back to the hotel. It was good fun, nipping in and out of the traffic, being asked to get out and walk at the slightest incline. We woke Lol and told him we had got 475 for the stones. He jumped up, wide-eyed, thinking we meant dollars. Although we had lost about £35 each, we shrugged our shoulders, put the kettle on and watched hundreds of ants working the floor and window ledge. Just before we turned in, a lizard ran down the wall and disappeared under the bed.

Friday 1 March

There was plenty of time for breakfast in the hotel before the train to Agra was due in. The servants never left us unattended and they saluted us with an open palm, the way soldiers in the Indian army salute English officers on old news footage. It made me feel a bit embarrassed and uncomfortable.

We squeezed on to the train, using our bags like fat bellies to keep going forward and avoid being pushed around. It was much busier than the Amritsar to New Delhi train and there were no seats available. We didn't mind too much. It was only going to be a relatively short ride and it was quiet, very quiet, and there were lots of beautiful women, dressed like birds of paradise. There were two young girls sitting by the window baring their midriffs and cleavages and being very feminine. I think they must have been sisters because they kept touching each other and giggling.

I spent half the journey reading and half looking out of the window. Everywhere was the greenest green I had ever seen and there were hundreds of colourful birds flying through the air and swerving through the trees, glorious in the sunshine. Even the more familiar looking hawks, kites and eagles were species I'd never seen before. It was wonderful not to be able to identify any of them, like learning to birdwatch all over again.

Four hours later we pulled into Agra station and stepped on to a noisy, crowded, fly-infested platform. We were taken to a cheap, clean hotel by rickshaw, powered by the legs of two skinny riders. These two guys worked like a comedy duo and we soon made friends with them. The hotel manager's son, Camel, was a young, good-looking, long haired Indian guy. He told us he had travelled half the world and talked with the cockiness of someone who had seen everything. I thought I'll bet he's had more women than Tony, Lol and me put together.

We ate a dinner of rice and very dark chicken then the two rickshaw riders took us to see the Taj Mahal. The ride through the countryside took twenty long minutes of steady pedalling and the sun shone all the way. By travelling at slow cycle pace, we became part of the lush greenery, tasting and smelling the herbs and spices and pollen in the air, instead of passing through the landscape, disconnected, at the speed of a van or train.

Agra was filthy and poor and overcrowded and yet the constant movement of happy people dressed in bright, rich colours made it fascinating. The Taj Mahal was more beautiful than I imagined and better organised than I expected. The contrast between the sublime ivory-white marble exterior of the mausoleum and the ordinariness of its surroundings made it appear as though the structure had landed from another planet. And there were even more women showing their midriffs and cleavages. We even got one of them to take the classic photograph of the three of us relaxing in front of the reflecting pool. It wasn't very original, but it was for us.

As the building began to turn milky white in the fading light, we set off back to our hotel and rode past fly-infested shops and fly-infested faces, the rickshaw missing cows, bikes and people by inches. The rickshaw stopped outside a good souvenir shop and between the three of us we bought one hundred dollars' worth of wood Buddha figures and bone elephants to send back home. We called at a jewellery shop and asked how much the stones we had sold in New Delhi were worth. The owner inspected the quality of the three turquoise rings we were wearing and told us he would have given us seven hundred rupees for everything. We looked at each other and shrugged. He wanted to buy the rings but we told him they were not for sale. They were part of us now – a symbol of our travels and solidarity.

At the hotel we paid the two rickshaw riders and gave them some of our old clothes we no longer needed before arranging to see them at eleven o'clock the following morning. We ate supper in the garden under low lights and a high moon. It was relaxing and peaceful apart from the constant chirp of cicadas. We thought they were crickets until Camel put us right. Back in our room, I kept my eye on the active ants and stealthy spiders. Lol thought he might have caught the flu and we all agreed we were tired and scruffy.

Saturday 2 March

We set off with our two rickshaw friends to the bazaar and bought a canvass bag for half the asking price. We probably still paid over the odds but we were getting better at this bartering game. We looked around a shop selling gifts made out of marble and ended up buying sixty dollars' worth of goods between us. Altogether I had spent $45 on gifts and was really low on cash now. We paid our two rickshaw riders and said goodbye. One of them was getting engaged that afternoon and we wished him good luck. Around five o'clock we saw his fellow rider staggering around the streets out of his mind. When Camel saw him, he became aggravated at the way 'these kinds of people spend their money on drink as soon as they get it even though their kids are starving'.

We spent the afternoon lounging around, packing, washing our hair and feet and talking about Agra. How we were fascinated by its parks full of parrots, hawks and colourful birds, and its smiling people and their dirty, dark, fly-covered faces. Every shop was infested with flies and nobody seemed bothered by them, they were just accepted. It got to eight o'clock and it was time to catch the express train to Madras. We were taken by rickshaw to the train station and as much as I hated myself for it, I couldn't help feeling self-important, sitting back like a lord, being transported through the streets above the crowds.

It was dark when we got to the station, though still noisy and crowded. There were distant hoots of trains, and flashes of wings as night birds flew in front of the street lights. As we waited for the train to arrive, an Indian woman opposite me started breastfeeding her child. Men wheeled their wares in barrows, shouting out the names of whatever it was they were selling. Shoe-shiners waited for business and there was a tangy smell of oranges and lemons in the air. It was still warm and there were sleeping bodies everywhere.

Boarding the train was orderly and there was no pushing and shoving getting to our compartment. The special sleeper we had booked and paid extra for back in New Delhi turned out to be nothing more than a reserved length of luggage rack and we laughed at ourselves for having being taken in again. We climbed up on to our sleeper and settled down to read. People were quiet and respectful. The constant, hypnotic click, click-clack of the train was interrupted by an occasional snore, a cough, a woman's voice. The man below us became agitated over something. He seemed a bit of a trouble causer and everyone avoided his eyes.

Be careful with this guy. Looks like there might be some action tonight. Don't get involved. It's late. The cockroaches are out. Click, click-clack. Click, click-clack. Like a lullaby. Gentle rocking of the carriageway sending me to sleep. Tony, please put your book down and turn out the light.

Sunday 3 March

We climbed down from the luggage rack and searched for seats to have breakfast. It was strange to think we had been travelling all through the night. If I squinted, the scenery through the window reminded me of Scotland but once I focused and saw the lush trees, the exotic birds and the beautifully dressed, straight-backed, majestic women working in the fields with the heat shimmering around them, I knew we could only be in India.

Yesterday, Lol shaved off his beard and this morning we told him he looked twenty-one not twenty-four. He seemed friendlier too. I wondered if by changing his appearance he was moving on from the past. I didn't say anything.

We had hardly eaten today, mainly oranges and coffee. It was too hot to eat. My right arm had got sunburned sitting next to the open window for hours. I hoped it wouldn't peel – I was just beginning to tan. My eyes were tired from reading and there was nothing to do so I climbed up on to the luggage rack and got into bed. A young wife with a baby in her arms had nowhere to sleep other than on the crowded floor. As she tried to get comfortable, I climbed down and offered her my sleeper. Her husband thanked me for the gesture but said they would be OK. He was really appreciative and I felt good even though nothing on the surface had changed.

It was dark outside. The fan was humming and everyone was quiet, half asleep. There was still the click, click-clack in the background. I thought about the driver a lot, how he managed day after day, night after night. I wished he would turn off the fans. It was like listening to a VW engine at four and half thousand revs. The heat, the wooden seats, the slatted beds, and the sweating bodies, made the compartment feel like a sauna bath. The constant swaying of the carriage made letter writing difficult, like being at junior school again.

Monday 4 March

Tony, as always lately, was up before me but Lol was dead. Or so I thought when I first looked at his grey, clean-shaven face as he lay asleep on the luggage rack. We were on the last leg of the train journey and the carriage was a little less crowded. During the morning a well-dressed Indian accidentally dropped his purse, and the two thousand rupees he had in it, down the latrine while the train was speeding along. Although he pulled the emergency cord immediately and the train stopped, he never found the money. I thought it was quite amusing really. I hoped some poor family found it.

Madras looked like New Delhi but it was even hotter and there were even more poor people on the streets. A young Indian lad volunteered to be our guide and found us a hotel. There was one room left and it only had two single beds but we didn't feel like searching around other hotels in the midday heat so we grabbed it. Our young guide then took us to the docks. The gates were locked and not due to open until the following day so it was back to the hotel out of the way of the heat and the beggars and the pestering rickshaw riders. The young lad followed us into our room and hung around for ages even though we had already paid him. We completely ignored him for most of the time and eventually he got up and left.

During the ride around that morning and afternoon I saw a few things that stuck in my mind and painted a picture of Madras. Hundreds of families in ditches under rag-made roofs, nitting each other's heads, washing their bodies with water from the street hydrants, brushing their teeth with their fingers. A well-dressed man walking along the busy pavement of the main street lifting up his dress and picking his bare arse for at least ten seconds. A woman with no arm and a mutilated leg, her flat left breast on view, holding out a beggar's cup in her good hand. A woman stopping in the middle of the pavement, squatting over a widening pool of urine.

That night I spewed up seven or eight times, finally retching bile. It must have been something I ate.

Tuesday 5 March

The noise in the street below our room window was driving me crazy. It was only six o'clock in the morning. I couldn't face breakfast and felt too ill to go out with Lol and Tony in the heat chasing around the harbour and booking office trying to find a ship bound for Singapore or Australia. The piercing sound of horns and shouting in the street below, the drone from the incessant room fan above, the heat and stuffiness all around, and the feeling of sickness were getting to me and I began to hate Madras.

Lol and Tony came back with no happy news other than they'd heard that a passenger ship bound for Singapore and Australia was stopping off at Colombo in Sri Lanka on the 25 March – twenty-one long days from now. It didn't make me feel much better. Lol had a quick sleep to recover from the hunting and Tony spent three quarters of an hour sunbathing on the roof between the open water tanks and flue outlets. They were heroes and they tried the harbour and booking office again later in the afternoon. On their return they brought even less information than they had that morning and none of us were feeling good.

The street noise was getting louder and some idiot down there had been playing the same six notes on a cheap flute over and over again for the last two hours.

I thought I ought to write home but I didn't feel up to it. Lol and Tony said it had been even hotter than yesterday. At last, the noise below began to die down and I started to feel drowsy. I wondered if we would ever get out of Madras.

Wednesday 6 March

I was feeling healthier the next morning and ordered breakfast before the others stirred. Lol was tired out from yesterday's exertion and he stayed in bed. It was hot outside. If thought if I stand still on the pavement in my bare feet for more than five seconds, I'll leave two footprints of skin.

On the way to the docks, which were even busier, noisier and more colourful than when we first arrived, Tony and I had to keep stepping into doorways and other shady places to escape the heat and we were tired out before we reached the dock gate. We got a port pass without fuss and entered the harbour area, overwhelmed by the number of ships and the variety of cargo being slowly loaded and unloaded in the heat.

One of the first ships we saw was British. We went on board and chatted to three English youths and drank coffee with them. They were merchant navy men and seemed good lads. Bad news though. Their ship wasn't going our way. We trudged on and had a light-hearted chat with the captain of another British ship but still ended up with no useful news. We walked under working derricks, our eyes fixed on the load dangling above our heads, clambered over heavy cargo blocking the pavement, and breathed in the aroma of tar on the roadway as it melted under the sun.

We tried shipping agency after shipping agency without luck. The heat was unbearable and I lost my temper when a couple of persistent Indians tried to sell us hashish and pestered us to change money. One of the captains we spoke to told us again about the Colombo to Australia passenger ship which made us feel a little better. The booking office outside the docks confirmed the liner would be calling at Colombo on 25 March and told us the approximate cost but they had no details about any vacancies.

My feet were sore from plodding in sandals and my exposed toes were burning. We gave up and came back to the air-conditioned coolness of the hotel restaurant on the ground floor. It was like walking into a dark cave and both of us laughed as we stumbled into tables and chairs until our eyes got used to the new light. Sun-worshipping Tony had been walking the streets bare-chested and he left his shirt tied round his waist as we ate fruit and ice cream. Half way through the meal, a middle aged, respectable looking Indian guy came over to our table and asked which country we were from. England, we proudly replied. Then he berated Tony for not wearing a shirt, saying he was bringing India to shame and asking would he behave like that in an English restaurant. I started to defend Tony and the irate man called me a bastard. I told him there was no need to swear and he went back to his table chuntering. Everyone else in the restaurant smiled apologetically. The angry man left and a guy he had been dining with came over and gave us cigarettes and apologised for the outburst. Three other men at the next table, one said he was a professor, came over and they too apologised for the angry man's behaviour.

Camel must have heard about the commotion downstairs in the restaurant and later that afternoon he told us about the hatred some Indians feel towards the British following the British Raj. He said some of his countrymen detested what they saw as the religious white supremacy of the empire which they felt was built on brutality and theft. I thought this wasn't in the version of history I was given at school and I was ashamed of what I'd said and Tony cringed at his own innocence. It was just as bad knowing that the man's colleagues felt they had to apologise for his outburst.

My turn to sleep on the floor. Immune to the bugs, now. Stare at the ceiling fan, slow and turning forever. Time to calculate. If we can't work our passage to Australia, and instead have to take the passenger liner from Colombo, we should just about have enough money to survive until we land in Fremantle. What a situation. Good job we have a sense of humour. Feel bad about a slight argument I had with Tony tonight. He's been unusually touchy, lately.

Thursday 7 March

I didn't know whether to talk to Tony this morning but I did eventually and we seemed okay. Outside, the heat was unbearable again. We went in search of food, sticking close to the walls of the buildings like rats to keep out of the sun, and anything more than a steady walk caused fatigue and sweat. We couldn't afford to buy proper food and today only had pop, ice-cream and soup. Tony reckoned there was no sense in going to Australia bearing in mind our financial status. I didn't say anything but deep down I half-agreed with him. Lol made his case for carrying on, saying we had come this far and he was sure we would find work in Australia. After debating for fifteen minutes, I sided with Lol and so on a majority vote we decided to keep going and see what happened. That was the first big decision we'd made where we had to resort to majority rule. It didn't feel comfortable.

A communist group marched by below our balcony shouting and waving and it was entertaining seeing them from above and then the flute player returned.

Friday 8 March

We visited the booking office straight after breakfast and they were fairly confident there would be three places available on the ship to Fremantle. We didn't celebrate in case we were tempting fate. We booked the train to Rameswaram which is on the southern tip of India from where we plan to catch the ferry to Sri Lanka. Tony confessed this morning he was on the point of returning home, probably overland by hippie bus. He sounded serious and I got the feeling he had been working on it for longer than we thought.

Our daily food intake consisted of two fried eggs and toast, soup and chapatti and maybe two more fried eggs again at night and four or five bottles of Limca throughout the day to lubricate the innards. There wasn't much else to do after eating other than alternate between lying down in the room and sunbathing on the hotel roof. Tony was tanning fast and still looked good from his travels in Spain. Lol was going red and I was half and half. They ribbed me about my bony chest so I ribbed Tony about his thin legs and Lol about his beer gut. When it got too hot on the open roof for me and Lol, we moved to the shade cast by the air-conditioning units and left Tony to bake.

The hours from five o'clock to seven o'clock in the evening were the longest. We watched a funeral procession go by on the street below. Singing, firecrackers and trumpets heralded the parade. Dancers and followers in colourful dresses clustered around a cart decorated with flowers as it wheeled the body, dressed in rich ornaments, through the noisy crowds. All the way through the loud procession the flute man never once stopped playing.

Tony was contemplating phoning his mom tomorrow to find out about Gloria in order to help him make up his mind whether to go to Australia or go back home through Europe. For a moment that night I thought about going home and I wasn't even feeling homesick or down. I kept thinking about all the worry I was causing my family, especially my mother. The night was a little strange somehow. It was a quarter past ten and none of us looked like going to bed. Something is in the wind, I thought. I was right. Tony decided to spend some time on the roof and I joined him. It was still and peaceful. Hawks and vultures circled above. Occasionally a car drove by and now and again the sharp sound of a bike bell sprang up from the street.

'I can't make up my mind whether to stay or go,' Tony said.

'What are you thinking?'

Tony lit a cigarette and said, 'I miss Gloria badly but I also don't want to give up on Australia now that we're so close. I know I'll regret it for the rest of my life if I don't go.'

'You can't do both, Tony.'

'I know. That's the problem.'

'What would you do if you did come to Australia with us?'

'I reckon we would be okay. We could tour the country on motorbikes. And then I wouldn't mind going to America and travel from coast to coast. I'm sure we'd do okay. It's a big country.' Tony took a deep drag on his cigarette. 'But I do miss being with Gloria.'

'I suppose you could always come to Australia later. It'll always be there. The thing is, will Gloria?'

I was trying not to say what I would do if I was in Tony's position but I was failing. I think I would have turned back if I loved somebody as much as Tony loved Gloria. But who knows? I loved and missed my family and that was hard enough.

'I suppose I could always do it later, as you say. But I might not get the chance again.'

Listening to Tony talking about his longing to turn back made me feel that I was ready for home. But I kept quiet and eventually Tony put his cigarette out.

'I'll stay,' he said. 'I'll give Australia a try.'

Saturday 9 March

I was disturbed all night long by Tony and Lol walking around, switching lights on and running water. Tony had been bitten all over again by the mosquitoes and he couldn't get to sleep without putting some cream on. They were both worn out and I volunteered to post our letters and call at the booking office. My new flip-flops were much better than my old ones and I walked at a silly fast pace, leaving every other pedestrian behind, dodging contact like George Best.

I did my duties and came back to the hotel tired out and thirsty. Tony and Lol went to the station for Tony's train ticket back to New Delhi. Yes, he has finally made up his mind. He is going back to Europe. He told us over lunch after hinting all morning. I had expected it. Tony didn't sound convincing last night up on the roof. I envied him going back home to a girl as lovely as Gloria and wished there was a good reason for me to return. But I thought I can't go back to no job after only four months, can I?

I had an idea to celebrate our splitting up by opening the bottle of wine Francois had given us in Kabul as a leaving present. Secretly, I ordered a table in the restaurant and put the wine on ice. It was mainly for Tony, of course, but also to celebrate Lol and me making a no turning back commitment to Australia. We enjoyed the occasion, although the food wasn't good, talking of our time together and the good relationship we had maintained. We smoked, drank the awful wine, and I felt a little sad but good as well. I hoped Tony would be all right. I also hoped Lol and I would be all right.

We went back to our room feeling like youngsters. There was a bit of horseplay and I locked Lol out of the room. He was only wearing his underpants and he was angry but only temporarily. It was a warm, sticky night again. I felt sorry for the waiter who brought us a soda to the room and I gave him a pair of my old shorts.

So, Tony is leaving for New Delhi tomorrow. Don't want to think about it too much. Could get upset. What can we buy him as a token of our friendship? Something will come to me tonight.

Sunday 10 March

The booking office confirmed the cost of the ticket from Colombo to Fremantle would be $253 each. That left me and Lol with the great amount spare of one dollar. My bank account back home at Lloyds was empty and it was no good asking my mam and dad for anything. They needed all their spare cash to pay the council rent, eat meat once a week and go out on Saturday night. Lol wasn't in a much better position than me having lost out on the sale of his bungalow. Luckily, Tony could now afford to lend us fifty dollars each giving us a few dollars to play with provided we existed on eight rupees a day until we boarded the ship on 25 March. That was sixteen whole days from now. We wouldn't be staying in a hotel that's for sure.

I was a bit down, knowing we had to wait around in Madras without any money and with the sickening prospect of living rough on a beach in Colombo waiting for our ship to arrive. Rationally, I told myself, I ought to be going back with Tony. I kept trying to forget how easy and sensible it would be. Now I was in debt and going to Australia where I would need around £250 to get back home. On the bright side, if I could get a well-paid job the problem would be erased inside two months and I would have a choice of what I wanted to do next. But I didn't like the idea of having to find a well-paid job immediately instead of continuing my adventure and travelling through Australia. Still, I left England with that prospect. I normally snatch at challenges like these so I put it down to the mood I was in. Let's hope so anyway.

Tony was nervous and excited about catching the train back to New Delhi that afternoon and he kept singing songs with 'going home' and 'back to you' lyrics. Lol appeared extra happy and excited while I was preoccupied with how to say goodbye. We left Tony reading in the hotel and took a rickshaw to the train station to look around the shops for a goodbye gift. We bought a wooden flute and wrote a simple message, 'If we could choose one person from all the world to live, travel and have fun with it would be you every time, Tony.'

On the way back to the hotel I rode the rickshaw and the Rickie sat in the back with Lol. We must have been conspicuous because everyone looked and laughed and one guy even clapped. I didn't think he was being sarcastic. A policeman threw some dark words at us but he never looked seriously concerned.

We arrived at the station at three o'clock and Tony boarded the packed train. He pushed his way to an open window and we shook hands for a long time, my throat tightening, Tony not daring to look at us. The whistle blew and the train steadily chugged out of the station. We waved goodbye and I swear Tony was in tears. I don't know how I managed not to shed a tear as well. Lol looked affected but he didn't say much. I hoped to God Tony would be okay.

Back at the hotel we ordered rice and milk. We had already spent five and three quarters of a rupee today which meant we only had two and a quarter left. I felt miserable and thought why didn't I go back with Tony?

I found a little detective book in the hotel foyer that I hadn't read. It was like getting a Christmas present. The solitude helped convince me I had made the right decision to give Australia a go and come back home if it didn't work out. I thought about buying a bible, a dictionary, or an engineering book if I had the money. Anything to fill the time.

Heart is bumping. See a clear image of a burnt body unravelling from a sleeping bag and sitting up in obvious pain. Have to open my eyes. Forehead is wet through. Take deep breaths. Must be seeing all those deformed Indians begging on the streets. It was the same the other day in Madras, when I was ill and hallucinating and that damn pipe player got inside my brain. I kept seeing beggars and gutter families staring at me in silence, expressionless, as though I was a freak. Then when I looked closer, I saw all of them were blind. Don't know what it is but something's got to me. Hope Tony will be safe. God bless him.

Wednesday 13 March

Last night I dreamt of arriving home. It was an anti-climax. When I met my mother, I put my arms around her and she just said, 'Hello. What's up with your hair?' and turned away.

There was a little bookshop round the corner from the hotel and I bought a tiny Webster dictionary for two rupees. I spent two happy hours going through the 'As'. Then I started reading Napoleon Hill's 'How to Sell Your Way Through Life' and didn't stop until page one hundred. Hill came over as a bit conceited and I didn't agree with everything he advocated, but he made me doubt some of my convictions which alone made it interesting. There were about a dozen words I couldn't understand and I looked them up in my little Webster. I wrote them down and tried to make sentences containing two or more of the words but after four sentences I felt too tired and turned in for the night.

Lol and I began packing our things, feeling a little more useful than we had during the previous few days of time-killing. We got some great news today. The tickets have arrived. We were a few dollars short in the end due to the exchange rate and lost ten dollars each on the transaction at Thomas Cook Travel Agency. Fortunately, two cheaper tickets, booked by an Australian couple having second thoughts about the voyage, became available and that saved us.

I did a personal record of thirty-two press ups. The sun tan was coming on and my body looked twice better. Unbelievably, an hour after those thirty-two press ups, I did thirty-three more. I put it down to the section on faith in Napoleon Hill's book.

We found a good bed compartment on the almost empty Rameswaram train at Madras Egmore station. I spoke a few polite words to three Ceylonese lads sitting next to us and it was in my mind to try and use them for assistance and shelter in Sri Lanka. This was not like me. I was becoming a classic traveller, always on the look-out for free gifts.

The train set off to Rameswaram on time and it felt good to be on the move again, although this time, of course, it was different. A few miles away from Madras the scenery became even more tropical before withering away to relatively barren terrain. We had spent and ate hardly a thing today and strangely I didn't feel any worse for it.

A vendor with a tray of coffee boarded the train at a rural train stop and I bought two coffees from him. I nearly lost five rupees when he 'forgot' to come back to our carriage with the change. He stood on the platform and laughed as I shouted to him to bring me my money. The train began to move and I ended up jumping off, snatching the five rupees from his top pocket, running bare-footed alongside the moving train and jumping back on again. The fox was still laughing as we left him behind at the station with his tray of coffees. Some of the passengers began to laugh at me as well. But I felt I was in the right and thought, bollocks to you, mate, we need every rupee we can get. To my surprise, an hour later at the next station the very same coffee vendor walked into our carriage laughing and tapping his top pocket. He belonged to the train and must have jumped back on at the last minute. Even I had to laugh and I paid for the coffees a second time. Later, another Indian with a tray came into our carriageway shouting, 'Acodring. Acodring'. We ignored him until we discovered he was selling a cold drink so we bought one off him to share.

It was quiet on the train and Lol and I were too tired to do anything except watch the magic of the night. Passengers without a sleeper began to settle down on the floor for the night. Something scuttled across the floor. I nudged Lol and flattened one, two, three and then four, three and half inch-long cockroaches with my new flip flops. An old woman smiled at my antics and nobody seemed concerned by the giant, brown creepy-crawlies. Within five minutes there were dozens of the things scurrying from dark corner to dark corner. I couldn't see me sleeping soundly tonight.

An old Indian guy sat with us for fifteen minutes and gave us a banana each when we told him we had no money. As I took the fruit from the kind old man, a young beggar pleaded for food from me. The three Ceylonese lads sitting at the side of us started singing native songs, tapping the seats in rhythm. It sounded fine and even Lol tapped his fingers. I felt like singing along and tried to imagine how powerful it would sound if everybody in the carriage joined in.

In the sleeper (luggage rack) Lol and I had to lock legs to stop falling out. That was falling out on to the floor, not falling out with each other. I had to get up once when the cockroaches started crawling up the bed post. Eventually I was too tired to worry about them anymore and I went to sleep.

Thursday 14 March

The luggage rack was unforgiving and looking down next morning at those still trying to get comfortable on the floor, it appeared that no one else had slept well, either. The train guard announced that we were twenty-five miles from Rameswaram and the sea ferry crossing to Sri Lanka. The final stretch of line was worth the previous night's discomfort, flanked as it was on both sides by the deep blue Palk Strait and eventually crossing over a curving, weather-beaten bridge before terminating at Rameswaram station.

We crossed half a mile of calm sea in a battered sailing vessel towed by a motor boat to reach the moored ferry. The heat was so intense I was tempted to dive in and swim the last few hundred yards. The open-sided ferry was only half-full and we found a quiet place at the front of the upper deck and gazed out onto the rolling, foaming ocean for the whole of the voyage, leaning against the side to dampen the sway, watching little rainbows appear out of the spray, the folding waves enveloping hundreds of flying fish. Three hours of peace and meditation.

August 2018 - The Traveller's Rest,
North of Ullapool

We follow the landlord into the bedroom and I put my damp bag down under the cold sash window. Tony puts his bag on the bed nearest the door and he looks happy enough. 'This'll be fine,' he says. 'Perfect.'

The landlord turns the radiator valve from frost to number one and says if we want to eat in the bar tonight, he can do chips sausage and egg, sausage egg and chips, or egg chips and sausage.

Tony says, 'Is there anywhere safe we can park the bikes for the night?'

'You can put them in the stables round the back,' the landlord says, backing out of the room. 'They'll be safe and sound in there. We've got security lights.'

'They're not gas, are they?' I say, and laugh but the landlord doesn't.

The wardrobe leans forward and there is a piece of folded cardboard wedged in to stop the door opening. As we pull off our leathers, we have to hop around on the wide, sloping floorboards to keep our balance. We bump into each other and Tony laughs when I get my foot stuck and fall on to my creaky bed.

'What a great little pub,' I say. 'I'm glad you spotted it. I didn't fancy pushing on to Lochinver in this weather.'

Tony taps the oak ceiling beam. 'This is not fake,' he says. 'It must have been an old coaching house originally, with it having stables round the back. I hope it's not haunted.'

'You don't believe in ghosts, do you?'

'I didn't used to but you never know,' he says. 'I wouldn't rule anything out, now. Nobody knows for sure what's out there.'

Tony seems to have gone spiritual since his mother died. As a non-believer I have to be careful what I say.

'That's true. Look well if a headless highwayman jumps out of the wardrobe while we're half asleep.'

'Or Lol.'

'Bloody hell, Tony. Don't say that. You've got me worried, now.'

'Whether it's a headless highwayman or whether it's Lol, they wouldn't waken me up tonight. I'm shattered. That was some stretch we've done today. All the way up from Glasgow.'

'It's a pity it rained so much. But at least when it stopped, we got some fine glimpses of lochs and mountains.'

We hang up our waterproofs over the bath to drip dry and Tony consults the road map.

'That big loch we just passed a few miles back there.'

'The one with all those little islands in it?'

'It's called Loch Sionascaig. There's a lake Sionascaig on Titan.'

Tony sees my blank look.

'You know,' he says. 'Titan, the moon.'

'Give over. There's no water on any moons.'

'Not water. Methane.'

'You know some stuff,' I say, still a bit sceptical. Tony does know some stuff.

He hands me the map and I put on my glasses.

'That storeman and that landlord were right,' I say. 'There is a lot of coast above Ullapool. You don't realise how big and remote it is until you actually get up here.'

9

Then Almost One: Sri Lanka

14-25 March 1974

It took an hour to get through customs at Talaimannar, Sri Lanka but the beautiful location made the wait a pleasure. We queued outside the customs office watching the sun go down, the waves roll in, and the dolphins play in the sea breeze.

A Dr Mohamad from Sri Lanka introduced himself as we were changing money at the adjoining train station to buy our tickets to Colombo. When he asked us what we did back in England, I told him we were Mechanical Engineering students. I had no idea why I said that and Lol kept a straight face. The doctor invited us to visit his home in Colombo with the offer of staying free of charge at a friend of his and we arranged to see him on Saturday at the hospital where he worked. I couldn't believe our luck. We were starting to scheme like freeloaders. Next step, begging.

We sat outside the station café with all the other passengers off the ferry, mainly Europeans and American travellers, and waited patiently for the train to Colombo. Skinny, flea-ridden dogs wandered in and out of the tables and travellers' talks would be interrupted by begging kids. Huge moths made the station lights flicker and the platform buzzed with night-flying beetles. At long last the train shunted noisily and slowly into the station, its single eye scanning the track ahead.

There were few passengers on the train and we tried to get some sleep in one of the quiet, dimly lit carriages. The slatted wooden seats felt like concrete and after a while we resorted to sleeping on the floor, ignoring the scurrying cockroaches. Each time we pulled into a station I was woken by noisy, clumsy Ceylonese passengers boarding the now packed train. A rumour was going around that there were thieves on the train and I went back to sleep on the floor with my passport wallet gripped tight between my legs.

Being stabbed in the eye by a thief, blood is dripping down my cheeks. Frightened and in pain. Hear myself moan. Sit up wide-awake to find a hippie shelling nuts on to my face.

Friday 15 March

Sleep was fitful and at half past six I decided to watch Sri Lanka wake up to the dawn. Lol didn't stir and I stood at the open carriage door breathing in the tropical warm air and the smell of lush vegetation. It made me light-headed, like being in a greenhouse on a hot English summer's day brushing pollen off the ripest of ripe tomatoes. The tropical flora at the track side raced by, slowing over the middle ground as though going the other way, until the forests in the distance barely moved in front of the rising sun. We passed through Kandy and bright-eyed, smiling school kids waved at the train as they skipped to school in neat uniforms, satchels swinging. Despite feeling dog-tired I couldn't take myself away from the open door. Lol joined me at half past seven when we stopped at a station and we drank coffee together, marvelling at the beauty of Sri Lanka.

Within minutes of arriving in Colombo, everyone disappeared, including Dr Mohamad, and we were left stranded at the station. We walked off in the direction everyone else had taken and after only two hundred yards we had to put our bags down, sweat running down our backs and clinging to our foreheads, too fatigued to go any further. Lol watched the bags while I attempted to locate a cheap hotel or at least find out where everybody had gone. The YMCA had a nine rupee per night bedroom without a fan. It didn't appeal. An old man led me on a wild goose chase for twenty minutes ending up where we started with nothing new but blisters. Dejected, I went back to Lol and asked him to have a go while I recovered. I slumped on my bag, looking around this foreign place and felt isolated and lost. Ten minutes later Lol returned, out of breath, with nothing good to report.

Depressed and burning in the heat we booked into the YMCA and it turned out pretty well. Although cheaper than a hotel it was still expensive considering there was no fan. But it did have a library and a gym, recreation facilities and a restaurant. Lol worked out that if we stayed there until our ship arrived, we would have six dollars to spare. Out of that six dollars we would have to eat and drink for ten days, send a cable to Lloyds back home asking for their address in Fremantle, and get through the nine days on the ship to Australia.

I showered, my skin renewed, then fell into a deep sleep. At half past seven in the evening, I was woken by the sound of clanging weights and ping pong balls being hit in the gymnasium next to our room. I had a quick look around the place, nodding to the players and keep-fit guys in a sort of brotherhood recognition. Lol stayed in the room. I think the sound of all the activity had tired him out. We'd not eaten all day so we went into a Chinese restaurant around the corner from the YMCA and had the cheapest soup on the menu. By the time we came back to the YMCA everything was shut. There was nothing to do but retire to our room to sweat. Lol stopped rubbing his feet together and I knew he had fallen asleep. I lay there wondering how Tony was doing. Eventually I got to sleep after wedging open the door and allowing the slight movement of air to cool my head.

Saturday 16 March

We caught the bus to the General Hospital where Dr Mohamad worked and found him in his dispensary. He gave us a guided tour of the many departments and we saw the making and fitting of false limbs, the VD clinic, and the canteen among others. The place was unhealthy in parts and unpolished but efficiently run. We watched a chiropodist dress a man's toe which had just had the ingrowing nail removed. The patient cried out a couple of times as Dr Mohamad talked us through the operation. The doctor was trying hard to impress us and I sensed he was making excuses for the roughness.

We walked for two hours around the hospital getting hotter and more fatigued. At last, it got to twelve noon, Dr Mohamad's finishing time, and we caught the bus to his home, which was surprisingly bare and shabby, situated on the ground floor of a big block of flats. His family and the friend he had told us about at the train station in Talaimannar, were welcoming and open and his wife made a delicious pot of leaf tea. We were humbled when the doctor's friend confirmed we could stay at his house free of charge for as long as we liked.

The doctor asked us to stay for dinner. It was a good meal but unusually we weren't very hungry and I think we might have insulted his family. I hoped not. We tried to make up by discussing English novels and text books with the doctor and his father for three quarters of an hour even though we were desperate to get back to the YMCA for some sleep.

Sunday 17 March

We booked out of the YMCA and even though we could now afford to eat a meal every day we were careful and only had chips, egg and tomato. We collected our sleeping bags and luggage and caught the number 103 bus to Dr Mohamad's friend's house. There were plenty of empty seats on the bus and I sat on my own behind Lol, feeling a little lonely, looking out of the window as the rain fell on a strange landscape. I didn't know why I was down. It wasn't the city. Colombo is picturesque in parts, with its natural lakes and fine lake-side houses and beautiful tropical gardens. Maybe it was because we were nearing the end of our journey.

From outside, our home for the next ten days looked promising but inside it was a disappointment. It was a veterinary surgeon's workplace converted into apartments at the rear. Our room was bare, scruffy and hot and smelled of cat piss. There were glass cabinets containing stuffed animals up against one wall. The four glass eyes of a freak two-headed calf watched us as we looked around for somewhere to bed down. There was nowhere to put our sleeping bags other than on the soiled floor. Through the cardboard walls we could hear screaming kids running around the hollow rooms next door.

It was only eight o'clock in the evening and there was nothing to do. I felt miserable and trapped and sensed Lol felt the same. I decided I wanted to leave and go back to the YMCA but Lol wasn't feeling well and he wanted to stay the night. It started to rain and all the other bad places we'd slept in came into my mind. I agreed I would stay the night and try to forget where I was.

A young man sharing our flat came in at nine o'clock and we talked out of politeness until he went to sleep on the floor. For an hour we listened to the animal and human noises coming through the thin partitions and watched mice scuttling under the glass cases and running down the cabinet legs onto the floor. Neither of us could get to sleep and so, still wrapped in our sleeping bags, we lifted ourselves up onto a little round table no bigger than a lorry wheel, our legs dangling over the edge, and two long hours later we were both fast asleep.

Monday 18 March

The grotesque crow of a cockerel two feet away from my head woke me up at six o'clock. Quickly and without smiling or uttering a word we packed our bags and slid out of the place. I suppose we ought to have said thanks to the owner but we just wanted to get into the fresh air and away. Our room was still available at the YMCA and we booked into our old room to the surprise of the man on reception.

Later that morning, before the heat of the day and the blinding sunlight became unbearable, we went to the quarantine office in Colombo to get the jabs we needed to enter Australia. The clinic was busy and we were worried about the state of the syringes but within fifteen minutes we were safely inoculated, all papers checked and back out on to the hot, blinding street again. On the way to the YMCA, we called at the Post Office and sent a cable to Lloyds Bank to set up an account each in their branch in Fremantle. We had done everything we could in preparation for a new life in Australia. The country was getting closer by the day. All we had to do, then, was find a job and a place to live.

While Lol had his usual afternoon sleep, I spent the afternoon in the YMCA library reading any English papers, magazines and books I could find. I called in the gym to watch some boxers training and got talking to an old Ceylonese coach who was fitter than I had ever been and had the typical character of an old boxer – hard, confident and gentle.

'That training looks hard,' I said when he took a break from doing sit ups. I counted a hundred.

'You have to train hard to box easy,' he said, wiping the sweat off his palms with a towel. 'Are you staying here, at the YMCA?'

'Yes. Me and my friend have just arrived. We're staying for a few days then we sail to Australia.'

'Come and train with us. You look as though you keep yourself fit.'

A lad was hitting a punch bag, throwing his shoulder into it and I was glad he wasn't hitting me. In the ring, two lads were sparring and they were fast and controlled.

I patted my belly and said, 'I used to keep myself fit. When I played football back in England. I miss it.'

'Do you box?'

'No, but I've always wanted to. My dad used to box in the army. I like the discipline side of it.'

'Many young men bounce into the gym wanting to learn how to fight. They are full of wild aggression. We teach them the value of self-control and show them how it is always better to walk away than to fight. But sometimes there is no alternative but to fight. To prepare for those occasions, the young men are taught how to overcome their aggressor.'

'I think I'd be lost training with all of you,' I said. 'You all look super-fit. But I'll see. Maybe later.'

Watching the young lads train hard and the old boxer encouraging them to work on their technique made me realise how much I missed and loved sport. I went back to my room and said to myself get fit and be a good soccer player.

Lol was still horizontal and not feeling well. I flopped into bed with a wet towel over my head, trying to cool down, and I hung between sleep and reality for two hours.

There was no glass in any of the windows in the YMCA, just heavy wooden shutters, and the annoying squawk of a jackdaw perched on the window ledge forced me up.

I returned to the library and spent an hour reading Dale Carnegie's How to Win Friends and Influence People. It had an almost magical effect on me and when I stood up to leave everyone in the library appeared to be in a better mood than they were when I went in.

It was too hot outside and not much better inside and we shuttled back and forth to the toilet block every half hour for a cold shower. Lol's guts were rumbling and he rushed to the toilet block. Twenty minutes later he came back and gently rolled onto the bed. I noticed there was something different about him. It was only when he put his pale arms behind his pale head that I realised he'd torn off his shirt sleeves. It was hot but I didn't think it was worth spoiling a good shirt to cool down, especially when it was his favourite – cream cheesecloth with a button-down collar.

'What's tha done to thi shirt?' I said.

Lol opened one eye.

'There wont any toilet paper.'

It was painful to laugh. Both of us had been out in the sun too long and our faces were tight and bright red. It was a good moment. We were getting on well together. It could have been the Dale Carnegie book.

Lol was feeling weak and I suggested we forget our dire money situation for once and go out for something proper to eat. The Chinese restaurant around the corner was packed with noisy French sailors, and we had bacon, egg and chips. We tipped the waiter the minimum we dared and Lol bought five cigarettes with his allowance and I bought a packet of biscuits with mine.

Back at the YMCA we met a mouthy man from England and his Australian girlfriend. He talked ten to the dozen about the ship to Australia, the one we were catching, and how they were planning to book a superior cabin, not a grubby little tourist class cabin (like ours), and he didn't seem to want to listen to anything we had to say. I thought he's obviously not read How to Win Friends and Influence People. On the way to our room to retire I met the old boxer again and we still held that peculiar respect between coach and student. What a great bloke I thought.

Would like to write home. Can't afford the stamps. What a measly allowance we've been forced to accept. I'm sure Lol's been nicking my biscuits.

Tuesday 19 March

Lol woke me at two o'clock in the morning to say he'd seen a rat nibbling my biscuits. We located the grey, frightened animal and trapped it behind a cabinet. I flushed it out while Lol bashed its head with a boot. We threw the thing out of the window and heard it thwack on to the road below. Lol couldn't get back to sleep but I couldn't keep awake.

We'd been doing too much sunbathing and I'd been feeling thirsty all day. Two rushed visits to the hole in the floor and a lie down cured me and I felt ten times better and even did thirty minutes more sunbathing.

The Chop-Suey we had for supper at the Chinese restaurant was tasty. Half way through the meal Lol stuck his fork into a dark piece of meat and said, straight-faced, that he'd noticed the dead rat below our window had gone. We walked back to the YMCA feeling good, whistling and tossing the room keys up into the humid night air. Lol said he needed some exercise to induce sleep so he set off to the docks walking at a swift pace. When he returned, I thought he'd been in a race the way he collapsed on to the bed. When his breathing returned to normal, he put his hands behind his head and looked up at the ceiling.

'I've been thinking,' he said. 'What about working in Australia for a year to get twelve hundred quid together and then go back home through America?'

The walk must have cleared his head, and the solitude of the environment in the YMCA was just what I needed to get my thoughts straight.

'Sounds okay to me,' I said. 'What would you do if I decided to come back early?'

'If I was settled,' he said, rubbing his feet together slower than usual, 'I'd stick it out.'

Wednesday 20 March

There was a bit of bother with rats again last night. The vermin stole some of the biscuits we left out as bait without being seen. Listening and watching for movement made it a long night.

The monotony of hot beach, toilet, cold shower, cold drink, wash clothes, was beginning to get to me. I didn't know whether I was feeling homesick, or just down and bored. It got worse. Lol was snoring and I tried to sleep but I was thinking too much of home and wondering whether I was doing the right thing going to Australia. Thoughts kept tumbling over in my mind and I was getting lower and lower. I looked across at Lol's dark shape fast asleep on top of the blankets in the bed opposite and nearly, oh so nearly, made a decision to turn back.

What should I do? The answer won't come. Everything is tied together. Complicated by my emotions. One minute, one decision, the next minute, totally opposite. Not opposite. Wrong word. Maybe it should be…

I don't know. I just don't know. Too bewildered. Too hot. Confused. Tottering on insanity. Falling asleep.

Thursday 21 March

I woke up the next morning and knew exactly what I should do. I was going back home the way I had come. I had all the basics arranged in my mind. First, phone Francois to see if Tony was there. If so, cancel my ticket to Australia and tell Tony to wait for me. If he wasn't there, travel back home on my own the cheapest way possible. I told Lol of my decision and waited for his response. I wasn't expecting him to laugh but he did.

'Where are tha getting t'money from to phone Francois, niver mind to go back home? The tickets to Australia are non-refundable.'

I burst out laughing because the alternative would have been to cry. Within a split second my mind switched from being set on going back home to shouting Australia here we come. There is a lesson in there somewhere I thought. Something to do with combining the heart and the head. Lol can do it. He is steadfast and I admire the way nothing deflects him from his goal.

Only four days to go. Fly baby fly.

Saturday 23 March

Last night was the worst I've had since leaving England. All night, I was turning over and over trying to get a comfortable position in the heat. In the end I resorted to a shower at half past two in the morning and swung the shutters open to coax some air into the room. I thought bollocks to the rats.

In the afternoon, I went back to the library planning to continue reading How to Win Friends and Influence People but someone had borrowed it. The librarian must have seen my disappointment and he asked me how long I was staying at the YMCA. 'No problem,' he said. 'You can borrow a book.' It was like winning the pools. There were plenty of English language books on the shelves and I found the Human Zoo by Desmond Morris.

Reading on the bed was heaven and I skimmed through the book and then read the first chapter. It offered clear, simple answers on why we do what we do when we interact with others, and it made human habits seem less complicated than I thought. Maybe it was reading about chimpanzees preening, I don't know, but for some reason I asked Lol if he would have a go at cutting my hair. My locks were down to my shoulders and much too heavy for the heat of Colombo. He cut the back and it looked fine. It was so good I had to have it cut all over to balance the style. Lol said he'd never cut hair before. I thought I wished you'd told me that half an hour ago.

Monday 25 March

When our last day in Colombo finally arrived, I was excited and anxious to get going. It was a good job we were not marching on our stomachs. Our breakfast wouldn't have fed a rat. We could only afford to share one boiled egg and a slice of toast. That left us with five rupees to buy and post one card home each and send a joint one to the gas depot. I sent my card to my friend

Ken who was looking after my bike in his garage back in Barnsley.

Ken.

Help! I'm desperate. I've no money left and I'll be in Australia on 4th April. If you still want to buy the BSA chopper you can have it for £200. A bargain! If you do buy it, can you make sure you let my mam have the money quick then she can send it over to my bank account in Fremantle.

See you later (maybe!)

Mike

The ship wasn't due in till three in the afternoon and Lol, in one of his quiet moods again, went for a walk and I killed an hour in the library. In the leisure section I found a good book on weight training and I copied out, on the back of an envelope, an exercise schedule and immediately felt fitter.

A young Ceylonese guy who I had met in the boxing gym bought our sleeping bags. We were rich again and could smell food everywhere we turned but by the time we'd changed the rupees into dollars and carted our travel bags off to the shipping department there was no time to eat. Never mind, I thought. It'll make tonight's dinner on the ship taste even better.

August 2018 - The Traveller's Rest, North of Ullapool

We take a shower and go downstairs for a drink and something to eat. Probably eggs, chips and sausage by the sounds of it. We're both hungry. We haven't eaten since Inverness apart from tea and a scone in the cedar-clad café in Achiltibuie.

Off to the right in one of the little rooms, a few youngsters are playing pool and fooling around. The taproom is empty except for the old guy with the grey beard. He doesn't look to have moved. He's still sitting on the bar stool and his black dog is still half-asleep at his feet. We sit at a table by the window and when we order chips, egg and sausage, the landlord tells us we have made an excellent choice. I stand with my back to the log fire for a few minutes to get warm. Tony never feels the cold. He says it's my circulation. Tony, as inquisitive as ever, picks up the local paper left on the next table and I try to open the tall cupboard at the side of the fireplace and have a nosey inside but the hinges are thick with paint and I leave it.

Half way through our meal, the young pool players leave and we hear their car rev up and race away down the dark lane into the night. It's now ten o'clock and there's only me and Tony and the old guy and his dog left in the place. The landlord comes out from behind the bar and sits on one of the bar stools to read his paper, again. He's either a slow reader or it's the evening edition. I notice him kick off his shoes and begin to rub his feet rhythmically the way Lol used to do. I nudge Tony and he tells me I'm becoming obsessed with our search.

We're just thinking of drinking up and going to bed when, without looking round, the old guy speaks.

'I hear you're looking for an auld pal of yours?'

I nearly choke on the last of my beer. The landlord must have said something to him. I put on my friendliest voice and try not to sound like a clandestine debt collector.

'We are. His name's Lol. I used to work with him at the gas board in Barnsley.'

The old guy finishes off his beer and bangs his glass down on the bar.

Tony says, 'We set off to Australia with him in nineteen-seventy-three. A long time ago. We think he might be renting a log cabin somewhere around these parts.'

The old guy says, 'There's a man from Yorkshire aboot your age staying in a lodge at a site not far fra here. I look after the groonds.'

Tony and I let go of our pint glasses and look at each other in disbelief. We join the old man at the bar.

'We could be lucky,' I say. 'It might be Lol.'

'Do you say the site's near here?' Tony says.

The old man still hasn't looked directly at us. His eyes narrow and his thick moustache, edged with froth, moves slightly which I take to be a smile aimed at the landlord.

'They look like honest boys', he says. 'It must be worth a pint to know where this site is.'

The landlord looks over the top of his paper and says, 'Aye. At least a pint.'

I pull out my wallet.

'Information first,' I say, grinning.

10

Food and Women: The Indian Ocean
25 March – 4 April 1974

We joined other passengers on the way to the harbour and became a slow stream of suitcases and rucksacks. There was no organisation and no urgency at the customs barrier. People sat on their bags in the queue and smoked and chilled and when another barrier opened most stayed where they were. Eventually we got through customs and walked towards our ship, smiling with excitement and relief. And what a sight it was. The ship was huge and you could almost feel the cool air of Europe still clinging to it. We walked up the gantry and a smiling crew member in an immaculate white uniform welcomed us on board with a hint of query in his eyes. I wondered if he could tell we had the dust of four months' road travel on our clothes. We stepped through the steel door, out of the tropical heat, and there was cooling air, and carpets, clean walls, ice water vendors, spick and span crew. And girls everywhere. There were diagrams on the walls showing the layout of the different decks, fire assembly points and lifeboat locations and there were coloured blocks showing a swimming pool, a restaurant, two lounges, three bars, a library, sitting areas, everything. Even our tiny third-class cabin which we were sharing with another passenger felt luxurious.

We claimed our bunks, too excited to unpack, and sat around upstairs in one of the lounges waiting for dinner. We smoked and talked and watched the harbour lights grow brighter as the sun went down. At last, the restaurant opened. The dining room was full and Lol and I were shown to our own table which was to one side and a bit out of it. All the tables were covered in starched, white cotton table cloths set with identical silver cutlery and every passenger looked well-fed and tanned.

And then the banquet began. I had only ever seen a feast like that in films. The food just kept on coming. Soup, chicken, stuffing, potatoes, veg, gravy, apple pie and custard, coffee and mints, followed by wine and brandy for those who could afford it. Nobody on the ship could have been hungrier than Lol and me and we never paused, even when we were distracted by the smiling waitresses, and we left nothing.

The restaurant gradually cleared and we joined everyone on top deck to wait for the ship to move off. She did at ten o'clock and we left behind the lonely lights of Colombo. Lol went for a walk on his own again, no doubt thinking about his ex-fiancée.

An Australian lad with hair so black we nicknamed him Sooty, was sharing our cabin and he told us the ship was full of women and everybody was 'shagging.' Lol rubbed his hands and smiled as he climbed up into his bunk. I rolled into my bed and dropped to sleep within minutes even though it felt as though someone was walking all over the mattress.

The sea was calm and flat the next morning and looked as heavy as mercury. Sooty loaned us some leaflets on Australia and told us how beautiful Perth was. We thought he was kidding when he said it snowed up on the mountains in the north of the country. I'd only ever thought about hot sun and huge fields of wheat. Sooty was never still, always preening in the tiny toilet mirror, always somebody urgent to see. He could have been a salesman for Australia and he made us feel good.

In the afternoon, after sunbathing and playing table tennis, we went back to the bunk for a rest. When I woke up it was seven o'clock and the cabin was empty. I went looking for Lol, feeling lonely and lost, hardly a penny in my pocket. He was already eating in the restaurant and we had a little argument about sticking together at meal times.

It was another excellent meal and the young waitresses looked as good as they did on our first evening meal. We were invited to a party in an Australian guy's cabin and listened to Leonard Cohen, which normally cheers me up but it didn't this time. I smiled at a couple of girls and got a response. I didn't take it any further. I was feeling tired, uncomfortably quiet, conscious of my chopped hair, and when it got to half past twelve Lol and I left the noisy party and went back to our bunk to sleep.

A nasty tempered Lol pushed past me to the bathroom the next morning. I could have turned on him, blaming me for wakening him up in the night to look for the clock. I wanted to have my breakfast on my own, get out of his sight, but he came into the restaurant and sat down at the table while I was half way through my bacon and eggs. He told me the reason he had been a bit tetchy lately was because his gums had started bleeding and he'd read that it could be linked to heart problems. I said I'd been feeling tired and edgy as well and we agreed we were both at fault. It was still no reason to be as nasty as he was. I decided to go for a stroll on the top deck to watch the ocean and get away from Lol for half an hour. He always seemed to be following me around since Tony turned back.

It was midnight and we were half asleep when Sooty and a giggling girl came into the cabin. I opened one eye but it was too dark to see anything. I could hear them climb up on to his top bunk and he started slapping her arse, by the lovely sound of it, and she giggled even more. The larking around went on for half an hour. Lucky man I thought and I pretended to be asleep.

Friday 29 March

We had been at sea for five days and today we were docking at Singapore harbour for one night. After sailing through clean blue waters all the way from Colombo it was a shock to see large amounts of debris floating on the sea as we slowly pulled into the harbour. Through the porthole I had an even bigger shock when I saw the skyscrapers, the massive anchored ships, the planes landing and taking off, and the busy port authority boats racing up and down the waterways.

Everybody was getting dressed up to go ashore for the evening and I watched the hippie lads, due to end their voyage here, tie up their hair into buns and shave off their beards to try to fool the authorities. Lol and I picked up our passports from the bureau and while the well-off took a taxi, we explored the streets on foot. We didn't see many westerners and the local Singapore men wore vests and baggy pants which seemed at odds with the glossy, open-fronted shops selling jewellery, watches, tape recorders and high fashion clothes. Everything looked the same. The bright shops, the skyscrapers, the big shiny cars, and the humid night air added to the feeling of being inside a huge store.

The next morning, we all gathered on the top deck, waiting for the big move off. Dock workers and tourists gathered below, looking up and waving, and we waved back as though we knew them all. Our ship was towed out by a small boat through the moored vessels and driftwood until we were far enough out of the harbour to go under our own power. We left Singapore's modern skyline behind and soon lost sight of the aeroplanes landing and taking off.

When I woke up the following day, I had a nagging pain down the right side of my face. It felt like a wisdom tooth. In the restaurant, I could only manage a bowl of cornflakes and by the time I got back to my cabin for a lie down I had a headache and a slight floating feeling in my stomach. Chuffing hell, I thought. We've been at sea for nearly a full week. I thought I'd escaped seasickness.

I didn't dare get up for dinner and only felt okay when I lay face-down. I wasn't going to admit how bad I felt but Lol must have seen the pain in my eyes and he fetched me some aspirin from the medical centre. He said I would feel better for some fresh air and he was right. I managed to get some tea and biscuits down and was upright long enough to hear we had crossed the equator during the night then it was back to bed. The ship was rolling a bit as we sailed past the island of Java. It might as well have been a traffic island for all I cared. Lol came to bed and told me some budding navigator had said there was an electrical storm over Java and the captain had announced he had brought in his stabilisers until the storm passed. That's why half the passengers were seasick.

Tuesday 2 April

Somehow, I made it to the restaurant for breakfast and swallowed half a bowl of cornflakes despite being on the verge of throwing up with every spoonful. It was a day when I could have done without feeling ill because we had to report to the doctor for an examination as part of the entry requirements for Australia. We stood in a long, long queue for over an hour just to have our hands and arms checked for signs of drug use or infection. With deep breathing and concentration, I managed to trap the soggy cornflakes in my stomach until the examination was over and then I felt sick again. My nose and jaw hurt like hell and the seasickness came and went in rhythm to the rolling of the ship.

At lunch I could only eat a pathetic Carr's Table Water biscuit and a small piece of cheese. The restaurant was busy and two girls joined us at our table. We'd seen them during the first few days at sea sunbathing by the side of the pool, watching them apply sun tan lotion to each other's back. I remember Lol saying we ought to go over and offer to do it for them and see what happened. Both of the girls were attractive, about our age, and they introduced themselves as Rebecca and Judith. They were English, a bit posh and a bit loud. Rebecca was tall and slender and the sun had brought out her freckles. Judith had black hair and darker skin and I couldn't decide which girl I preferred because I was more concerned with stopping my stomach from falling out with my head.

Rebecca, who was tucking into a plate of shrimps that I tried not to look at, asked me why I wasn't eating. I could feel my pale face turning pink but I persisted and managed to tell her about my suspected wisdom tooth. I didn't mention the seasickness – I didn't want her to think I was weak. Rebecca carried on eating, pulling the black-eyed heads off the squidgy pink bodies and nodding sympathetically in all the right places. Rebecca talked easily and seemed genuinely concerned about my health. I noticed Lol and Judith were talking to each other and it felt cosy. The turquoise rings we were wearing caught their attention and they laughed when we told them about Magic Mohammed and his brother Ali and the expensive leather jacket and the nonsense address in New Delhi.

When we, or should I say the other three, finished eating, the two girls stood up to leave. We smiled at each other's corny but friendly exit lines and agreed to meet up in the lounge before dinner. Lol and I shook hands when they'd gone and at that proud moment, I could have eaten a full English breakfast.

Later that afternoon, as Lol took his usual nap, I went up on deck in my football shorts and sandals to sunbathe and to get away from the smell of diesel fumes swirling around our corridor. I found a vacant sun lounger by the side of the pool and I'd only been on my front two minutes when Rebecca came over in her bikini, pulled up a sun lounger and lay down beside me. At first, I had to shield the sun from my eyes to talk to her, which gave me a chance to sneak a look at her freckled, bronzed body close-up. I couldn't believe how lucky I was to be so near to her and no Lol at my side. We talked for an hour and a half, mainly about her which was okay, and when we split up to get ready for dinner, I arranged to see her later in the bar of the Flower Room. I woke up Lol and told him how great I felt and he immediately asked what Judith was doing.

We showered, put on our best T shirts, combed our hair and beards, and climbed the two decks to the Flower Room. The place was quiet and the pianist in his black suit and straw pork pie hat was playing a soft jazz piece. Rebecca and Judith were sitting at a table on their own near the bar looking cool in their summer dresses, hair shining under the spotlights, pretending they hadn't seen us walk in.

We acted casually as though we were a couple of rich gentlemen on a cruise ship and asked the girls what they were drinking. We could only make the offer because ten minutes earlier back in our cabin we had ferreted through every pocket and bag we owned in search of hidden dollars and loose coins to find enough money to buy a round of drinks. Thankfully, they said they were okay and would buy their own. I thought what a relief. That means me and Lol can have a pint of beer tomorrow.

Rebecca and Judith told us they had met on the ship and were sharing a cabin. Judith was on her way to Melbourne and a new job. Rebecca had been away from home travelling for three years and was visiting relatives near Fremantle for a few months before touring Australia. The four of us were getting on well, each given the space to talk about travelling, Britain, and Australia. Before long, all the tables were taken and there was a good level of noise. The pianist had switched from jazz to a run of Beatles songs and a few people were on the dancefloor. I could have sat at the table talking all night and I was surprised when, after about half an hour, Judith stood up and said she wanted to circulate. Poor old Lol stayed with me and Rebecca for a few songs but he looked awkward, tapping the table out of time to Yesterday and after a few minutes he said goodnight and went back to our cabin on his own.

I spent the rest of the evening into the early hours of the morning with Rebecca, talking, dancing, laughing. We had a stroll around the ship and watched the waves breaking, and the moon's reflection shimmering on the surface of the water, and the stars twinkling in the sky. We braved the bow, holding on to the rail and when I said I felt like I was on a motorbike flying over the sea, Rebecca said that's just what she was thinking. She said she rode a Triumph 500 back in England. I couldn't believe it. I was in heaven. She saw me laughing and there was a strange silence and we kissed and boy was that good. Everything came together, all the romantic stuff you read about – the gentle swaying and rolling of the ship, the dancing fairy lights, the distant dance music coming and going.

We went back to Rebecca's cabin at four in the morning and talked nonsense and then I left after another soft kiss, singing all the way back to my cabin. As I gently closed the door, I heard Lol turn over in his top bunk.

'Good night was it, then?' he said in the dark.

'I think I'm falling in love.'

Lol went quiet and I thought he must have fallen asleep. Then out of the darkness he said, 'Thy 'as me sympathies.'

I slipped into my bunk and we talked about the way to treat a girl on the first night. Lol said he couldn't understand why I was so sensitive and hadn't given her one.

'Tha could never be guilty of rape,' he said.

He made it sound as though it was a weakness, which I thought was a bit below the belt. I wanted the discussion to continue but Sooty came in with what sounded like a new girl and they climbed up on to his top bunk, giggling and slapping arses.

Wednesday 3 April

The next morning, the ship was rolling and dipping but I was feeling much better and I ate my breakfast as first the ocean and then the sky filled the restaurant window. I met Rebecca for coffee and we sat on the deck at a table in the sun with the warm sea breeze blowing into our faces. Rebecca's eyes were bright and alert to everything that moved and yet they never seemed to shift from me. As soon as we finished our coffee, she stood up and grinned.

'Fancy a few laps around the top deck?'

I'd never been challenged to a race by a girl before and I smiled confidently. We set off running like young horses, belting around the funnel in our sandals, side-stepping strolling passengers, deck chairs and puddles, all the while trying to anticipate the rise and fall of the deck. I was surprised at how fast and athletic she was and after a few laps I had to slow down and eventually stop to get my breath back. I made an excuse to go back to my cabin and it took me half an hour to recover.

We met up again for a drink an hour before dinner and I put on my flat shoes instead of my sandals just in case she decided to do a hundred yards dash again. We shared a bottle of wine that Rebecca had brought all the way from England and although I would have preferred a bottle of Barnsley Bitter, it was very easy to drink. As we drifted back through the quiet corridors towards our respective cabins to get changed for the Captain's Dinner, Rebecca set off running again, switching the deck lights on and off and any other switch and lever she could find that wasn't behind glass or locked up.

'Come on,' she said. 'It's the last night. We're young and I feel mischievous.'

It was wonderful to be with a girl so full of life and I set off after her, zig-zagging down the corridors, knocking on doors, lifting telephones off their hook, jumping up to slap the ceiling. When we got to the stairs and I had to leave her, I was panting and I thought if only we were sharing the same table tonight.

The majority of passengers wore evening dress to the Captain's Dinner and the candle-lit restaurant hummed with excited conversation. I kept looking across to Rebecca's table and I caught her looking back a couple of times. The courses kept coming and I tried to eat a bit of everything but I was still feeling a little woozy and had to decline the cream pudding, alight with vodka, served individually to the delighted passengers by the gorgeous, friendly waitresses. Of course, iron-stomach Lol had everything including my complimentary half pint of Guinness and glass of vodka.

After the meal the four of us met up in the bar and Lol tried to get off with Judith again but he made the mistake of asking one of our waitresses for a kiss and Judith left saying she wanted to circulate. Rebecca and I danced and laughed all night and when it got to three in the morning, I walked her back to her cabin. It felt awkward and both of us were slightly embarrassed and ten yards from her door we kissed and said goodnight.

Early the next morning, our final day at sea, Lol and I went up on to the top deck to watch the sun rise. There were a few passengers around even at that early hour, leaning on the railings, coats and jumpers on, watching the little fishing boats in the distance ride the waves and the small racing yachts cross each other as they sailed the breeze. We were thinking about going back to our cabin to change into our warm jeans and jumper when someone pointed to the horizon and shouted, 'There she blows.' Lol saw land before me and then I picked out the dark shape against the grey sky and there it was. Australia.

When the bank opened, we changed our last few American dollars into Australian dollars before meeting up with Rebecca and Judith in the lounge. We talked about the voyage and the impending disembarkation. The conversation was polite, lacking the fun and spontaneity that had lit up our earlier dates. I think all of us were conscious of how close we were to saying goodbye.

Rebecca told me she was staying with her uncle on the outskirts of Fremantle for a while until she decided what to do. She gave me his address, already written out, which made me happy and when I kissed her goodbye it didn't feel like the end.

We got out of Rebecca and Judith's way to let them say goodbye to each other and queued up to be checked by the immigration officials from Fremantle. About fifty of them had boarded the ship, all dressed in identical uniforms, sitting in pairs on identical chairs behind identical desks. There were separate queues based on surnames and it was a slick operation. We showed them our documents and answered their firm and friendly questions and they smiled and said welcome to Australia.

We collected our scant belongings from our cabin and joined the other passengers queuing to disembark. As we got closer to the gangway, we could taste and feel the fresh cool air of Fremantle and both of us said how alive we felt.

'I wonder what Tony is doing right now,' I said.

'He'll be happy enough,' Lol said. 'He's in love.'

We stepped off the gangway into a new country and shook hands.

'We've done it, Lol. Four and half months of travelling and we've finally made it to Australia.'

'It's some achievement,' Lol said. 'And we've managed not to fall out. Although there were times when I could have smacked thi and I'm sure there were times when tha could have smacked me.'

That was the nearest I had ever been to knowing what was going on inside Lol's head.

August 2018 – Leaving the Traveller's Rest

During the night the floorboards in our bedroom creak and I hear an occasional scraping sound in the corridor outside. We are not disturbed by a headless highwayman or by Lol but when I get up, the first thing I do is check that the cardboard wedged in the wardrobe door is still in place. After breakfast, we stand at the front door and watch the rain pelt the puddles in the car park. We look at the map again and screw up our faces.

I say, 'It's about fifteen miles to those lodges. We're going to get wet through.'

'If it turns out not to be Lol at this cabin, I'm ready for calling it a day.'

'Me too. I think we've gone as far as we can.'

Inside the barn, we start up the bikes and pull on our cold waterproofs. The landlord, who has been watching from the back door of the pub, dashes across the yard to join us, the top of his white shirt turning grey in the rain.

'It's due to clear up later,' he shouts. 'Sunshine and the odd shower for the next two days.' He lights a cigarette, blowing the smoke out into the yard. 'All the way up the west coast.'

We say something about tough northerners not being bothered about the weather, pull on our helmets and shout our thanks. The landlord steps clear as we click into first gear and he wishes us the best of luck with our search.

11

Australia at Last

4 April – 12 September 1974

We followed the signs directing us to the Customs
Office and queued to have our baggage checked. We
each ended up in a private booth where our full names
had been written in black felt tip pen on little white
boards above a desk station. The impressively smooth
procedure took less than fifteen minutes and we picked
up our bags and stepped outside to look around for the
bus station. Our aim was to get to Perth and book into
a cheap hotel recommended to us by one of the ship's
cabin crew.

Passengers were still disembarking and I saw Rebecca
standing at the entrance to the car park on her own with
her bags at her side. As we crossed the road to see if she
was all right, a car pulled up and a man got out and put
his arms around her. Rebecca looked up and waved Lol
and me over. She introduced us to her uncle and asked
him if we could hitch a ride to the bus station in
Fremantle. Her uncle looked us up and down and didn't
seem too keen on the idea but I suppose he didn't want
to upset his niece so soon after welcoming her to
Australia. He dropped us off outside the GPO and
pointed out half a dozen hotels.

'You're better off trying to find a hotel here in
Fremantle rather than Perth,' he said without explaining
why and he never smiled when we said thanks and

goodbye. Maybe he thought we were hoping for a lift all the way to Perth. I wanted to kiss Rebecca but her uncle's wary eyes put me off.

There were plenty of young girls walking around Fremantle town centre which looked like a cross between America and England with its mix of pool rooms, milk shake bars and fish and chip shops. The pedestrianised paved area with its modern metal benches and big, open shop fronts reminded me of the plans I'd seen in the library on Eldon Street in Barnsley just before we left home showing how the new, modernised town centre would look. I don't remember it showing the overflowing litter bins and the gangs of young lads with their cans of lager and the old boys on their own drinking cider out of bottles in brown bags.

The banks were closed and we only had eight Australian dollars between us, hardly enough for a meal or a drink and nowhere near enough to feel secure. The first four hotels we tried were full, or so they said when we explained our financial position. Eventually we booked ourselves into the Federal Arms hotel opposite the bus station using our passports as surety. Too tired and too poor to enjoy a walk around the town centre, we showered and slept for two hours.

That night in the main drinking room of the Federal Arms the landlord introduced us to an English guy called Bob who had been in Australia for seven years. Bob looked as though he was attached to the bar, sitting on his high stool, his loose change scattered around his beer glass, and he gave us some advice on what to expect now that we were in Australia. He was a bit mouthy and a bit of a show off and we had doubts about his assurances and his authority on all things

Australian but we were wrong. The following morning, he turned up at the hotel as promised, drove us five miles out of Fremantle to the foundry where he worked, and by two o'clock Lol and I were each given a job as unskilled workers on $100 a week starting on Monday.

Things got better. In the afternoon, the £300 that Lol had sent home for arrived at the Fremantle branch of Lloyds bank. And it got even better. There was £200 waiting for me in my account. My old friend Ken must have bought my motorbike and my mother had done as I had asked and transferred the money to Fremantle.

We had a steak pie in the bar at the Federal Hotel, or Fed as everyone called it, and Bob introduced us to one his mates, an English guy called Reg. Reg had only been in Australia a few months and he lived in a flat on the outskirts of Fremantle. We shared a few midis with him and Bob and with each drink Reg got louder. Nobody else in the bar seemed to notice or mind and the landlord kept topping up the glasses and sliding the coins off the bar into the till.

Reg was a Londoner and by the end of the session I could hardly work out what he was saying, and I was sober, having declined the last few rounds. Lol was slurring his speech which made for some amusing exchanges of dialect and dialogue. It got to three o'clock in the afternoon and when Reg slammed down his glass on the bar, I was ready to turn in.

'Fack it. I'm pissed,' he said trying to focus on me and Lol. 'Why don't you two Yorkshire bastards come and share the flat with me. Split the facking rent three ways.'

I thought I'd misheard and I asked him if he was being serious.

'Course I'm facking serious. I trust you. Come on. I'll show you the facking place. What about it?'

Lol was rocking slightly on the bar stool and he managed a gormless smile.

'Shounds like a bloody good idea to me,' he said.

I was a bit worried when Reg picked up his car keys and drove us to his flat. I sat in the back and held on tight to my seat belt.

The building he pulled up outside was a modern two-storey block containing about a dozen flats. It looked clean, quiet and it wasn't too far from the town centre. Reg's flat was on the upper floor and it had a TV, a washing machine and a fridge. There were two bedrooms, each with a single bed and we took Reg up on his offer straightaway.

I turned to Lol and said, 'We'll have to take it in turns to sleep in the bed.'

Lol, trying to stand upright and steady in the bedroom doorway said, 'I'll feight thi for it.'

We had been in Australia for just over twenty-four hours and already we had a job, a place to stay and a flat-mate with plenty of stories to tell.

Reg looked to be in his mid-thirties. He was a chain smoker and breathed like a ninety-year-old miner. A romancer with a broken nose, he said he fled to Australia to escape some business colleagues in the motor trade in Lancashire. He bragged he had been a talented boxer in his youth and fought and hammered Terry Downs as an amateur. He claimed to have slept with a dozen women in the twelve weeks he had been in Australia and to prove his story (and his virility no doubt) he played us a tape of him 'shagging' one of them in the flat.

The following week, Lol and I started work as labourers at the foundry, getting up before dawn ready to clock on at half past six. I had been inside a foundry a few times before on call as a gas fitter back in Barnsley so I knew what to expect. I didn't mind the noise of the pneumatic hammers pounding the red-hot steel bars, or the smoke from the molten metal and furnaces coating my throat, or the heat that soaked my T-shirt within minutes. It was the unsmiling, constant supervision that was a shock after so many months of freedom. You had to pretend to be busy even when there was no work to do, and tea breaks were literally timed by a stop watch. Nobody dared look directly at the foundry clock or the supervisor as he walked past. All the workers had developed that subservient, sly look you sometimes see a beaten dog adopt when its master comes home from the pub drunk.

Lol was happy to be doing a job without any responsibility for once and he kept his head down. I didn't want to be treated like a dog and told the all-seeing supervisor I had more to offer than sweeping the foundry floor. On the second day he gave me the job of making the stoppers that control the flow of molten steel out of the ladles. It was exciting at first, watching to see if the stopper I'd made held tight before it was lifted clear to allow the molten steel to flow into the moulds. On the third day I was given a five-minute training session on how to operate an overhead chain lifting gear, and then given responsibility for moving heavy ladles around the foundry. Within an hour of the training, I accidentally got the swinging hook trapped under a steel girder which was holding back dozens of other steel girders weighing tons. I bent the girder and almost brought the lot down. The supervisor wasn't happy and we had words about the quality of the on-the-job training. On the fourth day, I assume as a form of punishment for talking back, he gave me the task of shovelling tons of coal from a pile round the back of the foundry. Working under the blue sky, within a hundred yards of the Indian Ocean, I wheeled the heavy black lumps back into the dark, dusty, noisy hell hole, wheelbarrow after wheelbarrow, shuttling back and forth between sun and hell.

On the fifth day, Friday, I phoned in to say I would be late, fabricating a story about the flat being broken into and having to wait for the police to arrive. Then I called at the Fremantle Gas and Coke Company showroom, persuading the sales manager to contact the works depot to see if there were any vacancies for a qualified gas fitter. The supervisor at the works depot interviewed me in the canteen that same day and after I correctly identified the type of water heater on the wall over the sink and its flue parts, I was offered and accepted a job as a technician, starting on Monday.

I was given my own van with all the necessary tools, including an electric drill, ladders and portable vice – stuff you had to book a week in advance back at my old depot in Barnsley and have delivered from the main store in Rotherham. Above all, unlike those poor wretches back at the foundry, I was treated like a human being.

The manager of the gas fitting firm, Alec McBride, a red-faced scot, was fair and firm. He gave me a month to get used to the different by-laws and types of material and appliances used in Australia. Most of the houses were single-storey buildings on stilts and the water and gas pipes ran under the property and sometimes over the corrugated tin roof. There was a mixture of galvanised steel pipe and copper pipe. The copper pipe, being thinner and harder than that we used back home, had to be bent and soldered in a way that was new to me. The other gas fitters were helpful but it took me longer than I thought and I never did master the changes. I made the big mistake of saying how much better (in my opinion) gas fitting was in England compared with Australia. I was turning into a whingeing pom. Eventually, Alec put me on a number counting job that involved knocking on hundreds of doors – doors that had been knocked on without success by other gas fitters for years – to gain access to meters and appliances, and each day felt like a week. But it wasn't all bad. It gave me the opportunity to meet plenty of customers, both Australians and immigrants.

The Aussies, young and old, had a simple philosophy summed up by their moto, she'll be right. Their days were split into four and controlled by the sun. Up before dawn and off to work, but go steady. Clock off at lunch time and enjoy the sun and sea for two or three hours. Late afternoon, finish off the work started in the morning. Early evening, light the barbeque and open the tinnies.

The immigrants were mainly from Britain and mostly from England. Many of those the same age as my parents had gone to Australia to escape post war austerity. Younger ones had emigrated to take advantage of the warmer climate and outdoor life. Some had emigrated to fulfil a sense of adventure. Nearly all had taken advantage of the £10 assisted passage scheme, the Ten Pound Poms as they were called, under the 'populate or perish' initiative by the Australian government. One immigrant, a forty-year-old man from Nottingham living in Australia for twenty years, was a Nottingham Forest FC fan and he told me the one thing he missed about England was being in the stands on a cold, rainy November evening watching a mid-week game, drinking Bovril with his mates and then going to the pub for a pint and a pie. A common dream among immigrants over sixty who had lived in Australia for most of their lives was to go back home to England when it was time to die.

Now and again, Alec would give me an installation job to do and it was good to be doing something constructive again. And then it would be back to door-knocking. Within a few weeks, I slipped into a habit of turning up at the yard to clock on, knocking on doors till midday then spending the afternoon back at the flat with the van parked out of sight before returning to the yard to clock off. I could have been sacked at any time. I wasn't happy with myself. It was as bad as stealing.

On one of those afternoons on my own in the flat hiding away from Alec, I thought it was about time I wrote to Rebecca. She replied straightaway and when Reg said I could borrow his car and his blue suede jacket, I arranged to take Rebecca to a drive-in movie in Perth overlooking the Swan River. We plugged into the sound system and hung our elbows out of the windows the way we'd seen American movie-goers do on TV. It was our first date on dry land, and we were both a bit nervous. I tried to shake out two cigarettes from my flip top pack of Marlborough, trying to act cool, and ended up ejecting half a dozen on to the dashboard. Freud would have laughed.

One evening we went to a racecourse in Fremantle to watch the harness racing, or trots as the Aussies call it. We bet on every race and the excitement was worth losing twenty dollars apiece. Over the next few weeks, we were invited to a few parties and sometimes it felt good and sometimes it was a strain on both sides. Our kisses lacked passion, something was missing, and I decided to treat Rebecca as a good friend, telling myself that that was no bad thing.

Rebecca's uncle turned out to be friendlier than he first appeared but I couldn't make him smile. He had that kind of humour where he never laughed at his own jokes. And he had a habit of offering words of wisdom as we watched TV, never taking his eyes off the screen. Rebecca would look at me and we would pull faces. And he always treated me with suspicion. Rebecca's aunt was just as protective of her niece but the more we got to know each other the more she seemed to trust me.

Rebecca and I talked about going to Russia on the Siberian Express together or buying a motorbike each and riding east across the Nullarbor Plain to explore as much of Australia as we could. We were both excited by the idea of another adventure and I arranged to call round to discuss the plan in more detail. A few days later, Rebecca's aunt opened the door to let me in and I could tell from her face there was something wrong. She said Rebecca wasn't feeling well and took me upstairs. Rebecca was in bed suffering from pains in her kidneys and she looked pale and weak. I only stayed a short while and when I kissed her goodnight, I thought she was going to cry. Later that week, her aunt phoned to say they had taken her into hospital with suspected hepatitis and the doctor had advised that all her close contacts get vaccinated as a precaution. Her aunt said Rebecca was thinking of going back home to England when she was fit enough to travel.

Rebecca was in hospital for a fortnight and then spent five weeks convalescing at her uncle's. I took her flowers and cards but I began to see the visits as a duty and we drifted apart. One day I got a letter from her saying she was flying home and I replied wishing her good luck. I never called round to see her again and I wasn't proud of myself.

With Rebecca gone, the idea of motorcycling across Australia faded and I ended up doing what I vowed not to do. It was all down to my big mouth. I had been bragging to one of my new work mates, a great guy originally from Leeds, about having played football in the Yorkshire League back home and I gave in to his calls to go training with a team called Cockburn United who were in the second division of the Western Australian Soccer League. The squad was diverse, made up of players from Australia, England, Scotland, and Eastern Europe. It was good to be getting fit again and socialising with players and their wives and girlfriends. Everyone linked to the club loved the Aussie way of life. After every game it was back to someone's house for a barbeque, beer, wine and optimistic talk about life in Australia.

As soon as I got clearance from the Football Association, and my boots arrived from home (I don't know how much it cost my dad in postage), I was selected for the team at centre half and played in every game for the rest of the season. I'd never played as well nor enjoyed my football as much and I won the man of the match so many times it became an embarrassment. A scout from a first division club wanted to sign me for his team and said I was good enough to play for the Western Australian state side.

I was in love with the game again and trained every day. I even borrowed a ball from the club and put it on the bedside table in the flat so I would see it as soon as I woke up. My dad said he took a lot of pride in telling all his mates down at the New Lodge Working Men's Club that I was playing for a club on the Australian pools. I didn't tell him the team was no better than the one I played for in the Sunday league back home, but it really was on the national pools and it regularly appeared in match reports in the Western Australia Chronicle.

Lol and I settled into the flat and got to know Reg a bit more. I could see why he had a broken nose. One time we saw him bluff his way into a skilled welding job at a prestige engineering company despite admitting to us that he had only ever welded rusty car chassis. He lasted a day. One night at half past twelve he came into the flat pissed up, banging into the furniture and swearing, and phoned his ex-girlfriend in Lancashire, pleading with her to come over and marry him. He couldn't remember anything about it the next day. One afternoon down at the Fed he tried to bargain with a bloke at the bar to let him sleep with his fifteen-year-old daughter.

A couple of months after landing in Fremantle, Lol fell in love with a bright, attractive aboriginal Australian girl called Karen and she moved into the flat. She brought some light back into Lol's life and at first it was all good fun and he was happy. That was before they both started drinking all day long and inviting others back to the flat for overnight stays. Empty beer bottles and stale food began to accumulate in every room and stuff went missing including the kitty money and my flying jacket. The jacket was only a cheap version, not real sheepskin, but it had been in my possession all the way from home and it meant a lot to me. And then Lol and Karen started fighting each other, fists and nails. Karen would run off and Lol would look lost for a few days then jump in his car, drunk, and bring her back to the flat in the early hours of the morning and they would have it off on the bedroom floor at the foot of my bed out of Reg's sight.

One noisy night the neighbours in the flat below called the police and a few days later Reg received a letter from the owner of the apartments telling him he had to quit the flat within seven days. Reg went straight round to see the man. When he came back, he told me the guy had made a derogatory comment about 'the coloured girl and her coloured friends'. We talked about the racist language and agreed the owner was out of order and if he wasn't careful, he could be done for discrimination. We didn't say anything to Lol or Karen, partly to protect Karen's feelings and partly to stop Lol from going round and thumping the guy. Reg went back and argued his case and the threat was never carried out but it led to him telling Lol and Karen that if they didn't quieten down and say goodbye to the freeloaders, they had better look for another flat. I felt guilty for agreeing with him, especially when Lol put his arm around Karen and neither of them would look at me. But I had had enough. I hadn't come half way round the world through eleven countries by van, plane, train and boat to be kept awake all night long by the sound of doors slamming and drunken fighting. Reg knew if things didn't quieten down then I was away.

Things improved for a few weeks but then one by one the freeloaders slipped back in. One night, when Reg had gone down to the Fed for his usual evening session, I came back from training and I was looking forward to some quiet time. I opened the door and Lol and Karen and half a dozen of their friends were lounging around, feet up, watching TV and drinking. There were beer cans and full ashtrays all over the place. I thought if Reg comes home early tonight there'll be a riot.

One of the lads in the group, a big guy with ginger hair, was wearing my jumper. When he saw me staring at him, he took it off and laughed. Lol giggled and offered me a can of beer. I was desperate for a bit of time on my own and I went to the bedroom out of the way before I lost my cool. Luckily it was my turn to have the bed.

An hour later I heard people leaving and gradually all went quiet. A few minutes later the bedroom door opened and Karen's best friend, an aboriginal Australian girl called Jo, jumped in bed beside me in her jeans and T-shirt, saying she had nowhere to sleep. I had already worked out that Lol and Karen were trying to ease Jo into the flat. She had been staying over more and more and once I even found her waiting outside the door in the rain when there was no one in. I felt sorry for her. She had sad eyes that looked as though they had run out of tears and Karen treated her like a slave.

Jo was good-looking and I was tempted by the closeness of her body but I knew what was going on.

I thought do they think I've fallen off the back of a bus. I told Jo she was welcome to share the bed for the night and then I turned over. I couldn't be bothered to work out why I did what I did.

Over the next few days Lol and Karen tried to control the inflow of people but they failed and after a few more warnings from Reg, and little sympathy from me, they gave up and one Sunday moved out. Later that day, Jo rang asking to speak to Karen and Lol. They'd not told her they had moved out and, right or wrong, I gave her their new address. When she said goodbye, she thanked me for bearing with her and for helping her out in her time of need. I put the phone down and swallowed hard.

Lol and Karen's flat was in a rough part of Fremantle and it was the start of a downhill slide. Lol packed in the foundry job and finished up unemployed and on benefits. Whenever they came back to borrow something off me or Reg or watch the television, they reeked of beer and usually one or both had a black eye. Sometimes they would stay for hours and then sit looking out of the window and Reg, having been drinking all night himself, would throw me his car keys and I would end up running them back to their flat. Nobody was happy and eventually they stopped calling round.

Reg, not the most honest man I ever met, was always looking to change job for some reason. His latest ambition was to go up north to Kalgoorlie and try prospecting for gold for six months and earn 'big' money. He asked me if I fancied joining him. We could earn a couple of thousand dollars each, he said, and I was tempted. I'd seen the pick-up trucks covered in red dust returning home to Perth and Fremantle after months in the gold fields and it sounded rugged and romantic. But I knew that living in a shack in the outback with Reg for half a year would be a bit different to sharing a flat in Fremantle where I could walk away any time I wanted.

I was undecided and then as usual Reg went off the idea and he put his non-drinking time and energy into a flurry of applications for all kinds of jobs from car dealing to boat building. After many failed interviews he successfully applied to become a prison warden at Ermine jail and a miracle happened. His behaviour altered almost overnight. He cut down on the drinking and womanising and he stopped bragging so much about his fantastic exploits. Whenever he had an essay to write as part of his prison training, we would debate the subject and he would ask me to read his first draft and correct the spelling. He told me about a lecture he had attended in the prison classroom concerned with the fight for civil rights of Aboriginal people by Charles (Charlie) Perkins, an Australian aboriginal. Reg said it had opened his eyes.

'Guess in which year the aboriginal Australians won the right to vote?' Reg asked me.

'No idea,' I said. 'Beginning of the century?'

'Nineteen-sixty-bladdy-seven,' he said. 'Seven years ago.'

One of the essays Reg was given as homework was titled, 'The Reality of Life for Aboriginal Australians'. It was so sensitively written I couldn't believe it was by the same Reg who only a few weeks earlier had tried to get Karen into bed while Lol was out looking for her. Or maybe that proved how sensitive he was. I couldn't help liking Reg and I wanted him to make a success of the prison job. I did wonder how long the change would last.

Throughout those months I kept in touch with Tony and when I got a letter from him one day in July saying he and Gloria were planning a tour of Europe in October I made up my mind to leave Australia and meet up with them. It would be a fitting end to return home together. The time felt right. I had earned enough money to pay for the return journey, the football season was almost at an end, Reg was moving to Ermine and giving up the flat, Rebecca had flown home, and Lol was lost.

My plan was to sail east and so complete a round the world trip, via New Zealand, Tahiti and the Panama Canal, then disembark at the port of Vigo, Spain to rendezvous with Tony and Gloria. I liked the idea of undertaking the second half of my round-the-world trip on my own and I spent weeks wondering whether I should call on Lol and tell him. There had been a distance between us ever since he left the flat, and he wasn't the same man that set off in the van with Tony and me back in November last year. I thought if I tell him, what do I do if he says he wants to come back with me? I can't say no. Would we be like strangers? And how would I feel if he said I was the last person in the world he wanted to travel with?

But I knew I couldn't just leave without saying anything and a month before my departure date I called on him to tell him my plans. I trudged up the four floors to his flat and knocked on the door. As I waited in front of the spyhole trying not to stare into the glass eye, three Aboriginal youngsters, not much more than toddlers, ran down the corridor screaming and laughing as a dog jumped up at them and tried to bite their nappies. An old Aboriginal man, sitting on a stool drinking beer outside his flat, kicked out as the children ran past and the dog scurried back whimpering.

The lock turned in the door and Lol shouted come in. When my eyes got used to the darkness and the cigarette smoke, I saw there were still no carpets down and the couch Lol and Karen were curled up on had sunk even lower. There were empty beer bottles and cigarette packets on the floor and the place stank of piss and stale ale and I felt sorry for both of them.

'I'm going to Europe, Lol,' I said before he could ask why I had come. 'Tony and Gloria are travelling around Europe and I'm going to meet up with them in Vigo, Spain. I've booked my ticket on the ship. It leaves on the twelfth of September.'

Lol didn't say anything. There was banging on the floor above and a man yelled and a woman screamed something in reply. Lol and Karen didn't move. I thought I hope Lol isn't thinking he can book a last-minute ticket. Surely there wouldn't be enough time.

I so wanted to travel on my own but the more I looked around the flat the more I wished he would get out of there and find his old self again even if that meant coming back with me. Then I saw Karen grip Lol's hand and I watched the way she looked up at him and I remembered what he had said about Tony being okay because he was in love.

Lol finished his beer and he took a long time placing the empty bottle on the floor. Then there was a hiss-hiss as he levered the top off another two beers.

'Good luck,' he said. 'I'm staying here in Australia,' and he passed a bottle to Karen and put his arm around her. 'We're planning to go fruit picking in Melbourne, aren't we love. See what happens.'

Two weeks before the ship was due to leave Fremantle, Lol came round to the flat with Karen. They were holding hands and their eyes were red and not from drinking. Karen was wearing Lol's turquoise ring.

'I've changed me mind,' he said. 'I'm coming back with thi. I've booked me ticket.'

August 2018 – The lodges

Tony is riding in front and when he sees the sign pointing to the self-catering lodges he signals and we ride down a narrow lane towards Loch Broom just outside Ullapool. Half a mile down the lane we come across a spread of evenly spaced lodges, about twenty, set into the wooded hillside, tiered to give each a full view over the loch. The homes are grander than I had imagined, more like ski chalets than log cabins with their steep roofs, verandas and hot tubs. They face the low morning sun as it rises above the loch. There is a vehicle, partially concealed by pine trees, on every drive. I can see a couple of Range Rovers, a red two-seater vintage sports car, a variety of hatchbacks, and a few four-wheel drive pick-ups. We park at the entrance and I can tell Tony is impressed.

'This is a bit upmarket,' I say.

'Just a bit.'

Tony pushes his sunglasses up into his hair. If there's a good-looking woman on site, he will have sensed her.

'Where shall we start then?' I say. 'Do you want to split up and we'll take half each?'

'They'll think we're selling dusters.'

'Come on then. Let's stick together and work round each one until somebody calls the police.'

We get half-way round the hilly site without being threatened or told to bugger off. Even a Dutch couple on holiday believe our story. We ring the bell on the tenth lodge and wait. A young woman opens the door and we run through our script, apologising for disturbing her and explaining the reason for our call. She smiles and tells us this is our lucky day.

'I'm Andrea' she says. 'Lol's me dad. He's in the lodge next door.'

12

Back the Other Way

12 September – 7 November 1974

Lol and I left Fremantle sailing east in order to complete our round the world trip. Compared to the sparkling ship we travelled on from Sri Lanka, the vessel heading for Europe looked as though it was coming to the end of its useful life. Corrosion had penetrated large areas of the white paint on the railings and lifeboats streaking everything brown. The engine didn't look in great condition either with dense black smoke blowing out of the twin blue funnels. Worse still there were hardly any young women on board and far too many young men.

When I woke up on the first morning, I thought I'd gone to bed on a trampoline by mistake and Bill, the old man from England who was sharing our bunk, was using it for his early morning exercise (I knew it wouldn't be Lol). The ship was swaying and creaking and I was seasick for two days almost all the way through the Australian Bight to Melbourne. I couldn't get out of bed and Lol kept me supplied with seasickness tablets. He seemed miserable at my debility.

It was late evening when we docked into the Port of Melbourne. On the quay, ropes were drumming tunelessly on the flag poles and the flags were flapping and wet. A few passengers got off, most carrying luggage and not coming back. The rest were wrapped up against the wind, cameras bulging under raincoats.

Lol was eager to go ashore but I didn't feel well enough so he went on his own. Somebody had left a cowboy book on a cushion on the top deck and I took it back to my cabin. I'd never read a cowboy book before, my dad read nothing else, and I was surprised how enjoyable it was. I had almost finished reading it by the time Lol returned.

'How was Melbourne?' I said.

'Okay. I sent a telegram to Karen and told her I loved her.'

There were tears in his eyes and I felt thoughtless and selfish for imagining my illness had been the cause of his misery.

'I'm sorry, Lol. I should have known you were still thinking about Karen.'

'Don't worry about it.'

He climbed into his bunk and turned off the light so I put the cowboy book down and switched off my light as well. I could tell his eyes were still open, staring up into the dark. We'd lived together for so long we could sense these things.

'Lol. What would you do if I fell overboard and drowned?' The answer came back almost before I'd finished the question. 'Fly back to Fremantle tomorrow to be with Karen.'

The next morning, my head and my stomach were behaving themselves and I went for a walk around Melbourne with Lol. There were lots of girls, shops, offices and fast cars. The city's buildings and roadway system reminded me of Leeds and looking back I realised how small and beautiful Perth was. We both bought a pair of Levi's, a T-shirt and a waistcoat and posted a card to the gas depot. Lol saw a girl he had met earlier on the ship when I was confined to my sick bed and he went for a walk with her.

I stopped at a café for a beer, the first in days, and got talking to a lovely young Italian waitress working there. Her eyes were as dark as her hair, and her smile was natural and untrained. Whenever it was quiet, she would stroll over to where I was sitting, place a hand on my table, the other on her hip, and ask me all sorts of open questions – where was I from, where had I been, where was I going, who was I travelling with – and I would soak up the warmth of her attention. After a couple of cold beers, and an exchange of life stories – I told her things I'd never told anyone before – it was time to leave for my ship. She flipped over a page of her little notepad, wrote down her name and address, and handed the sheet to me. I borrowed her pad and warm pen – it felt like I was holding her finger – and wrote down my name and my address in Barnsley. It was strange giving my details to someone I had only known for half an hour. Like sending a message in a bottle. Of course, I knew the reason she was being so friendly was in part to get a good tip but I still felt on top of the world all the way back to my cabin.

As the time drew near for the ship to leave the Port of Melbourne, passengers started throwing streamers down to the hundreds of people gathered on the quay to cheer us off. It was a carnival atmosphere and people were wiping away tears of laughter. Everyone became a comedian and a dancer and a contender for champion streamer-thrower. When the ship began to inch away it seemed like the thousands of coloured streamers linking those on land with those on deck would never snap.

By the time we sailed into Sydney harbour, I was eating everything the kitchen could put in front of me. The harbour, where we saw the sun rise over Sydney Harbour Bridge and later that day took a guided tour of the Opera House, was unlike anything I'd ever seen before. In some ways it was as much of a culture shock as when we drove our van across the Bosporus Bridge into Istanbul.

Two days away from Wellington, we were having a quiet drink and smoke in the ballroom when we noticed two attractive girls, one blonde and one dark-haired, drinking on their own. The blonde girl went to the bar and I emptied my glass and found the courage to stand at her side and say hello.

'It's quiet in here, isn't it?' I said. I've never been good at chat up lines.

'Yeah it is. I'm hoping it's going to get livelier later on when the DJ comes on. He plays some great dance music,' she said.

She had a lovely, open smile and spoke with a broad Australian accent so warm it was like the sun coming out.

'Where are you bound for?' I said.

'Ponta Delgado.'

She picked up her two drinks and paused and I couldn't get over how confident I felt.

'I should know where that is,' I said.

'It's the biggest island of the Azores.'

'Oh. Right,' I said trying to sound as though I knew exactly where she was talking about and at the same time wishing I had taken more interest in geography at school.

'I'm going there for a year to do some voluntary work with my friend, Lorraine. We're both nurses.' She looked over to her table and Lorraine waved.

'Me and my friend, Lol, over there are getting off at Vigo,' I said and left a long enough gap to test her geography. 'Spain.'

'Yeah,' she said. 'I know where it is.'

We both smiled, slightly embarrassed at how nice we were being to each other.

'Well. It's good to meet you. My name's Jennifer.'

'My name's Mike. I'm sure we'll see each other again between now and Vigo, Jennifer.' I consciously used her name, remembering the word of advice from Dale Carnegie about a person's name to that person being the sweetest sound. It felt awkward.

'I'm sure we will,' she said and when she joined Lorraine, I could see they were talking about us. I hoped it was complimentary and was glad Lol was there to witness it.

The next day I was ironing my new jeans in the little laundry room at the far end of our deck when a girl about my age squeezed passed and began ironing her dress. Susan introduced herself straightaway. She was from New Zealand, due to get off the ship at Wellington at the end of a long voyage from England. Susan was a bit heavy, not really my type, but when she took off her big glasses, no doubt to take a closer look at my unshaven mug, she was quite attractive. Inside five minutes she asked me if I wanted to join her at the cinema that night and I was amazed at how easy it all went.

The picture was hilarious and a bit smutty and I felt conscious of laughing out loud at some of the more ribald scenes. We had a quick drink in the bar and went back to my cabin to see if old Bill was still out. I knew Lol would be out. He never came back before midnight. He never said where he had been or who he had been with and sometimes it looked as though he had been crying again. Luckily, Bill was still out and after a bit of teasing on both sides we stripped off and got into bed. I felt as randy as hell and I was swallowing my spit with excitement. After a bit of fumbling on my part – you'd think after nearly a year I'd have been like a stallion – she took the lead, climbed on top and we made it before Bill came back. I could have cried with enjoyment and I think I loved her at that moment.

Bill came in around midnight as I was reading in bed.

'You look happy, young man,' he said, clicking on his own bunk light.

'And so do you, Bill, you old stop-out. Have you had a good night?'

Bill sat on the edge of his bunk and groaned as he took off his shoes.

'I've had an absolutely wonderful night, thank you. I spent the whole evening talking and dancing with a lovely lady. We hit it off straightaway. She's a widower and a few years younger than me. Mind you, who isn't?' he said and we both laughed. 'She's an Australian lady. She boarded the ship at Fremantle. I told her I had had my eye on her the moment I first saw her.'

Bill went into the bathroom to put on his pyjamas then he climbed into his bunk.

'She's a handsome, lovely lady. What a night we've had. She's disembarking at Wellington and then travelling to Auckland to attend her granddaughter's wedding at the weekend.'

'You're both getting off at Wellington, then,' I said and raised my eyebrows at Bill. 'You never know. You might meet up with her again.'

Bill pulled the blankets up to his chin like a child and his eyes widened.

'She's already asked me to accompany her to the wedding.'

The next day I saw Susan chatting up another guy and she waved to me. I went back to the laundry room smiling at the free love and as I ironed my new T-shirt I thought of Jennifer's golden Australian accent.

When the ship docked at Wellington, I was feeling seasick again and my wisdom tooth was acting up. I thought why does my tooth only hurt when I'm on a ship? It felt as though I had a dagger in my jaw.

I managed to get up on deck with Lol and wave Bill and his new woman friend off, then I had to sit down against one of the lifeboats on the other side of the ship and take deep breaths of fresh air while Lol went to fetch some painkillers for me. It was quiet on that side of the ship and just as I was thinking my exaggerated breathing was going unnoticed, Jennifer and Lorraine appeared strolling along arm in arm.

'Are you feeling okay?' Jennifer said.

By this time, I was sweating and probably looked about to be sick. I wiped my brow and concentrated on my breathing.

'I think I've got a wisdom tooth coming through.'

Jennifer put her hand on my forehead, checked my pulse and slowly shook her head.

'Don't buy any green bananas.'

I loved the way Jennifer smiled at everybody she met and I loved even more the special way she smiled at me.

She liked me and I liked her and we weren't sure or cared which came first. I couldn't get her out of my mind and we began sunbathing by the pool, our arms and thighs brushing against each other whenever we shared a drink or a magazine article, or looked at a photograph. Each new wonderful day began with an intimate phone call recalling the previous night's encounter. We were together every minute except for the official mealtimes where we were forced to sit at our designated tables. The only benefit of dining apart was the opportunity to catch up with Lol before going our separate ways for yet another day.

During the daytime Jennifer and I stayed in her cabin making love and sleeping in each other's arms. At night we danced in the disco, walked on the decks and talked under the stars until three or four in the morning.

I thought about my time with Jean back home. Sex with Jean had been great. She taught me a lot, but it was the only attraction between us. We knew it and enjoyed it and it didn't stop us going out with others. With Jennifer it was different. One night under the stars we talked about sex and love and I told her I had an old-fashioned romantic view of intimacy. She said it was the best thing anyone had ever said to her. She went quiet and at first, I thought she was looking out to sea thinking about what I had said. I meant it and I hoped she wasn't secretly disappointed in me. Then she held my hand and told me how, as a teenager she had been abused by her uncle. When my anger subsided, I told her I thought I loved her and we hugged each other and laughed.

I had never felt so close to anyone before. I was totally in love, babbling on about getting married and having kids, and acting like a jealous teenager when she danced with other guys. For days we hardly saw anything outside of our own little burrow. One afternoon while we were dozing in her dark, windowless cabin, far beneath the sunshine and life above, Jennifer sat up and flicked on the bunk light.

'We really need to get outside during the day and get some sleep during the night like normal people,' she said. 'We're missing out on so much.'

She was right. I noticed how dark she was under her eyes and I knew I must have looked the same. I felt the roll of the ship. The cabin was just a cabin. I had lost it. From that day on we engaged in everything the ship had to offer, something that didn't come easy to me. We danced in a Greek show on stage in the ball room in front of a hundred passengers, joined Lol and a girl he had started seeing, in a fancy-dress parade on the main deck, and took part in a pantomime dressed as pirates where we ended up being thrown into the swimming pool. It was scary at first, learning new parts and making my feet do strange movements to strange music. But Jennifer and Lorraine were like two old stage hands and they had an answer for my awkwardness.

'Let yourself go,' Lorraine said.

'You're too stiff,' Jennifer said. 'Relax. Just jump in. You'll love it.'

They were right. Once I stopped thinking about how I looked, I was away. First, I volunteered to be games coordinator and organised a men's five-a-side tournament. Five big, friendly Aussie rugby players were drawn against my weedy team of soccer players and we had great fun tackling each other. It was funny to see twelve and a half stone frames knock sixteen stone frames all over the deck. It's all about timing and balance, we told them. I was relieved when there wasn't time to organise a rugby tournament.

Next up was the women's five-a-side soccer tournament. Jennifer and Lorraine put a team together and everyone chased after the ball as though it was on fire and their job was to stamp out the flames. The girls didn't care who was watching and I loved the way Jennifer laughed whenever she or Lorraine tripped up. Inevitably, the ball finished up in the South Pacific.

I had travelled three quarters of the way around the world and it took two fun-loving Aussie girls to set me free from my inhibitions.

The ship called at Pepette, Tahiti, which was as hot and humid as Madras, and Jennifer went offshore with Lorraine and some of her other girlfriends. Lol had gone sightseeing with his girlfriend and I was feeling sorry for myself. I missed being with Jennifer. I thought is this what love is like?

I considered hiring a motorbike to cheer myself up but decided to save the money and instead walked around the town centre on my own admiring the stalls on the street market and the mountains and the greenery all around.

In the disco that night we danced to the DJ's rock and roll records and held each other close for the final few romantic numbers. We'd both had more than usual to drink and it was as though there were just the two of us on the floor. The next morning, I woke up at the side of Jennifer in her single bed in the darkness. I tried to ease my dead arm from under her shoulder and check my watch. I couldn't remember how I had got there. We had agreed to sleep in our own beds following her plea to get out more and we had been sticking to the rule. Sleeping apart had not been as difficult as I thought it would be. Things were settling down between us and infatuation had been replaced by a bit of common sense and clear thinking.

There was some commotion outside the cabin, like someone moving heavy furniture, and Jennifer tried to turn over.

'What's that?' she said.

I pulled my arm free and saw it was only five o'clock.

'I think we're sinking,' I said.

We got dressed and sneaked out of the cabin without disturbing Lorraine. A night security man patrolling our deck told us the noise was coming from the floor below. The crew were getting ready to navigate the Panama Canal, he said, and he led us through a gate marked private to show us what was happening.

A door had been opened in the side of the ship and we could see a square of early morning daylight and flashing torches. A gang of black men were clambering through the opening from a little boat bobbing against the doorway. They were hauling ropes and chains and light machinery into the engine room, all the while shouting instructions to the ship's crew who were arguing back and complaining.

When the gang finished whatever they were doing, the little boat left and the door was sealed. We thanked the security man and climbed up to the top deck. There were a few passengers out already, watching the ship close in on the mouth of the canal as the sun came up. As usual there was an expert, a middle-aged English man in a baseball cap, white socks and sandals, carrying an expensive camera around his neck complete with an assortment of huge lenses. He knew exactly what was happening and what each worker was doing. I'd seen him before. He dined on the table next to Lol and me, and he was just the same there, taking over the conversation, never listening. I was glad he wasn't on our table. That would have tested my understanding of How to Win Friends and Influence People. At first, the man's running commentary attracted an audience but gradually the passengers found something else to do and he was left talking at his wife who stood nodding by his side.

After breakfast we went back on top deck and Lorraine joined us. It was light now, and there were hundreds of black men in white vests on the banks on either side of the canal working hard and skilfully to guide the ship through the canal while hundreds of white passengers looked on. The workers operated the massive locks and cranes, pulling on heavy ropes and chains, resting and staring at us in between duties. I wondered how much they earned in a week and how that compared to the wage I received as a foundry labourer in Fremantle.

Our passage through the canal was slow and delicate. At times, there were only inches between the sides of the ship and the canal walls and we were warned to keep our hands off the guard rails and not lean out. We were completely helpless throughout the whole operation – true passengers. By mid-morning, Jennifer and Lorraine, like most of the other passengers, went below to get something to eat but I was fascinated by the scale and delicacy of the manoeuvre and I watched every inch of progress.

I wondered why some of the banks on the locks and passageways were made of nothing more than packed earth. I thought maybe it was a safety feature to prevent expensive damage should a ship scrape the wall. Or maybe it had been too expensive to clad the sides in concrete or timber. Or maybe it was a deliberate plan to leave the walls as earth and so make it easier and cheaper to widen the canal for future, bigger ships. Maybe I should have asked the expert.

Our first port of call after navigating the canal was the island of Curacao, which is part of the Kingdom of the Netherlands. Jennifer and Lorraine planned to visit the sanatorium there and asked if I wanted to join them. They had heard about the hospital and wanted to see if it was possible to take a look around the mentally handicapped ward. The official on the reception desk said he would be honoured to let us visit the children and when he opened the ward door my stomach turned. The kids, mostly orphans, were in rows of metal cots, their hands tied to the bars with leather straps to stop them climbing out or scratching themselves.

One young boy, aged about eight or nine, had a very badly disfigured face with bulging eyes, a dwarfish head and horrible teeth. He was smiling at me, rocking in his cot and I just held his hand and smiled back and tickled him. He looked straight into my eyes and his gaze touched me. I thought what will happen to him and all these other children? Day after day, night after night locked away in this hospital? How would children like these survive without a hospital like this to look after them? I thought about my five weeks in hospital and the magpies flying in and out of their nests and I felt ashamed of my self-pity.

The young boy's smile faded as we reached the exit door and he began to rock from side to side, restrained by the leather straps. I sensed he knew we were leaving for good and I blinked away a tear. Jennifer put her arm around my shoulder and said, 'You get used to it.'

By the time Jennifer left the ship with Lorraine at Ponta Delgado things between us had cooled a little. No specific incident caused the temperature to drop. No new lover came on the scene. We still spent most of our time together and we promised to write to each other, making vague plans to meet up in Europe next summer. She gave me a fountain pen with her name on and I gave her my turquoise ring. I don't think either of us believed we would see each other again. I suppose it was a holiday romance, a port of call at a beautiful place, but no less real for that and she will be in my memory forever.

*

Four weeks after sailing out of Fremantle the ship pulled into the port of Vigo. A small crowd had gathered on the quay and as we drew near, Lol spotted Tony's long blond hair and then I saw Gloria's radiant smile. We waved and shouted at each other and I almost cried with joy. They were both a beautiful shade of brown and Tony didn't look any different from the day he waved us goodbye at Madras train station. We hugged each other and it was good to be back together again.

The four of us walked around Vigo telling each other how well we looked and how great it was to have met up as planned. We finished the walk with a coffee outside a café overlooking the moored ship, its funnels smoking in readiness. I couldn't get over Gloria's broad accent. I hadn't heard a woman speak with a Yorkshire accent for almost a year and it left me feeling warm and sad at the same time. I looked around the dock. We were the only ones there and we waved goodbye to the ship and the friends we had made.

Gloria said, 'Thanks for looking after Tony. I can't tell you how much I worried about him when he was away.'

She put her arm around his waist and I noticed she was wearing Tony's turquoise ring.

There was just enough room in the back of Tony's little blue Vauxhall van for Lol and me to sit side by side without getting cramp. We travelled east across Spain heading for Benidorm where we planned to spend a couple of weeks on a campsite used by Tony and Gloria a few weeks earlier. The days travelling in the cramped van were long and uncomfortable and we stopped every two hours to stretch our legs. The cheap hotels we used helped our recovery and there was a brief easing of discomfort when we visited El Escorial, historical site of the King of Spain. But there were crowds everywhere and coaches from all over Europe and we didn't stay long.

We finally arrived at Los Olivos campsite in Benidorm and put the tent up in the rain and tried to get to sleep on the cold hard floor. The weather was consistent – rain during the night, warm and sunny during the day. On one of those drizzly evenings the campsite flooded and the tent began to feel like a sinking boat. The four of us put on our driest clothes and set off for a stroll along the deserted shoreline. The tide was going out and nobody spoke. The weight of our feet squeezed the sand dry and it felt like we were making tiny impressions on the world. I handed out the cigarettes to Lol and Tony.

'What's your story then, Tony? What did you get up to when you left me and Lol at the train station in Madras?'

'Oh, I had some great fun. When I got back to New Delhi, I stopped at that same hotel we stayed in. Just for one night.'

'Was Camel still there?' I said.

'He was, but thankfully I didn't see that angry bloke in the restaurant this time.'

'I still feel bad about that,' I said.

'Me too. Anyway, after a night in New Delhi I flew to Kabul and spent two days with Francois at his place.'

Lol said, 'Did Tipp attack you?'

'No. He's only attracted to you.'

I don't think Gloria knew why we were laughing but she joined in.

'Sellick was there. And then Pascal came round for an hour, as well. It was great.'

I said, 'Did you call round at the Ansari to see Mali and Charman and Algy?'

'Yeah, I did. I had a cup of tea and a brownie with them. They're all doing well. I told them you had carried on.'

I was happy for Tony and I felt a bit envious that he had met up with all those good people again.

'Then I caught the hippie bus at Kabul bus station. It was on its way back to Europe.'

Tony reminded me and Lol about the famous hippie bus that went back and forth between Europe and Asia picking up and dropping off wandering travellers and those carrying eastern goods to sell back in the west. He told us how he narrowly avoided arrest at the Turkish border when the passenger he had been sitting with throughout the whole trip was caught carrying a knife and a bag of heroin.

'You were brave, Tony,' I said. 'Going all that way on your own.'

'It didn't feel like I was being brave when I was doing it. All I had to do was sit there and read and chat if I wanted to. It was good. I can see why some hippies spend all their time going backwards and forwards from Europe to India. Life seemed to slow down on that journey. It was so peaceful. It made you feel, I don't know, spiritual.'

Lol said, 'Was it 'far out man?''

He said it in inverted commas to show he was taking the micky.

'When we got to Greece, I jumped off the hippie bus and caught local buses and trains and finally hitchhiked my way to Switzerland. And I met up with Elizabeth at the hotel where she was working.'

Tony had been calling Gloria by her new name ever since we met them in Vigo. He said he preferred to use Gloria's middle name, Elizabeth, sometimes shortened to Liz. He didn't say why and Gloria didn't seem to mind. I think it was the first time I'd come across anyone switching to their middle name. Maybe it was a sign of how their relationship was developing. The new name suited Gloria and it didn't take Lol and me long to adapt.

I said, 'I'll bet that was some reunion when you two met up again.'

Liz said, 'It was. He looked like a starving hippie.'

'We stayed at the hotel for about six weeks,' Tony said. 'It was a cool place, wasn't it, Liz?'

'Very grand. I loved being there,' Liz said. 'It was good work experience.'

'It was very exclusive. We saw a few film stars going in and out while we were there and one day we saw David Niven standing on the steps drinking champagne. He was just standing there on his own looking super cool.'

Liz said, 'And we saw Bert Reynolds with a gang of people. The hotel manager told us they were making a film nearby and they were the film crew.'

'And I tell you what,' Tony said. 'The place was buzzing with Ferraris and Porsches.' He nodded to himself as though he had inside information about each individual car and its owner.

'Then when Elizabeth's contract ended, we caught the bus back to England and after a few months of hanging around in Barnsley we bought the little van and came to Spain and here we are.'

Liz said, 'And what did you two get up to when Tony left you?'

We told them about our time in Sri Lanka and how we sailed to Australia and worked together for a short while and how Lol went his own way and moved out of the flat. I didn't say too much about the episode with Karen and I was surprised when Lol opened up.

'Yes. I went off the rails a bit in Fremantle,' he said.

I kept quiet not wanting to show I agreed with him.

Tony said, 'What do you mean?'

'Drinking. Loafing around. Fighting with Karen.'

Liz's face went from a smile to a frown and Lol looked away.

'Don't ask me why. It just happened. I think I got lost.'

Everyone went quiet and found something to look at in the sand.

'Anyway,' I said, flicking my cigarette butt into the sea. 'Apart from that it was a great laugh. Especially coming back on the ship. Both of us got involved in a play and got dressed up as pirates, dancing and diving into the pool and generally acting daft.'

'We had a fantastic time,' Lol said. 'And the weather was great nearly every day.'

We told them about the beautiful places the ship had called at on the return journey and I told them how impressed I had been with the Panama Canal.

'When we got through the canal, we stopped for a few hours at Cristobel port. It's a tiny place, a bit frightening at first with all those black faces staring at you but it turned out to be as friendly a place as I've ever been to. A guy I'd seen a few times on the ship got off there. Wait for this, Tony. He was standing there on his own, I thought he'd lost something, and then a huge crane swung round with this big wooden crate dangling from it. They lowered it on to the dockside then this guy broke it open with an axe and inside was this big Triumph twin motorbike.'

'Very nice,' Tony said.

'He kicked the beast up and rode off into the sun. I didn't half envy him.'

Liz started up a separate conversation with Lol, asking him if he was missing Karen, and they dropped back a little and we couldn't hear them above the sound of the waves.

Tony lit up another cigarette and said, 'If I'd gone to Australia with you instead of turning back, I reckon we would have ended up travelling through America.'

'I reckon we would,' I said.

'We would have done okay. I'd love to go to America one day in a camper van or on a bike. But it'd be no good going with Elizabeth. She'd want all the comforts and mod cons.'

I thought I detected a hint of regret in Tony's voice. We both took a deep drag of our cigarettes and waited for Liz and Lol to catch up with us.

'Well,' Liz clapped her hands and gave that lovely smile again. 'What have you two learned after all this travelling around the world?'

I waited for Lol to say something but as usual he wanted me to go first.

'It's definitely changed me,' I said. 'It's true what they say about travelling broadening the mind.' Tony and Liz nodded. 'Meeting so many different people from so many different places just makes you realise how many good people there are around the world, once you look beyond the stereotypes. We hardly met a bad guy anywhere. We got done a couple of times but nothing serious.'

'That's true.' Tony said. 'Even that guy on the hippie bus with the knife and the heroin was fine with everybody.'

I said, 'And even when things didn't go to plan, like when we got stuck in Afghanistan because the Pakistan border was closed, we got through it and finished up meeting some great people and having a brilliant time. I think the lesson there for me is know what you want and just keep going, even if sometimes it feels like you're taking a step backwards.'

'And what about you, Lol?' Liz said and her smile was so warm I could have hugged her again.

Lol rubbed his finger as though he was feeling for the turquoise ring he'd given to Karen.

'I've learned this much. There's less pain when you're on your own.'

The collar on my jacket was cold and wet and I could sense Tony and Liz had had enough of looking back. Lol never mentioned the girls he'd met on the two voyages and there was no point in me telling them about my time with Rebecca in Australia or how happy and daft I had been these past few weeks on the ship with Jennifer. I could hardly believe it myself. I wondered how Jennifer was coping in the Azores and I was sad for a moment, knowing I would probably never mention her again to anybody else.

As the days shortened, we left Spain and drove north up the east coast into France, our plan being to stop off in Paris and call on Francois. We arrived in the capital on a cold November night and drove around the streets looking for our old friend's address. We were doing well before we got lost. Liz could speak a bit of French and she asked a pedestrian for directions. When she turned round, she was beaming. We had stopped just fifty yards from Francois' street, Rue du Faubourg Montmartre. Luckier still, the hotel right in front of us had vacancies and we booked in for two nights.

The next morning, I phoned Francois from the hotel. He must have been surprised to hear my voice and he sounded excited. It felt strange to be talking to him once again after all those months and he told us to come straight round to his apartment. When he answered the door wearing a sloppy suit, his beard and hair much shorter than it had been in Kabul, I was a little disappointed. His apartment was untidy and full of character like Steptoe's house. Of course, Liz had never met Francois. I could see she wasn't too impressed and

Tony looked a bit embarrassed. But somehow after only half an hour it was the Francois we'd known in Afghanistan – cool, confident and wise.

He served us coke and cider in bowls, he had no glasses, and asked us how long we were intending to stay in Paris.

Tony said, 'We plan to stay for a couple of nights. We want to walk the beautiful streets and see the main attractions of the city.'

'You must stay here.'

He followed us to the hotel and cancelled our second night, telling the irate manager in a no-nonsense way to send him the bill if he wasn't happy. If one of us had tried to cancel, we would have grovelled and apologised and still ended up staying.

Back at the apartment, Francois told us he was going to a party and would be returning in two days' time. I smiled to myself and thought nothing has changed.

'Make yourselves comfortable and enjoy the apartment,' he said.

'That's really good of you, Francois,' Lol said. 'Would it be okay to take a bath? I think we're all ready for a good soak.'

'Of course. You can even share a bath, if you would like. I know how much the British like to save water. Wait. I have a cartoon to show you.'

He took a magazine from a pile on a desk in his study and inside was a cartoon of a middle-aged British couple sitting opposite each other in a bathtub of water. The man and woman were very straight-backed and serious-looking and on the bathroom wall there was a picture of the Queen and a London bus. Francois, translating the caption, said, 'Drought in Britain: couples encouraged to share a bath.'

To us this seemed like a sensible approach and we didn't get the joke.

'You see,' Francois said, laughing. 'That's why it is so funny.'

Somehow, we all squeezed into Francois' mini and he took our silly big grins and wide eyes on a guided tour of Paris. It would have cost us hundreds of pounds if we'd had to pay and it wouldn't have been anywhere near as special. In between pointing out the important landmarks, Francois told us which restaurants were worth visiting and where the best cafes were located. After an hour, I stopped trying to take it all in and rested my head against the window, smiling to myself.

When we got back and Francois left to go the party, we had a snoop around his apartment and kept getting lost. There were six rooms and that wasn't counting the study, bathroom and the separate bathroom.

'This is fantastic,' I said.

'It's not bad, is it,' Tony said. 'A massive apartment in the centre of Paris and it's our home for the next two nights.'

We didn't have enough money to pay to see the sights. Instead, we walked the streets, kicking fallen leaves, stopping to point out an unusual door entrance or a dazzling shop display, racing Tony up the steps to the Sacre-Coeur while Lol and Liz shook their heads and laughed. We were a unit, carefree and happy, feeling Paris loved us as much as we loved Paris. And when our legs tired, we sat outside a cafe, drinking strong coffee, pretending to like the taste of our Gauloises cigarettes. Young couples at every table kissed and caressed and

I reminded Lol about the time we were in the King George Hotel in Barnsley and a young lad put his arm around his girlfriend in the lounge and the landlord shouted over, "Hey. We'll have none of that in here."

When Francois returned from his party and it was time to leave, we said goodbye, promising to keep in touch, and after dipping our croissants in our bowls of coffee for luck, we drove out of Paris to Calais. The ferry crossing was choppy but by keeping my eyes on the horizon I managed not to be seasick and my wisdom tooth stayed quiet. The white cliffs of Dover came into view and we held a minute's silence and hugged each other which felt like the right thing to do.

The land was green and pleasant all the way to Canterbury and we looked around the cathedral city for somewhere to spend the night. Every hotel we tried was full or too expensive and we gave up our search and decided to drive through the night all the way to Barnsley. When we joined the M1 it was like driving on to an endless runway with its rumbling sections of grey concrete, and the grumpy, charmless service station we stopped at for a coffee to keep us awake, added to the dreariness. Tony asked me to take over the driving and we counted down the blue signs and the mile markers appearing in our headlights out of the night as we drove north. Through the rear-view mirror, I could see Lol and Tony had fallen asleep and as we passed the exit sign for Leicester, Liz's head began to nod at my side and she too fell asleep.

I slipped into the middle lane, overtaking a line of lorries as they climbed a steep section of motorway, and for the first time I began to picture in detail what it would be like coming back to my home town, to my home estate. Soon, I thought, I'll be driving past people I know, cars I know, short cuts I know, shop windows I know, pubs I know, houses I know. Will there be a ton of coal outside the neighbour's house waiting to be taken in? Will I be too late for the pie and pea man in his little caravan kitchen? Will any of the old folk in the bungalows opposite have died? Will that busted football still be wedged high up in the neighbour's apple tree?

Then I'll be walking down the path of our house to the back door past the front door that I went through without lingering a year ago to begin the journey. How different will those last few strides feel? Or will they feel the same, like coming home from town on an ordinary Thursday morning in an ordinary November? And what was wrong with that? Had I become a snob? Had I always been a snob?

But I knew I'd changed. I knew that for sure. My self-confidence had grown and I felt stronger, less aggressive. Before I went away, I often felt on the edge of things, never totally comfortable around others. Now, having met so many fascinating people – regardless of where they were from or what they looked like or how they spoke – in so many wonderful places, I felt at ease with myself. And those hard times on the road – the nights in the freezing van, the grim hotels, the sweltering streets of Madras, and the airless YMCA in Sri Lanka with its wooden shutters and hungry rats where I nearly turned back – those times had taught me how to turn the negative feeling of loneliness into the positive feeling of tranquillity.

Above all, the journey had given me a different perspective on my family, my home town, my country, and their place in the world. Now, somehow, it all felt together. Connected.

It was a strange feeling. I couldn't wait to knock on the back door and hug my mother but the closer I got to home and the nearer the end of the journey, the more the feelings I'd had before my travels began to resurface. The boredom. The wanderlust. The compulsion to look over the wall. Maybe this is how it'll always be, I thought. On the road for ever.

I looked through the rear mirror at the sleeping Lol and Tony, two people who'd taught me the value of true friendship, and I wondered what thoughts and feelings they had. I knew we'd probably never talk about it.

Liz stirred and Tony and Lol woke up and there it was – a big blue and white sign saying Welcome to Yorkshire.

It was too early to go home and we rested at Woodall services near Sheffield and drank coffee and smoked more than usual. Even Liz had a cigarette. It was nine o'clock when we turned off the motorway at Birdwell and cars still had their headlights on in the grey morning light and pedestrians passed each other in colourless coats, collars up, heads down. We drove through Stairfoot and Monk Bretton to Lol's parents' bungalow and parked opposite the kitchen window. Lol picked up his travel bag and as he walked down the drive, his dad came to the front door, unsmiling. He looked at Lol as though he was a cold-call salesman, his eyes switching from his son to Tony's van and back. Lol didn't turn round and the door closed.

I asked Tony and Liz to drop me off at the edge of my estate and I walked the last few hundred yards home. No one saw me go down the path. I opened the door into the new conservatory at the back, the one my dad had built and written to me about, and I smiled. It was no more than a porch, a few sheets of corrugated plastic nailed to a wooden frame. The big, rough timbers he'd used to bridge the four-foot gap between the back door and the outside toilet and coal house were like pit props.

My elder sister, Sandra, screamed when she saw me and she held onto my mother's arm in shock. My mother and my younger sister, Anne, were sitting at the kitchen table and there seemed to be kids running around all over. I embraced my mother then my sisters and they cried and I almost cried with them. My little brother, Jonathan, ran into the kitchen and I picked him up and he said he was four.

I put my bag down in the hallway and the house felt tiny and claustrophobic, not much bigger than the van. I felt slightly depressed and I think it showed. My sisters stood up to make room for me at the table, and to stare at me, and my mother's hands were shaking as she filled the teapot.

Sandra said, 'What happened then? Come on tell us.'

'We're gagging to know what you got up to,' Anne said. 'What was it like in Australia?'

My mother could see the worn-out look on my face as she poured my tea.

'Let him get in, first,' she said. 'There'll be plenty of time later for storytelling.'

We talked about the letters we had exchanged and how much they had meant to us and I gave my mother another hug.

'Has my dad gone to work, Mam?'

'No. He's on nights. He's down at the pigeons. Do you want me to ring the Royal and tell them to send him up?'

'No. Don't do that. I'll surprise him.'

I walked the mile and a half to the ring of pigeon huts behind the Royal Arms Hotel. There were a few flyers around, leaning inside their hut doorways, looking up at the sky, hardly saying a word, not a smile in sight. One flyer shepherded his pigeon towards his loft, giving nothing away about the bird's performance in training. I couldn't see my dad anywhere but his hut door was open and someone shouted:

'Hey up Joe. Your lad's back.'

My dad appeared, stooping in the hut doorway, a slate blue pigeon in his big hands, its wings pinned gently and securely to its side.

'Well, I can't believe it,' he said, smiling, a hint of embarrassment on his face as his fellow flyers looked on poker-faced.

He fastened the pigeon back in its pen and we hugged each other. Someone shouted:

'Put im darn. Tha dun't know weer is bin.'

My dad looked older and poorer than I remembered with his mucky hands and shoes, flat cap and worn-out jacket and I thought a year is a long time for a miner.

'I'll buy you a pint, Dad, when you've finished training.'

'I've done,' he said, locking the hut door. 'They've been up and fed and they're all back in.'

And we went into the pub patting each other on the back.

August 2018 – The reunion

As we walk with Andrea along a track through the pine trees to Lol's nearby lodge she tells us they block book three lodges every year for all the family. Andrea has a key to her dad's lodge and she lets herself in.

'He'll have a right shock when I tell him. Just wait here a minute while I fetch him. Dad. Are you decent? There's somebody here to see you.'

Andrea disappears into a room off to the right at the end of the hallway and we stand on the ramp outside the open front door, smartening ourselves up like somebody on a first date. The bare floorboards in the entrance are painted flat white to match the walls and sleek radiator. Heat flows out of the door, warming our faces. There are muffled voices from the back room and we watch the door handle for any sign of movement. Higher up the hill, a middle-aged couple are folding down the hood on their red vintage sports car. It's going to be a good day.

The room door opens and a few seconds later an old man appears holding on to a walking frame. It's Lol's dad – the grey face, the broad concave chest, the little beer belly, the white forearms. He rests the frame and stares at us and we laugh at the suspicious look in his eyes.

'Don't you recognise us, Lol? It's your old travel buddies.'

It takes him a few seconds to speak.

'Chuffin'ell. It's Mike and Tony.'

Andrea smiles and says, 'Let 'em come in then, Dad.'

'You haven't changed a bit, Lol,' I say shaking his hand.

'Thy as. Thi eyes have gone.'

His voice is weak and I have to watch his lips. Andrea smiles at her dad's humour and she invites us into the main room. The window is big and square and we look down over the pine trees out on to the loch as though we are suspended in mid-air.

Andrea brings in the tea and biscuits and says, 'My dad's not been so well, have you, Dad?'

'I've had a triple heart bypass and I've got diabetes and Parkinsons.'

'You've had it tough, Lol,' Tony says.

'I'm alright. Me family looks after me.'

We talk about the good times we shared all those years ago on the road. I feel a tear well up and I can hear from Tony's voice he is feeling the same. I ask Lol if he ever wished he'd stayed in Australia.

'I'd have been in prison, if I'd stopped theer.'

Lol's memory and wit are sharp but he tires quickly and Andrea brings him his tablets and a glass of water. A young girl, Lol's great grandchild, dances into the room and when she sees me and Tony, she sits at Lol's feet to hide her shyness and he rubs her hair while we catch up.

After half an hour, Lol's eyes are heavy and I nod to Tony. We get up to leave and tell Lol how wonderful it's been to see him again and to meet his family. We shake hands and Andrea writes down her dad's mobile number and we promise to get over to Barnsley and celebrate our reunion. Lol is asleep by the time Andrea shows us out.

Tony and I wait until we reach our bikes before shaking our heads and looking back.

'Wasn't that great, seeing the old boy again.'

'It was,' I say. 'We've done well. The three travellers. Together again.'

Appendix - equipment

My mother's old carving knife for self-defence (I never told her)

Two jerry cans for spare petrol (to look the part)

Two sets of spare wheels and tyres (to look the part even more)

One tow rope and an army folding spade for digging our way out of trouble

One fan belt, four sparkplugs, spare points and fuses and a set of feeler gauges (to prove we were handymen)

One gallon can of Castrol engine oil (but we forgot the funnel)

One tool kit comprising items 'borrowed' from the gas board including a hammer, two screwdrivers, an adjustable smooth jaw spanner, a pair of adjustable grips, a tube spanner, a set of Allen keys and a roll of insulating tape

AA itinerary and VW manual

First aid kit

Ten of our favourite 8-track tapes

Twelve toilet rolls, half a dozen boxes of Swan Vesta matches, a dozen tablets of Fairy soap, two bottles of Fairy washing up liquid, four bottles of shampoo, two dozen cans of beans, two dozen packets of soup, six packets of Marvel powdered milk, a pack of Oxo cubes, a hundred PG tips tea bags and two jars of Nescafe instant coffee.

Thanks

My thanks go first to Tony and Lol for making the journey so wonderful and enriching. I hope I have captured the essence of that adventure in the book. I'd also like to thank all the good people we met on the road between here and there for the colour and variety they brought.

For giving up their time to read the manuscript, I'd like to thank my former work colleagues and good friends, Ken Child, John Metcalfe, Trevor Nordon and Mike Wren. A special thanks to Jeff Halden for his suggested amendments and for the beautiful artwork on the front cover.

The greatest of love and thanks to my wife Diane for her never-ending encouragement and understanding. And love and gratitude to my sisters Sandra, Anne and brothers David and Jonathan for their advice, enthusiasm and support. In addition, I'd like to thank Jonathan for getting on to me over many years to write up my travel diaries.

And last of all, I would like to thank my mother and dad for their love which I carried with me and always will.